MOLIÈRE

Molière

Reasoning with Fools

MICHAEL HAWCROFT

OXFORD
UNIVERSITY PRESS

OXFORD
UNIVERSITY PRESS

Great Clarendon Street, Oxford OX2 6DP

Oxford University Press is a department of the University of Oxford.
It furthers the University's objective of excellence in research, scholarship,
and education by publishing worldwide in

Oxford New York

Auckland Cape Town Dar es Salaam Hong Kong Karachi
Kuala Lumpur Madrid Melbourne Mexico City Nairobi
New Delhi Shanghai Taipei Toronto

With offices in

Argentina Austria Brazil Chile Czech Republic France Greece
Guatemala Hungary Italy Japan Poland Portugal Singapore
South Korea Switzerland Thailand Turkey Ukraine Vietnam

Oxford is a registered trade mark of Oxford University Press
in the UK and in certain other countries

Published in the United States
by Oxford University Press Inc., New York

© Michael Hawcroft 2007

The moral rights of the author have been asserted
Database right Oxford University Press (maker)

First published 2007

British Library Cataloguing in Publication Data
Data available

Library of Congress Cataloging in Publication Data
Data available

Typeset by Laserwords Private Limited, Chennai, India
Printed in Great Britain
on acid-free paper by
Biddles Ltd., King's Lynn, Norfolk

ISBN 978-0-19-922883-6

1 3 5 7 9 10 8 6 4 2

For my parents
with thanks and with love

Preface

This book is about a single aspect of Molière's dramatic technique, but it is one which lies at the heart of long-standing critical controversies over the interpretation of his plays: do they aim to do more than make us laugh? The book focuses on those characters commonly known as *raisonneurs*, who engage in sustained dialogue with some of Molière's most memorable and most foolish protagonists, including Arnolphe in *L'École de femmes*, Orgon in *Tartuffe*, Alceste in *Le Misanthrope*, and Argan in *Le Malade imaginaire*. The *raisonneurs* who engage with such star roles in Molière's comedies have been variously interpreted either as exponents of wisdom or ridiculous bores. This book argues that new light can be shed on the words and actions of these problematic characters by detailed contextual analysis of the dramaturgical and comic structures in which they operate. They have never before been accorded such exhaustive treatment.

The body of the book is composed of close readings of the plays in which the *raisonneurs* appear. I engage not only with the text of Molière's plays, however, but also with those critics who have written centrally on these characters. The perspective adopted throughout is specifically that of the seventeenth-century audiences for whom Molière wrote, since there is ample contemporary evidence that Molière constructed his plays and performances so as to maximize audience laughter. Not all subsequent actors and directors have sought to perform Molière primarily for laughs: their interpretations are not the subject of this book, though the *raisonneurs* would inevitably look different, viewed in their perspective.

Despite many claims made in the last sixty or so years that Molière needs to be understood as a man of the theatre, I am convinced that the dramaturgical and comic structures deployed by the dramatist have still not been fully identified or explored. This book is only a minimal response to this perceived gap. By applying a dramaturgical analysis to the roles of the *raisonneurs*, it aims to show how such an approach is a necessary preliminary step to crucial matters of interpretation. There are certainly critics who have approached the *raisonneurs* with theatrical considerations in mind, and they might be surprised by these claims; but like others who have tackled the *raisonneurs*, these critics focus their interpretations on a few select passages rather than on the entirety of their roles.

My choice of a highly contested subject matter inevitably inflects the tenor of the book towards polemic. I hope all those critics with whom I disagree will accept my gratitude for the stimulation and provocation they have provided. I should single out my two close colleagues, Richard Parish and Jonathan Mallinson, who appear in the chapters on Cléante and Philinte respectively. I should also mention Noël Peacock and his article of 1981 advancing a comic interpretation of the *raisonneurs'* role. It is my sustained engagement with this article while teaching Molière, at first to support its findings and ultimately to question them, that led me to write this book.

The Introduction sets out the terms of this Preface more fully, and the first chapter surveys the history of criticism of the *raisonneurs* before explaining my analytical approach. Readers will make more sense of the rest of the book if they read these two opening parts first. The chapters on individual plays, however, though written to be read throughout, are so subdivided as to make partial reading possible. They are in effect linear commentaries on the *raisonneur* roles, and while I argue that the roles need to be interpreted as part of a theatrical continuum, which my analyses aim to conjure up, my use of sub-headings will enable readers readily to locate discussions of those parts of the roles that interest them most.

I have written the book with fellow academics and students in mind, but my analysis of each play contains the seeds of a theatrical production. If actors and directors had time to read books like this, I should like to think that this one would have useful things to say to them about possibilities for interpreting the roles of Molière's *raisonneurs* and his foolish protagonists.

I should like to thank the University of Oxford and the Warden and Fellows of Keble College, Oxford for granting me a whole year's sabbatical leave, which made the writing of this book possible. I am grateful for invaluable practical assistance offered by Jane Olds, the Fellows' Secretary at Keble College. I should also like to thank Robert McBride for sending me a version in French of his article on the *raisonneurs* that appeared in a Japanese-language edition of Molière's plays in 2002. The staff at Oxford University Press, especially Andrew McNeillie, Clare Jenkins, Jacqueline Baker, and Susan Beer, have been unfailingly helpful and encouraging in the later stages of the book's genesis. For practical help with the index I am grateful to Alex Midha. And finally I must thank Russell Goulbourne, David Maskell, and Olive Sayce, whose careful readings of the book in typescript have made it better than it would otherwise have been. My parents have never ceased to offer support of other kinds and it is to them that I dedicate this book.

Michael Hawcroft

Contents

Note on References

All references to Molière's plays and references to many of the texts surrounding the initial performance and publication of these plays are to the Pléiade edition of his *Œuvres complètes* by Georges Couton, 2 vols. (Paris: Gallimard, 1971). Short references to plays take the form, for example, '3. 6' (meaning act 3, scene 6) or '(1223)' (meaning line 1223). Page references to this edition take the form '*OC*, I, 1445' (meaning volume I, page 1445).

Introduction

Je me sens en humeur de disputer contre vous.[1]

According to Bray, 'Molière ne pense qu'à nous faire rire', but for Defaux, 'Molière est la pensée même.'[2] These are the opposite poles around, and between, which most Molière criticism moves.

A decisive issue in this ongoing critical controversy is the significance to be attached to Molière's so-called *raisonneurs*. These are characters like Chrysalde in *L'École des femmes* and Cléante in *Tartuffe*. Certain critics think they are the vehicle for a message that they believe Molière wants to convey to his audience. This is the view that led to their baptism as *raisonneurs* in 1890 by the critic Brunetière.[3] Others see them as pompous posers, who are themselves the object of Molière's comic scrutiny.

When Dandrey's article 'La Comédie du ridicule' was published in 1993, it was accompanied by a transcript of the debate that followed his paper when it had been delivered in the context of a conference.[4] The debate turned to the topic of the *raisonneurs* and pitted Dandrey's views against Biet's. Biet is sceptical of the value of what the *raisonneurs* have to say and thinks that they are often held up to ridicule:

---

[1] Sganarelle in *Dom Juan* (3. 1).

[2] René Bray, *Molière: homme de théâtre* (Paris: Mercure de France, 1954), p. 37; Gérard Defaux, *Molière ou les métamorphoses du comique: de la comédie morale au triomphe de la folie* (Lexington: French Forum, 1980; 2nd edn, Paris: Klincksieck, 1992), p. 25.

[3] Ferdinand Brunetière, 'Études sur le xviiᵉ siècle 4', *Revue des deux mondes*, 100 (1890), 649–87.

[4] Patrick Dandrey, 'La Comédie du ridicule', *Littératures classiques*, supplement (1993), 7–23.

Ces personnages, qui sont théoriquement des personnages de bon sens, sont souvent eux-mêmes atteints par un certain type de ridicule [...] Je ne crois pas qu'on puisse faire confiance à ces raisonneurs. Or, il se trouve assez souvent qu'on leur fait un peu trop confiance dans les écrits critiques.

(p. 22)

Dandrey, however, is inclined to take the views expressed by the *raisonneurs* seriously:

Mais si on prend Béralde, si on prend Ariste, si on prend Philinte etc, je crois que dans l'ensemble, quand même, on peut les prendre au "sérieux", avec beaucoup de guillemets.

(pp. 22–3)

Summing up, Dandrey admits the difficulty of the problem: 'Le problème des raisonneurs, c'est une immense question, c'est difficile' (p. 22). This books aims to make a contribution to the understanding of this problem. It proposes a new approach to the interpretation of the role of these characters that combines a focus on both dramaturgical and comic structures in the light of known performance styles adopted by Molière and his troupe of actors in the seventeenth century.

The book's ambitions are both modest and immodest. Modest, in the sense that the focus might appear narrow; it is exclusively on the *raisonneurs*, to whom no whole book has so far been devoted (though numerous articles and chapters have). Immodest, in the sense that it claims to offer an approach which suggests limitations in approaches previously adopted and has implications for the interpretation of Molière's comedies more generally.

I need to insist on the novelty of the approach that I have adopted. Colleagues have sometimes been sceptical about whether there is anything new to be said: 'Hasn't Fargher said that?', 'Didn't Defaux deal with the *raisonneurs*?' Fargher thinks them risible fools;[5] Defaux the eloquent exponents of humanist wisdom. Reading the critics on the *raisonneurs*, I was increasingly struck by three problems. One was that many critics who express quite contrary opinions to those of their predecessors do not often engage with their predecessors' views.

---

[5] Richard Fargher, 'Molière and his Reasoners' in *Studies in French Literature presented to H. W. Lawton*, ed. J. C. Ireson (Manchester University Press, 1968), pp. 105–20.

So what happens when these views are set alongside each other? I was also struck by the way in which critical opinion is formed on the basis of a small number of passages and quotations (nearly always the same ones). So what if *all* the lines spoken by the *raisonneurs* are used as the basis for an interpretation of their role rather than a select few? And finally I was struck by the predominantly reductionist approach of most critics, who treat the *raisonneurs* as a group that apparently lends itself to one global critical assessment. But what if each *raisonneur* is assessed separately in the context in which he appears? Chapter 1 is a survey of the contributions of critics since the end of the nineteenth century, and illustrates the problems to which, in my view, their work gives rise.

It is the need to address these problems that has shaped the method of presentation adopted in this book. Each *raisonneur* is discussed in a separate chapter, which allows the particular circumstances of a given play to prevail in the interpretation of his role rather than a perceived need to form a single overall assessment of the *raisonneurs* collectively. Chapters 2–6 each consider the entirety of the role of a *raisonneur*, and are structured as a linear exploration of the role as the play develops. To avoid the perils of selective interpretation and to give a sense of dramatic performance as a developing continuum, the chapters have been written as a sustained critical commentary on those scenes in which the *raisonneur* is implicated. I have tried to write in such a way as to conjure up the text fully so as to spare readers from having to move constantly between my commentary and the text of the play, but readers will certainly find it useful to have Molière's text close to hand. In addition, I have constantly quoted the views of other critics. This allows their contradictory views to be set alongside one another in the face of the textual evidence; it allows me to create a dialogue between them that is sometimes missing in their own writings. I also quote previous critics in order to make clear how my own approach and findings differ from theirs.

My approach, sketched out in this Introduction and discussed more fully in the last section of Chapter 1, makes recurrent appeal to the notion of dramaturgy. In one sense it is inspired by Bray's famous claim that there is no such thing as a *raisonneur* in Molière's plays and that every character fulfils a dramatic function (p. 32). Bray was writing specifically against the view that the so-called *raisonneurs* are

Molière's mouthpiece, and many subsequent critics, especially those who find the *raisonneurs* themselves the subject of comedy, would claim to be inspired by Bray's claim. But what neither Bray nor these subsequent critics have done is to examine the function of each of these characters in the context of the dramatic action to which they contribute.

I use the word dramaturgy in order to refer specifically to Molière's art as a constructor of dramatic actions. Molière certainly wanted to make audiences laugh—this is the achievement on which he resoundingly congratulates himself in the *Critique de l'École des femmes* and this is why my readings are constantly attentive to comic structures. But he needed a vehicle in which to deploy his comic techniques, and that vehicle is a dramatic action. It has never been fashionable to think of Molière as a maker of plots, since his comic techniques predominate and can leave the plots looking rather threadbare. But his plays do (mostly) have plots. They have a climactic action (often, but not always, a marriage) which is the result of the efforts of characters working against a number of obstacles. Characterization and dialogue in Molière's plays can be understood in terms of its contribution to the dual (and sometimes overlapping) aims of prompting laughter and advancing (or delaying) the dramatic action. As Bourqui has pointed out, a dramaturgical study of Molière is lacking ('travail d'envergure encore jamais entrepris').[6] This book will not fill that gap, but will exploit the notion of dramaturgy as a way of approaching the roles of the *raisonneurs*.

Molière often (though not always) identifies quite clearly the contribution to the dramatic action that the *raisonneur* is there to make. Béralde, in *Le Malade imaginaire*, for instance, comes to speak to Argan with the sole aim of promoting Angélique's wedding to Cléante. I shall argue that if the words of the *raisonneurs* are read in the light of their allotted role within the dramatic action and with due attention to Molière's constant deployment of comic techniques, their words and actions can be understood afresh. Béralde emerges as neither humanist sage nor eccentric fool. He deploys a range of rhetorical devices and arguments that might shake Argan's

---

6 Claude Bourqui, *Les Sources de Molière: répertoire critique des sources littéraires et dramatiques* (Paris: SEDES, 1999), p. 13.

superstitious dependence on his doctor just enough for him to let his daughter marry someone who is not a member of the medical profession. While Molière derives comedy from Argan's reaction to Béralde's speeches and from Béralde's ironic mode of expression, the speeches themselves are determined first and foremost by his role in the dramatic action, which is to say whatever he can do that might help the cause of Cléante and Angélique. His speeches are rhetorical strategies rather than coherent visions.

The dramaturgical approach, therefore, offers a wider perspective in which to view the apparently sententious utterances of the *raisonneur* and his interaction with the foolish protagonist. It seems to me that, by looking at these aspects of their role in isolation from the broader context of a developing dramatic action, critics have limited the evidence on which they have based their assessments of these characters.

I should comment on my use of the word *raisonneurs*. What I mean by it is that body of characters whom modern critics have so designated. Anybody who reads these critics will realize that the concept of the *raisonneur* is a highly unstable one. Not only do critics attribute very variable characteristics to the role; they do not even agree on the characters to be so designated. For the purposes of this book I have looked in detail at those five to whom almost all critics have accorded the designation: Ariste in *L'École des maris*, Chrysalde in *L'École des femmes*, Cléante in *Tartuffe*, Philinte in *Le Misanthrope*, and Béralde in *Le Malade imaginaire*. In the Conclusion, I attend to other characters who have sometimes attracted the same label and discuss the role in the context of Molière's dramaturgical strategies more generally. The approach, the evidence and the argument of this book all reinforce the critical instability of the term *raisonneur*. So my use of it should be interpreted as ironical. It identifies for readers familiar with Molière criticism a variable group of problematic characters, whose variously alleged similarities it is apparently not easy to sustain.

That said, readers prefer orientation to disorientation at the beginning of a book. So while insisting on the need to avoid reductive interpretations and on the variety of ways in which Molière integrates these characters into the dramaturgical and comic structures of his plays, I shall help readers by saying first that I

do not, in general, think that the *raisonneurs* are themselves comic
characters, though they are vital, and varied, elements in the plays'
comic structures; and secondly that, though I do not dismiss their
occasionally sententious utterances as ridiculously pompous, I do not
believe that their role is to expound the wisdom of humanism or
honnêteté. In the readings that follow, sententious utterances—and
all other utterances—emerge as rhetorical strategies deployed by
the *raisonneur* in a dramatic engagement with an interlocutor and
engineered by Molière to underpin a play's dramaturgical and comic
structures.

1

The *Raisonneurs* and the Critics

Monsieur, cette matière est toujours délicate.[1]

The so-called *raisonneurs* have preoccupied most critics of Molière since the beginning of the twentieth century, and rightly so, since an understanding of their function is central to any interpretation of his plays. Almost no critic fails to take a stand on them. This chapter presents chronologically and schematically the conflicting opinions on the *raisonneurs*, and introduces critics with whom the following chapters will continue to engage. The final part of the chapter explains the dramaturgical and comic perspectives adopted for the textual analyses in the remainder of the book.

SEVENTEENTH-CENTURY DEFINITIONS

The ghost of Molière might be surprised by the fuss to which the *raisonneurs* have given rise. His pronouncements on comedy do not identify them as a character type, and do not use the term *raisonneur*. In so far as the word was used in the seventeenth century, it had connotations quite different from its modern critical senses. In the *Dictionnaire de l'Académie* of 1694, *raisonneur* has a pejorative definition. It means a tiresome, verbose bore who uses bad arguments: 'Il ne se prend ordinairement que de la mauvaise part, et ne se dit que d'une personne qui fatigue, qui importune par de longs, par

---

[1] Alceste in *Le Misanthrope* (341).

de mauvais raisonnements.'[2] Molière uses the word in this sense in his plays.

In *Le Misanthrope*, Acaste uses it in a satirical portrait of the non-appearing Damon: 'Damon, le raisonneur, qui m'a, ne vous déplaise, / Une heure, au grand soleil, tenu hors de ma chaise' (577–8); and Célimène continues the portrait, making it clear what the weaknesses of the *raisonneur* are:

> C'est un parleur étrange, et qui trouve toujours
> L'art de ne vous rien dire avec de grands discours;
> Dans les propos qu'il tient, on ne voit jamais goutte,
> Et ce n'est que du bruit de tout ce qu'on écoute.
>
> (579–82)

In *L'Avare* the tyrannical miser Harpagon uses the term to reprimand his servant La Flèche for speaking out of turn: 'Tu fais le raisonneur. Je te baillerai de ce raisonnement-ci par les oreilles' (1. 3). In *Le Médecin malgré lui* the feminine form is used cynically and pejoratively by Lucas of his wife Jacqueline in order to undermine her common-sense advice to their employer Géronte about the desirability of marrying one's daughter to a man she likes: 'Mêle-toi de donner à téter à ton enfant, sans tant faire la raisonneuse' (2. 1). In *L'École des femmes*, Arnolphe calls Agnès a 'belle raisonneuse' (1546) to evoke her insubordination, when she expresses her preference for the youthful Horace. All these occurrences confirm the pejorative connotations of the word. It is used to mock or to express irritation. The characters it refers to—the absent Damon, the servant La Flèche, the peasant's wife Jacqueline, and the seventeen-year old *ingénue* Agnès—do not add up to any single character type.

---

[2] This definition is discussed in Richard Parish, '*Le Misanthrope*: des raisonneurs aux rieurs', *French Studies*, 45 (1991), 17–35, p. 34, n. 4. For an excellent account of the term *raisonneur* and its cognates in dictionaries and in Molière's plays, see Harold Knutson, 'Yet Another Last Word on Molière's *Raisonneur*', *Theatre Survey*, 22 (1) (1981), 17–33. His 'last word' is precisely to discussion dictionary definitions of the word.

MORALIZER

Indeed Damon, La Flèche, Jacqueline and Agnès are not the characters to whom the term *raisonneurs* was applied when it was first used by the critic Brunetière in 1890 to identify a character type deployed by Molière allegedly as a way of expressing his own philosophy for the benefit of the audience. Given the amount of ink that has subsequently been spilt over this term, Brunetière's own use of it is remarkably cautious. He uses it only once, places it between hesitant *guillemets*, and, while claiming that the characters in question express Molière's message, insists that they express only a part of it: 'En fait, les "raisonneurs" de son répertoire ne jouent pas le rôle du "chœur" dans l'ancienne comédie; ils n'expriment qu'une partie de sa pensée seulement.'[3] The five characters he most obviously discusses in this connection are: Ariste in *L'École des maris*, Chrysalde in *L'École des femmes*, Philinte in *Le Misanthrope*, Cléante in *Tartuffe*, and Béralde in *Le Malade imaginaire*.

However tentative Brunetière's view that there is a character type which acts, to some extent, as the dramatist's mouthpiece, it was adopted by his successors, Faguet and Michaut. But all three critics give somewhat differing accounts of the character in question and the supposed message. Brunetière believes that Molière's message is 'une philosophie de la nature' (p. 654): 'fils de Montaigne et de Rabelais [...] nul n'a été plus libre que Molière, plus dégagé de toute croyance, plus indifférent en matière de religion' (p. 686); and he identifies the proponents of this message as Cléante, Philinte, Ariste, and Béralde (pp. 657, 676). Faguet, who takes up the term *raisonneur* and applies it specifically to Ariste in *Les Femmes savantes*, derives a different message from Brunetière, a message of social conformity and moderation:

N'être pas méchant, mais n'être pas bon, n'être pas vicieux, mais à n'avoir qu'une vertu traitable et une sagesse avec sobriété; en un mot être médiocre,

---

[3] Ferdinand Brunetière, 'Études sur le xviiᵉ siècle 4', *Revue des deux mondes*, 100 (1890), 649–87, p. 671.

toujours médiocre, médiocre en tout, médiocre avec obstination, impla-
cablement médiocre.

> Voilà la morale de l'expérience.
> C'est exactement celle de Molière.[4]

The latest of these three critics, Michaut, is very confident about
Molière's use of the message-bearing character type, and identifies a
more varied and larger group than Brunetière:

> Jamais Molière n'a dissimulé son opinion personnelle; toujours, au contraire,
> il a chargé un de ses personnages, et quelquefois plusieurs, de le représenter
> et de l'exprimer très clairement. Dans *Les Précieuses*, c'est La Grange et, à
> certains égards, Sganarelle; dans *L'École des maris* Ariste, dans *L'École des
> femmes* Chrysalde, dans *Le Tartuffe* Cléante, dans *Dom Juan*, Elvire, le Pauvre,
> dom Carlos et dom Louis, dans *L'Amour médecin* Filerin, dans *Les Femmes
> savantes* Henriette et Clitandre, dans *Le Malade imaginaire* Béralde.[5]

After some hesitation, he decides to incorporate into the group
Philinte, 'qui est, sans conteste, le porte-parole de l'auteur' (p. 228).
All of them, for Michaut, are 'représentants du bon sens' (p. 227). The
approach of Brunetière, Faguet and Michaut needs to be understood
in the context of the educational system of the Third Republic, which
used the works of Molière to create the myth of the state, turning
ancien régime values into the secular and bourgeois ones that the
Republic promoted.[6] But even beyond the Third Republic and for
writers with very different political and religious values, the myth of
the authoritative *raisonneur* will prove tenacious. Writing in 1958,
François Mauriac conjures up these characters in almost apocalyptic
terms: 'Les raisonneurs de ses pièces monteront un jour à la tribune
de la Convention. Ils sont tout près d'enfler la voix.'[7]

---

[4] Émile Faguet, *En lisant Molière: l'homme et son temps, l'écrivain et son œuvre*
(Paris: Hachette, 1914), p. 132 (for Ariste, see p. 46).

[5] Gustave Michaut, *Les Luttes de Molière* (Paris: Hachette, 1925), p. 227.

[6] Ralph Albanese, *Molière à l'école républicaine: de la critique universitaire aux
manuels scolaires (1870–1914)* (Saratago, CA: ANMA Libri, 1992) (esp. pp. 124 (on
Brunetière), p. 135 (on Faguet), p. 141 (on Michaut)). See also C. E. J. Caldicott,
La Carrière de Molière entre protecteurs et éditeurs (Amsterdam: Rodopi, 1998),
ch. 1.

[7] François Mauriac, *D'un bloc-notes à l'autre 1952–69*, ed. Jean Touzot
(Paris: Bartillat, 2004), p. 442 (first published in *Le Figaro littéraire*, 24 May
1958).

DRAMATIC FOIL

Whether the mid-twentieth-century suspicion of authorial intention was exercising its influence, or the rise of the so-called New Criticism, there was a groundswell of opinion against the view that Molière used characters to express his opinion, and the critical pendulum swung in the opposite direction. The *raisonneurs* were written out of the script, and for some critics Molière became a brilliant creator of plays and performances with minimal intellectual content.

The most vigorous expression of this reaction is to be found in the work of Moore and Bray.[8] Moore's ground-breaking work swept aside the approaches and interpretations of his predecessors by taking as his starting point 'the abandonment of all assumptions regarding [Molière's] philosophy and his emotions, thus allowing us freedom to interpret comedies as comedies and their author as an artist' (p. 5). This stance leads Moore to make the following comments on the *raisonneurs*: that they express sober, colourless views; that these views are those of Molière's average spectator, and not his own; that such characters exist for an aesthetic, not an ideological, reason (p. 74). This is how he sums up their aesthetic function: 'They ensure symmetry and roundness of comic presentation. Excess is the more distinguishable if its opposite is exhibited at the same time. Sense shows up nonsense, sobriety offsets bad temper' (p. 74). Moore does not go so far as to say that Molière himself has nothing to say to us. But he is insistent that we do not hear it from any single character: 'The author's view (if this be the right expression) is in the all-embracing conception of a situation in which all characters of his play are set' (p. 126). And he does not think it easy to determine what that view is: 'We may not be able to say with any certainty what Molière thought about religion, nature or marriage' (p. 133).

Bray goes even further than Moore and throws the baby out with the bathwater. For him there is no reason to suppose that Molière had anything to tell his audiences. He was simply an artisan of the

---

[8] W. G. Moore, *Molière: A New Criticism* (Oxford: Clarendon Press, 1949); René Bray, *Molière: homme de théâtre* (Paris: Mercure de France, 1954).

stage whose concern was to entertain. The existence of the *raisonneurs* is owed, in his view, to a body of critics who thought that Molière must have had a message to convey to the audience and that it must have been a sensible one. Bray categorically denies the existence of any such character type: 'Il n'y a pas de *raisonneurs* dans le théâtre de Molière' (p. 32). Every character has only a dramatic function: 'Chaque personnage est exigé par sa fonction dramatique, non par une prétendue fonction morale inventée par la critique' (p. 32). Bray does not deny that there are ideas in Molière's theatre, but sees them as kaleidoscopically complex, expressed by a huge variety of characters, both sane and crazy, and he attaches no special significance to those spoken by the *raisonneurs*:

> Il y a dans ses comédies nombre d'idées, portant sur toutes sortes de questions qui se posaient devant son temps; mais ces idées ne sont pas contenues dans les seuls discours des prétendus *raisonneurs*. Elles ne sont pas l'apanage des personnages de bon sens: les ridicules, les passionnés, les maniaques, les vicieux ont aussi leurs idées. L'artiste qu'est Molière n'est pas plus proche des uns que des autres.
>
> (p. 36)

Except for those expressed in the polemical *Critique de l'École des femmes* and *L'Impromptu de Versailles*, written explicitly to defend *L'École des femmes*, Bray finds no authorial ideas and he inquires no further into them.

The studies of Moore and Bray have generally been thought to have had a salutary influence on Molière studies. They have led to a much better understanding of his work as writer, actor, and manager. But these two critics did not have the last word on the *raisonneurs*. Indeed they have probably nourished studies of this character type. Despite their scepticism about the word, they both use the word *raisonneur* much more frequently than the predecessors whose work they are criticizing. And since Moore and Bray, scholars have continued to grapple with the problem of these apparently unfathomable characters. The polarization between on the one hand the *raisonneur* as spokesman and on the other the *raisonneur* as having a purely dramatic function, which is to offset the folly of the protagonist, has led to a variety of nuanced views, but all of them can be situated with respect to this basic dichotomy.

COMIC IRONIST

Liberated, as they saw it, from the need to take the *raisonneurs* seriously and propelled by a mission to explore their aesthetic function, some
critics have gone further than Moore and Bray. Fargher, Herzel and
Peacock have all, in different ways and to different degrees, found that
the *raisonneurs* not only offset the folly of the protagonist; they are
themselves comic creations, at whom Molière wanted his audiences
to laugh.[9] Fargher was the first to spell out his belief in the comic
properties of the *raisonneurs*, beginning with Philinte, who, he claims,
is 'a prey on occasion to minor folly' and therefore 'a comic figure in
his own right' (p. 106). It is a pattern Fargher finds repeated elsewhere:
'to a greater or lesser extent, all Molière's reasoners conform to a basic
pattern, which is farcical' (p. 106). Fargher does not quibble with the
use of the word 'reasoner', since he is happy to identify in Molière a
body of characters whose role he sees as being to give advice; but he
interprets the term ironically and pejoratively (as it was interpreted
in the seventeenth century). He believes that Molière's *raisonneurs*
become ridiculous because of the way they give their advice (p. 106).
They give it 'inopportunely' (p. 108), they speak with 'excess'
(p. 108), they are 'besotted with their own sagacity' (p. 109), they
are 'inept' or 'platitudinous' (p. 110). For Fargher, there is only one
voice of 'self-evidently true and acceptable' doctrine in Molière's plays
(p. 113), and that is the voice of Louis XIV reported by his official in
the last scene of *Tartuffe*, penetrating the criminal deceit that would
otherwise have brought the action to a catastrophic conclusion.

Like Fargher, Herzel thinks it wrong to claim that there are no
raisonneurs in Molière, since there are 'obvious similarities between,
at a minimum, Ariste, Chrysalde, Cléante, and Béralde' (p. 565).
Herzel is ready to acknowledge differences between these characters.
He finds, for instance, that an early *raisonneur* like Ariste in *L'École*

---

[9] Richard Fargher, 'Molière and his Reasoners' in *Studies in French Literature
presented to H. W. Lawton*, ed. J. C. Ireson and others (Manchester University Press,
1968), pp. 105–20; Roger W. Herzel, 'The Function of the *Raisonneur* in Molière's
Comedy', *Modern Language Notes*, 90 (1975), 564–75; Noël Peacock, 'The Comic
Role of the *Raisonneur* in Molière's Theatre', *Modern Language Review*, 76 (1981),
298–310.

des maris expresses a social norm, against which the folly of Sganarelle
can be best appreciated (p. 568), and that Molière's last *raisonneur*,
Béralde in *Le Malade imaginaire*, expresses Molière's own views on
doctors (p. 567). But the most insistent pattern he identifies echoes
Fargher's. It is of the *raisonneur* who speaks 'out of fear' or with
'self-importance' (p. 569), who is 'long-winded' (p. 569) and a 'bore'
(p. 570). Herzel sums up Molière's comic handling of the *raisonneur*
as follows: '[he plays] the tyrant off against another figure, opposite in
some ways and claiming a smaller share of the audience's attention,
but equally ridiculous' (p. 570). By acknowledging that the views of
the *raisonneurs* are often expressions of a social norm and claiming
that Molière invites audiences to laugh at these characters, Herzel
opens up the way to restoring to them an ideological role, but a
subversive one. Herzel's vision invites us to see the *raisonneurs* not as
the literal spouters of Molière's views but as the tool by which Molière
prompted audiences to question the values of his contemporary
society. This is a line of argument, however, that Herzel does not
pursue.

It is Peacock who most vigorously and most persuasively puts the
case for a comic reading of the *raisonneurs*. He takes up the views of
a group of critics who also followed in the footsteps of Moore and
Bray, including Lawrence, Eustis, and McBride.[10] These critics believe
that the words of the *raisonneurs* are basically sensible, but they go
further than to say that their role simply highlights the folly of the
monomaniacs. They present the *raisonneurs* essentially as ironists. All
of them stress the irony deployed by the *raisonneurs* at the expense of
the protagonists. For Lawrence, they 'engage the comic character in
combat and [...] inundate him with irony without fear of a beating'.[11]
For Eustis, they are like the detached and ironical observers in

---

[10] Francis L. Lawrence, 'The *Raisonneur* in Molière', *L'Esprit Créateur*, 6 (1966),
156–66; F. L. Lawrence, *Molière: The Comedy of Unreason* (New Orleans: Tulane
Studies in Romance Languages and Literatures, 1968) (ch. 2 of this book is a version
of the author's article); Alvin Eustis, *Molière as Ironic Contemplator* (The Hague,
Paris: Mouton, 1973); Robert McBride, 'La Question du *raisonneur* dans les *écoles* de
Molière', *Dix-septième siècle*, 113 (1976), 59–73. The comic view of the *raisonneur* is
also held by Jeanne Haight (though without supporting analysis) in *The Concept of
Reason in French Classical Literature 1635–1690* (University of Toronto Press, 1982):
'the arguments of these characters are also often ridiculous' (p. 49).

[11] 'The *Raisonneur* in Molière', p. 157.

some Greek comedies, causing the protagonists 'to say even greater absurdities than they would otherwise' (p. 185). For McBride, both Ariste and Chrysalde determine the comic perspective in which the audience is intended to view the dramatic action; but Chrysalde is distinguished by the markedly ironic tone he adopts towards Arnolphe. He is the 'spectateur ironique' of Arnolphe's folly (p. 68).

In celebrating the comic role of the *raisonneurs*, Peacock takes on board the ironic stance that these characters adopt, but in addition makes the point that they are also the victims of Molière's irony (p. 299). In support of this claim, he elaborates points made embryonically by Fargher and Herzel. He begins by situating the *raisonneurs* with respect to the comic theory sketched out in the *Lettre sur la comédie de l'imposteur*, inspired by Molière, if not written by him. It is a theory of the ridiculous that has often been applied to Molière's protagonists, but never, before Peacock, to the *raisonneurs*:

> Si le ridicule consiste dans quelque disconvenance, il s'ensuit que tout mensonge, déguisement, fourberie, dissimulation, toute apparence différente du fond, enfin toute contrariété entre actions qui procèdent d'un même principe, est essentiellement ridicule.
>
> (*OC*, I, 1178)

For Peacock, the *raisonneurs* believe they are coherent; and they invite the audience's laughter because Molière the dramatist fragments that coherence with powerful ironies. They may think they give good advice, but they give it in such self-congratulatory or self-righteous tones that they cannot be taken seriously (p. 305). They may look on the folly of the protagonists with pellucid irony, but they are comically blind to any failings of their own (p. 306). They try strenuously to help, but prove risibly ineffectual (p. 307). Peacock follows Moore's lead but the distance he has travelled is considerable and his conclusion distinctive:

> The role of the *raisonneur* is more of a complement than a foil to the main character, and, in a more subtle form, the reverse side, as it were, of the *imaginaire*'s folly. If this role represents the norm of the plays in which the character appears, it is a comic, theatrical norm, a secondary, ironic manifestation of the incoherence evident within the main character, and different from the reality of the audience.   (p. 309)

So powerful was the trend for interpreting the *raisonneurs* ironically or comically that in 1994 Shaw summed up the matter as follows: 'The *raisonneur* theory is now largely discredited. It is accepted that characters like Philinte, Chrysalde, and Béralde are not simply spokesmen for the author.'[12]

HONNÊTE HOMME

If I have dwelt on Peacock's views, it is because the proponents of a reaction against the trend set by Moore and Bray do not in their bibliographies and discussions seem familiar with his work. The work of two influential French scholars, Defaux and Dandrey, seems at first glance to take us back full circle to a view of the *raisonneur* as the voice of reason and more specifically of a humanist-inspired seventeenth-century *honnêteté*.[13] Both offer different visions of Molière, Defaux tracing an evolution in his plays from moralistic comedy to comedy rejoicing in human folly, Dandrey seeking instead to demonstrate a constant preoccupation through all the plays with the depiction of the ridiculous. But both write against the approach to the *raisonneurs* adopted by Bray, Moore and their followers. Both take seriously what the *raisonneurs* have to say.

In approaching the *raisonneur* as some kind of sage or *honnête homme*, however, Defaux and Dandrey do not at all wish to reassert the readings of Brunetière, Faguet or Michaut. While these earlier critics had thought that the *raisonneur* was Molière's spokesman, they had, in their various ways, derived a message, suitable for schoolchildren, of social conformity to the secular and bourgeois tenets of the Third Republic. Defaux and Dandrey, by contrast, rely, for their approach, on an overall reassessment of the moral stance

---

[12] David Shaw, 'Molière and the Doctors', *Nottingham French Studies*, 33 (1994), 133–42, p. 140.

[13] Gérard Defaux, *Molière ou les métamorphoses du comique: de la comédie morale au triomphe de la folie*, Lexington: French Forum, 1980, 2nd edn, Paris: Klincksieck, 1992, and 'Un Point chaud de la critique moliéresque: Molière et ses raisonneurs', *Travaux de linguistique et de littérature*, 18 (1980), 115–32; Patrick Dandrey, *Molière ou l'esthétique du ridicule*, Paris: Klincksieck, 1992.

of Molière's comedies made in the 1960s by Morel, who resituated
the dramatist's apparent message of social conformity and mediocrity
in the context of seventeenth-century theories of *honnêteté*.[14] In the
Nicomachean Ethics, Aristotle had defined virtue as the mid-course
between two opposing vices.[15] It is a definition that was taken up by the
Latins, Horace, Cicero and Seneca, and that infused humanist writing
in the sixteenth century. 'L'archer qui outrepasse le blanc faut,' says
Montaigne, 'comme celuy qui n'y arrive pas'.[16] The same approach
to virtue pervaded seventeenth-century writing on behaviour, both
religious and secular. François de Sales in his *Introduction à la vie
dévote* recommends that one should 'fuir les deux extrémités'.[17] The
abbé de Bellegarde in his *Réflexions sur le ridicule et sur les moyens
de l'éviter* claims that 'tout excès est vicieux' and that 'le grand art
de plaire consiste à trouver le milieu entre trop et trop peu: ce
tempérament fait la perfection des vertus humaines'.[18]

By means of such recontextualization, Morel invites us to look at
Molière's mediocrity, the golden mean, in an early modern, rather
than a modern, perspective. Seen thus, mediocrity is not about easy
and convenient compromises. It rather represents '[le lieu] de la
perfection dans une sérénité conquise'.[19] It is historical change that
explains our modern misconstruction of the mediocrity that is the
goal of the seventeenth-century *honnête homme*: 'Le juste milieu de
l'honnêteté n'apparaît fade qu'aux époques où cette essentielle vertu
[...] ne se trouve plus à la base de la vie sociale.'[20] Hence Morel's
injunction to approach Molière's comedies through the eyes of two

---

[14] Jacques Morel, 'Molière et la dramaturgie de l'honnêteté', *L'Information littéraire*,
15 (5) (1963), 185–91 (reprinted under the title of 'Molière et les honnêtes gens' in
his *Agréables Mensonges: essais sur le théâtre français du XVIIe siècle*, Paris: Klincksieck,
1991, pp. 277–88); and his 'Médiocrité et perfection dans la France du xviie siècle',
Revue d'histoire littéraire de la France, 69 (1969), 441–50.

[15] *L'Éthique à Nicomaque*, ed. R. A. Gautier and J. Y. Jolif, 2nd edn (Louvain-la-
Neuve: Peeters, 2002), I, 2, 1107 a 2, p. 45.

[16] Montaigne, *Essais*, 3 vols., ed. Pierre Villey and V.-L. Saulnier (Paris: Presses
Universitaires de France, 1965), i, p. 198 (bk i, ch. 30).

[17] Saint François de Sales, *L'Introduction à la vie dévote* in his *Œuvres*, ed. André
Ravier and Roger Devos (Paris: Gallimard, 1969), p. 219 (iii.30).

[18] L'abbé de Bellegarde, *Réflexions sur le ridicule et sur les moyens de l'éviter* (Paris:
Jean Guignard, 1696), p. 368, p. 369.

[19] Morel, 'Médiocrité et perfection', p. 449.

[20] Morel, 'Molière et les honnêtes gens', p. 288.

self-evidently sensible characters in his polemical play *La Critique de l'École des femmes*: 'Si [...] nous assistons à la comédie avec les yeux de Dorante ou d'Uranie, ceux de la raison, de la politesse et de cette sorte de naturel qu'inspire l'honnêteté, nous nous tiendrons au point exact d'où s'organise la perspective comique.'[21] This is also the view of Howarth who says of all the characters he describes as *raisonneurs*: 'It would surely not be unreasonable to see their urbane, civilised manner, and the way of life they practise, as an illustration, if not of the aristocratic ideal formulated by the Chevalier de Méré, at any rate of the code of *honnêteté* as it was accepted by some of his less exacting contemporaries.'[22]

Shored up by his vast knowledge of humanist scholarship, Defaux goes further than Morel and Howarth, claiming that the *raisonneurs* are the purveyors of humanist wisdom: 'Ariste, Chrysalde, Uranie, Cléante, Elmire et Philinte parlent exactement comme leur siècle. Ils en expriment toute la sagesse adulte. Sagesse qui a d'ailleurs d'incontestables lettres de noblesse.'[23] So Ariste speaks just like seventeenth-century treatises on civility (p. 100), Chrysalde is characterized by 'le bon sens et le sérieux fondamental' (p. 103), Cléante by 'sa lucidité et son fin discernement' (p. 105). Defaux mocks Bray for blithely dismissing the thinker in Molière, and points out the contemporary evidence for serious moral implications in his comedies. He quotes for instance the claim in the *Lettre sur la comédie de l'imposteur* that ridicule is 'l'une des plus sublimes matières de la véritable morale'.[24] While agreeing with Moore that the *raisonneur* does indeed show up the folly of the protagonist, Defaux believes that this aesthetic function is all the more effective because of the ideological function that the role also fulfils. Because the *raisonneurs* are the repositories of such time-honoured wisdom, they are better placed to highlight folly than if their common sense was merely banal. Defaux sums up his view of their role with his characteristically persuasive Ciceronian phrasing:

Le *raisonneur* est le personnage qui, par son caractère *raisonnable*, son idéal de mesure et de médiocrité, son 'naturel', son 'honnêteté' et sa lucidité,

---

[21] Morel, 'Molière et les honnêtes gens', p. 287.

[22] W. D. Howarth, *Molière: A Playwright and his Audience* (Cambridge University Press, 1982), p. 246.

[23] Defaux, *Molière ou les métamorphoses*, p. 93.

[24] Defaux, 'Un Point chaud', p. 118; *OC*, i, p. 1173.

assure sur scène la présence de la norme: celui à partir duquel s'organise, indiscutablement, la perspective comique, s'affirme avec force la vocation didactique de la comédie, sa nature essentiellement morale; celui donc auquel le spectateur, pour lequel la pièce est écrite, s'identifie spontanément, riant quand il rit, approuvant ce qu'il approuve, condamnant ce qu'il condamne.[25]

The *raisonneur* is a thoroughly admirable character and dramatically necessary for that very reason. Defaux could scarcely give a more resounding response to Bray's claim that 'Il n'y a pas de raisonneurs dans le théâtre de Molière' when he writes: 'Il suffit pourtant de relire les comédies pour s'apercevoir que les raisonneurs existent, qu'ils raisonnent d'abondance.'[26]

Like Defaux, Dandrey also admires the *raisonneurs*, but above all for the critical lucidity that dominates their discourse. He thinks of them as a dramatic device akin to the chorus in Greek tragedy. They pass sensible judgements: 'Comme le chœur, le raisonneur s'offre à l'auteur pour relayer une opinion empreinte de sagesse.'[27] He thinks that some of them clearly express Molière's own opinions: 'Cléante, Béralde, Dorante dans *La Critique de l'École des femmes*, Brécourt dans *L'Impromptu de Versailles* peuvent être considérés sans conteste, pour partie et totalité de leur rôle, comme des porte-parole de Molière' (p. 199). Whether they are expressing views that are specifically Molière's or not, they are, according to Dandrey, the channel through which the moral vision of Molière's plays is conveyed, and it is a vision of rational lucidity. This is Dandrey's constant refrain: 'le raisonneur est parole incarnée, philosophe posté aux carrefours de l'action et armé de sa seule dialectique pour adapter les principes absolus de la raison à la relativité des sujets rencontrés par l'intrigue' (p. 192), 'Une lucidité rationnelle éclairant une conduite raisonnable, entendons modérée et 'philosophe', voilà à peu près ce qu'à travers les prônes de ses raisonneurs prêche la comédie de Molière' (p. 200), 'le raisonneur met le ridicule à l'épreuve de la lucidité' (p. 200), 'le raisonneur de Molière est fils de Montaigne' (p. 201). For Dandrey, the *raisonneurs* embody a message, though it resides not in the content of their speeches, but in the lucid manner in which they face up to issues.

[25] Defaux, *Molière ou les métamorphoses*, p. 109.
[26] Defaux, 'Un Point chaud', p. 118.
[27] Dandrey, *Molière ou l'esthétique*, p. 189.

His view is close to that of Calder, who sums up the *raisonneurs* as follows: 'To bring his honest and urbane spectators into the very heart of his actions, [Molière] provided them with lucid and modest spokesmen on stage [...] The *raisonneurs* themselves lay no claim to special wisdom; their only talent is to have a good uncluttered view of the things around them.'[28]

DRAMATURGY AND COMEDY

The evolution of criticism on the *raisonneurs* can be summed up as a double antithesis. Brunetière's, Faguet's and Michaut's view of them as serious spokesmen for Molière is opposed by Moore's and Bray's view of them as fulfilling a dramatic role with no ideological function. Later critics first of all refined the approach of Moore and Bray into one which stressed the comic nature of these characters, occasionally witty and ironical, often self-important, long-winded, ineffectual, quick to see the failings of others, and slow to see their own; then Defaux and Dandrey restored to them a serious ideological function as lucid commentators, informed by centuries of wisdom, taking the stance of the seventeenth-century *honnête homme*, with which Molière would have expected his audience to sympathize.

These starkly opposed views are critically teasing, not to say frustrating. For Peacock, Chrysalde becomes intoxicated with his own role and takes his ideas to absurd proportions (p. 305), but for Defaux he speaks pure gold.[29] For Herzel, Cléante is a 'ridiculous, meddling bore' (p. 570), but for Defaux he is 'non seulement le porte-parole de l'honnêteté du siècle, mais encore—mais surtout—indiscutablement celui de Molière lui-même' (p. 104). For Mallinson, between Alceste and Philinte 'one is not able simply to take sides',[30] but for Forestier 'toute la sagesse humaniste proclame que c'est Philinte qui a raison'.[31]

---

[28] Andrew Calder, *Molière: The Theory and Practice of Comedy* (London: The Athlone Press, 1993), p. 92, p. 206.

[29] Defaux, *Molière ou les métamorphoses*, p. 102.

[30] Molière, *Le Misanthrope*, ed. Jonathan Mallinson (London: Bristol Classical Press, 1996), p. xix.

[31] Georges Forestier, *Molière en toutes lettres* (Paris: Bordas, 1990), p. 148.

How can such blatantly contradictory views co-exist? And, more crucially, why is there no (or so little) dialogue between the proponents of the different views? For it is the case that the vigorous advocates of one view do not much (if at all) engage with the arguments of those who take another view. So, for instance, Peacock's sophisticated argument about the applicability of the concept of ridicule to the *raisonneurs* and his identification of their alleged character weaknesses are ignored by Dandrey, who argues for their honey-tongued lucidity. Equally, however (and for good chronological reasons), Peacock's resolute defence of the comic role of the *raisonneur* (published in 1981) does not respond to Defaux's equally resolute defence of their ideological role as embodiments of *honnêteté* (article and book both published in 1980). The critical debate on the *raisonneurs* starts to look like a *dialogue de sourds*.

Although I shall engage with the opposing views of the *raisonneurs* throughout this book, my contribution to the debate will not be to negotiate some perilous route between them. All criticism focused on the *raisonneurs* has been conducted in articles or discreet parts of books, and has therefore, of necessity, been highly selective in the deployment of evidence and argument. It seems to me that it is, in part, the consistently high degree of selectivity that has entrenched the widely divergent views.

One example will illustrate the problem: Cléante's long speech in *Tartuffe* 1.5 explaining the difference between true and false devotion. Herzel finds Cléante comically long-winded (p. 569). But what evidence does he offer? He does not quote from the speech to support his view. He tells us that it is 57 lines long, that Orgon does not want to hear it, that 'there is no reason to suppose that the audience does either', and that 'it seems clear that Molière was aiming here at one of his favourite effects, using a long-winded and impertinent speech to provoke a silent display of comic impatience'. Defaux, on the other hand, wants us to take Cléante seriously and, by way of support, he quotes three passages from this speech.[32] One is a reflexion on the desirability of mediocrity and Defaux quotes some lines from Boileau's fourth satire that make the same point. The other two concern the identification of religious hypocrisy and Defaux quotes

[32] Defaux, *Molière ou les métamorphoses*, pp. 104–8.

some phrases from Molière's prefaces and *Placets* written in defence
of the play, which also advertise the importance of distinguishing the
hypocrite. What neither Herzel nor Defaux does (Herzel not even
remotely) before passing judgement on the role of Cléante, is to look
closely at the words he speaks within their dramatic context. Both
illustrate the limitations of selective interpretation without adequate
contextualization. Hence, as a corrective, I shall offer close linear
readings of every *raisonneur* role, considering each one individually
in its entire dramatic context, rather than reductively and selectively.

A sustained dramaturgical approach to the *raisonneurs* has not
been attempted before, but its seeds can be found in some of the
contributions to the critical debate already outlined. When Bray
said 'Chaque personnage est exigé par sa fonction dramatique,
non par une prétendue fonction morale inventée par la critique'
(p. 32), he was implicitly inviting (though did not himself offer) a
dramaturgical reading of the role of every character, not only the
raisonneurs. Peacock says he will focus his article on the 'interplay
between the *raisonneur* and the main character' (p. 298), though in
practice he is keen to demonstrate their comic role and so quotes
isolated lines rather than looks at the continuum of theatrical representation. Dandrey is sensitive to the dramatic context in which
the *raisonneurs* speak. He repeatedly says that their lucid wisdom
is geared to their situation: 'le raisonneur ne demeure [...] pas
extérieur au flux de la dramaturgie', 'sa fonction consiste surtout
à approprier l'expression de la norme impérieuse qu'il édicte aux
situations relatives à propos desquelles il fait agir son esprit de
logique, de distinction, de modération' (p. 190). While these critics
acknowledge the importance of dramatic context, their conclusions
are not in practice based on substantial analyses of characters' verbal
interactions in this context. This is the gap that this book aims to
fill.

My approach to Molière's dramaturgy is specifically historical.
In fact another reason for the manifest divergences between critics
might be a tacit *parti pris* for or against a historical approach to
Molière. If the printed texts of Molière's plays are interpreted without
reference to the historical context in which Molière himself wrote
and performed them, they can be made to signify more varied, and
hence more critically discordant, things than if they are interpreted

Mile End Library
Queen Mary, University of London

Get help finding things in the library qmul.ac.uk
to check your loans & holds or to renew

Borrowed items 12/10/2012 13:55
XXXXX3232

Item Title	Due Date
Alan market and societies	18 10 2012
	05 11 2012
* Molière : bourgeois et libert...	09 11 2012
* Molière : Le Bivoir amentio...	09 11 2012
* Molière : L'école des femm...	19 10 2012
* Molière : reasoning with fig...	19 10 2012

* Indicates items borrowed today
PLEASE NOTE
If you still have overdue books on loan
you may have more fines to pay

Mile End Library
Queen Mary, University of London

Go to http://catalogue.library.qmul.ac.uk
to check your loans & holds or to renew

Borrowed items 12/10/2012 13:55
XXXXXX3232

Item Title	Due Date
Mes mauvaises pensées	19/10/2012
* Rivalry and the disruption (	09/11/2012
* Molière and modernity : ab	09/11/2012
* Molière, bourgeois et libert	09/11/2012
* Molière : traditions in critici	09/11/2012
* Molière, L'école des femme	19/10/2012
* Molière : reasoning with fo	19/10/2012

* Indicates items borrowed today
PLEASE NOTE
If you still have overdue books on loan
you may have more fines to pay

with that historical context in mind. There is a simple
this. Molière inscribed some aspects of the original pe
like gesture and tone of voice, into the written text; but
original performance is not so inscribed, and this gives modern critics
and modern directors the scope to interpret speeches in different ways
from those in which they would have been interpreted by Molière
and his own troupe of actors. However, even if many specific aspects
of the original performances are lost to us, there is enough evidence
about Molière's approach to the construction and performance of
comedy to justify reading the roles of the *raisonneurs* in this historical
perspective.

All contemporary evidence about Molière and comic performance
indicates that he wanted to make audiences laugh. When he started
writing for the Paris stage, it was not at all obvious that audience
laughter should be the absolutely core aim of the comic dramatist.
In *La Critique de l'École des femmes* he insists on the importance of
laughter. The characters in the play who are critical of *L'École des
femmes* refer to the laughter it provoked in order to attack it:

Il ne faut que voir les continuels éclats de rire que le parterre y fait. Je ne veux
point d'autre chose pour témoigner qu'elle ne vaut rien.

(Le Marquis, sc. 5)

Ne descend-il point dans quelque chose de trop comique et de trop outré au
cinquième acte [...]?

(Lysidas, sc. 6)

The play's defender Dorante celebrates the arousal of laughter
as Molière's greatest and hardest achievement: '[Dans les pièces
comiques] il y faut plaisanter; et c'est une étrange entreprise que celle
de faire rire les honnêtes gens' (sc. 6). Dominique Bertrand identifies
Molière's prominent concern with laughter as a source of originality:
'En soulignant combien le rire est essentiel à la comédie, Molière s'est
montré novateur et il a fait effectivement scandale.'[33]

Contemporary evidence makes it clear that Molière saw not only
the verbal construction of his plays as a source of laughter, but also the
manner of their physical and vocal enactment on stage. In particular, it

---

[33] Dominique Bertrand, *Dire le rire à l'âge classique: représenter pour mieux contrôler*
(Aix-en-Provence: Publications de l'Université de Provence, 1995), p. 215.

is clear that Molière, who typically reserved the biggest and most comic roles for himself, was a highly skilled comic actor.[34] His contemporary critics repeatedly criticized him for copying the exaggeratedly comic actions and gestures of the performers of the Italian troupe with whom he shared the Palais-Royal. One of the characters hostile to Molière in La Croix's dialogue *La Guerre comique*, published in 1664 in the wake of the controversy over *L'École des femmes*, suggests that Molière's skill lies in no more than adding some French words to the very physical performance style of the Italians:

Ses pièces sont-elles si belles? C'est son jeu qui pipe et qui les fait paraître. Le bourgeois ne se lassait de ne voir que les postures et les grimaces de Scaramouche et de Trivelin, et de ne pas entendre ce qu'ils disent. Molière est venu et les a copiés, Dieu sait comment; et aussitôt, alors qu'il parle un peu français, on a crié: 'Ah! l'habile homme! Il n'a jamais eu d'égal.' Il est forcé en tout ce qu'il fait; ses grimaces sont ridicules.

(*OC*, i, 1141)

Later, Le Boulanger de Chalussay, in his play *Élomire hypocondre* (1670), explicitly links Molière's desire to provoke laughter with his imitation of the Italians:

Élomire [= Molière]
Veut se rendre parfait dans l'art de faire rire:
Que fait-il, le matois, dans ce hardi dessein?
Chez le grand Scaramouche il va soir et matin.
Là, le miroir en main, et ce grand homme en face,
Il n'est contorsion, posture ni grimace,
Que ce grand écolier du plus grand des bouffons,
Ne fasse et ne refasse en cent et cent façons.

(*OC*, ii, 1238)

Evidence about the endless variety of postures and grimaces adopted by Molière suggests how much of his comedy is lost to the printed page, even though the illustrations of Pierre Brissart for the posthumous 1682 edition of his plays can, if treated with caution, be helpfully

---

[34] See W. D. Howarth, *Molière: A Playwright and his Audience*, ch. 1, and H. Gaston Hall, 'Molière's Roles Written for Himself', *Australian Journal of French Studies*, 33 (1996), 414–27.

suggestive when they depict characters originally played by the drama-tist. But if the specific details of Molière's individual performances are for the most part irretrievable, we can at least imagine in general terms the comically physical style that characterized his own acting.[35]

Consideration of performance styles is interesting in the context of the *raisonneurs* precisely because Molière himself did not play the *raisonneur* roles; he played the foolish protagonist—Sganarelle, Arnolphe, Orgon, Alceste, and Argan—with whom the *raisonneur* has to contend. What is even more interesting from the point of view of the following analyses is that, while Molière was alert to comic performance styles for actors other than himself, he did not envisage that every role should be performed for laughs. In *L'Impromptu de Versailles*, which shows Molière rehearsing his actors and giving them advice about delivery and action, he certainly tells Du Croisy how, comically, to speak the lines of a pedantic poet and Mlle Béjart how to adopt the haughty gaze of a prude. But Brécourt, who played Molière's sensible defender Dorante in *La Critique de l'École des femmes*, is explicitly not to play his role, that of an *honnête homme*, for laughs:

Pour vous, vous faites un honnête homme de cour, comme vous avez déjà fait dans *La Critique de l'École des femmes*, c'est-à-dire que vous devez prendre un air posé, un ton de voix naturel, et gesticuler le moins qu'il vous sera possible.

(sc. 1)

In other words, in contradistinction to the comic grimaces and postures that he himself so readily assumes in order to keep his audiences laughing, Molière envisages alongside, and as a contrast, an entirely poised performance. This evidence strongly invites us to read his *raisonneurs* as roles that should be performed in this way, especially in view of the discourse of *honnêteté* that Defaux finds in their speeches. The contrast between poised patience and gesticulating impatience reinforces the comic effects that the words themselves invite. We know that Ariste in *L'École des maris* and Chrysalde in

---

[35] See John Powell, 'Making Faces: Character and Physiognomy in *L'École des femmes* and *L'Avare*', *Seventeenth-Century French Studies*, 9 (1987), 94–112. On Molière's attitude to the actor's voice, see Charles Mazouer, 'Molière et la voix de l'acteur', *Littératures Classiques*, 12 (1990), 261–73.

L'École des femmes were originally played by L'Espy, then the old man of the troupe. The only surviving contemporary comment on his performance is that, contrary to expectations, he was 'inimitable' as Ariste. Cléante and Béralde were both played by La Thorillière. Mlle Poisson's eighteenth-century memoirs, if reliable, conjure up something of his appearance: 'C'était un très gracieux comédien, quoique d'une taille médiocre, mais il avait de beux yeux et de belles dents.'[36] She also comments on his consistently cheerful disposition (which did not help when he was playing tragedy). As to Philinte, he was played by one of the most reliable members of Molière's troupe, La Grange. According to Herzel, his 'contemporaries were unanimous in their praise of his vitality and his unstudied grace—qualities that they associated with both the actor and the man'.[37] Though detail is clearly lacking for the original performance style of these roles as compared to the amount of contemporary information evoking Molière's own style, this fact is in itself telling, and could be taken to confirm that foolish protagonist and *raisonneur* were performed in highly contrasting ways. The nature of this contrast will be explored in the detailed analyses contained in the following chapters.

Molière's central preoccupation with laughter affects not only the performance, but also the construction of his plays, all aspects of which are embraced by the term dramaturgy. Modern criticism has attempted to reorientate studies of seventeenth-century theatre towards the dramaturgical and away from the ideological. In a study of Corneille's tragedies, Forestier has argued forcefully and polemically that interpretations that disregard dramatic structure are built on shaky foundations.[38] At its most basic, a dramaturgical reading attends, for instance, to how the dramatic action of a tragedy has been constructed so as to lead to the denouement both plausibly and

---

[36] See Roger W. Herzel, *The Original Casting of Molière's Plays* (Ann Arbor, Michigan: UMI Research Press, 1981): Ariste (p. 42), Chrysalde (p. 46), Cléante (p. 54), Béralde (p. 79). He quotes Mlle Poisson's comments from her 'Mémoires pour servir à l'histoire du théâtre', published in the *Mercure de France*, May 1738 (p. 832), on p. 12.

[37] Roger W. Herzel, '"Much depends on the acting": The Original Cast of *Le Misanthrope*', *Publications of the Modern Language Association of America*, 95 (1980), 348–66, p. 355.

[38] Georges Forestier, *Essai de génétique théâtrale: Corneille à l'œuvre* (Paris: Klincksieck, 1996). See also his 'Dramaturgie racinienne (petit essai de génétique théâtrale)',

with appropriately tragic effects on the audience. The dramaturgical function turns out to be primary in determining what characters say and do. The question arises as to whether such readings of Molière's comedies might also prove fruitful in offering new insights into the words and actions of his characters.

In the case of Molière, however, there is a strong prejudice against taking plot construction seriously, since his comic purposes are generally thought to militate against a close attention to plot. Writing specifically about the construction of *L'École des femmes*, Conesa says: 'loin d'être linéaire, la progression dramatique de l'œuvre se présente plutôt sous forme de spirale'.[39] Going further than Conesa, Bourqui has recently argued that Molière took more from the Italians than a comic performance style, claiming that his whole dramaturgical technique is governed by a principle of comic digression, learnt from the succession of lazzi, or routines, that dominated the comic plays of the Italian performers.[40] Whereas drama in the Aristotelian mould develops a forward-moving plot in a linear style, Bourqui claims that the sinuosity of the arabesque more accurately conjures up the digressive construction of Molière's plays (p. 153), 'un nombre de scènes quasiment indépendantes maintenues ensemble par une intrigue lâche', as he says elsewhere.[41] The insight is a valuable one, since it puts the emphasis firmly on the technical virtuosity of Molière as a comic writer and performer, and Bourqui shows how numerous dialogues and actions are developed, with enormous skill, for the manifest purpose of stimulating laughter.

Littératures classiques, 26 (1996), 13–38. The way had been paved by H. T. Barnwell, *The Tragic Drama of Corneille and Racine: An Old Parallel Revisited* (Oxford: Clarendon Press, 1982).

[39] Gabriel Conesa, 'Remarques sur la structure dramatique de *L'École des femmes*', *Revue d'histoire du théâtre*, 30 (1978), 120–6 (p. 126). See also his '*Le Misanthrope* ou les limites de l'aristotélisme', *Littératures classiques*, 38 (2000), 19–29, and especially his comment that 'l'intrigue de comédie […] se présente […] comme fragmentée, accidentée, voire gratuite par endroits' (p. 20). Roger Guichemerre's consideration of ludic gratuitousness more generally in Molière's plays takes Conesa's views further in 'Gratuité et développement ludique dans les comédies de Scarron et Molière', *Littératures classiques*, 27 (1996), 281–9.

[40] Claude Bourqui and Claudio Vinti, *Molière à l'école italienne: le lazzo dans la création moliéresque* (Paris and Turin: L'Harmattan, 2003), ch. 3.

[41] Claude Bourqui, *La Commedia dell'arte: introduction au théâtre professionnel italien entre le XVIᵉ et le XVIIIᵉ siècles* (Paris: SEDES, 2000), p. 140.

And yet the plays are not simply a succession of unrelated or minimally related comic routines. Molière was well aware of the importance of dramatic structure. Dorante speaks up for *L'École des femmes* by saying that it pleased its audiences, and when he is faced with the charge that it might have broken the rules, he defends its 'exposition du sujet', 'nœud' and 'dénouement', three key components of a traditional dramatic action (*La Critique de l'École des femmes*, sc. 6). Molière's plays are held together in some kind of plot, even if it is loosely configured. Andrews, writing, like Bourqui, on the influence of the Italians on Molière, sees that comic routines are not necessarily in conflict with the development of a plot: 'such jocular units can actually do the job of advancing the plot rather than always being digressions from it'.[42] Molière's plays do tell a story, and if his comic purposes mean that he readily digresses from the story to incorporate routines likely to prompt laughter, the characters' words and actions will to some extent be determined by the need to advance the story (or at least to create the illusion that the story is advancing). This is why the analyses that follow will attend to both the dramaturgical and comic structures, to both of which the *raisonneurs* contribute.

By way of defending the moment-by-moment readings of the *raisonneur* roles that make up the body of this book, I can do no better than refer my readers to Dr Johnson contemplating how best to recommend Shakespeare. He insists that the dramatist is most effectively appreciated not through outstanding passages, but through the gradual progression of element after element:

It was said of Euripides that every verse was a precept; and it may be said of Shakespeare, that from his works may be collected a system of civil and œconomical prudence. Yet his real power is not shewn in the splendour of particular passages, but by the progress of his fable, and the tenour of his dialogue; and he that tries to recommend him by select quotations, will

---

[42] Richard Andrews, 'Arte Dialogue Structures in the Comedies of Molière' in *The Commedia dell'arte from the Renaissance to Dario Fo*, ed. Christopher Cairns (Lewiston, Queenstown, Lampeter: Edwin Mellen, 1989), pp. 142–76, p. 148. See also H. T. Barnwell's comments on the importance of plot in *Le Malade imaginaire* in his *Molière: 'Le Malade imaginaire'* (London: Grant and Cutler Ltd, 1982), pp. 28–9.

succeed like the pedant in Hierocles who, when he offered his house to sale, carried a brick in his pocket as a specimen.[43]

In exploring the role of the *raisonneurs*, this book will attend to 'the progress of the fable and the tenour of the dialogue', assessing the contribution of each brick to the construction of the whole edifice.

[43] Samuel Johnson, 'Preface to Shakespeare' in *The Yale Edition of the Works of Samuel Johnson*, vol. 7, ed. Arthur Sherbo (New Haven and London: Yale University Press, 1968), p. 62. The reference comes from Gary Taylor, *Moment by Moment by Shakespeare* (London: Macmillan, 1985), p. 14. Taylor's approach to Shakespeare is to consider how the succession of discrete moments creates pleasure (p. 2).

2

L 'École des maris: the raisonneur as brother and sparring partner

Nous tâcherons demain d'apaiser sa colère.[1]

ARISTE AND THE CRITICS

In *L'École des maris* (1661), Ariste is the brother of the protagonist, Sganarelle, though twenty years older and in his late fifties. He has given rise to less controversy than the other *raisonneurs*, perhaps because this is a less frequently studied and performed play than the others. But the spectrum of opinions expressed about him is none the less wide: from exponent of wisdom to elderly buffoon. There are those who think of him as the repository of serious ideas. Even Bray says that he expounds 'des idées sages', though doubts that these ideas are Molière's own.[2] Herzel too, who is quick to find other *raisonneurs* comic, thinks that 'a case can [...] be made for seeing Ariste [...] as the incarnation of correct ideas'.[3] Defaux is in no doubt that Ariste, whose name derives from the Greek word meaning 'excellent', is intended to command the sympathy of the audience for his 'conformisme prudent, son respect des usages et sa philosophie du juste milieu'.[4] Gossman, on the other hand, thinks

---

[1] Ariste in *L'École des maris* (1112).
[2] René Bray, *Molière: homme de théâtre* (Paris: Mercure de France, 1954), p. 33.
[3] Roger W. Herzel, 'The Function of the *Raisonneur* in Molière's Comedy', *Modern Language Notes*, 90 (1975), 564–75, p. 567.
[4] Gérard Defaux, *Molière ou les métamorphoses du comique: de la comédie morale au triomphe de la folie*, (Lexington: French Forum, 1980; 2nd edn, Paris: Klincksieck, 1992), p. 71.

he expresses 'not, apparently, a very elevating doctrine' and Peacock finds him positively comic, as do Fargher and Eustis, both of whom agree with Sganarelle's description of him in the play as 'un vieillard insensé' (253).[5]

Calder's description of the opening of the play, and of Ariste's role in it, puts the emphasis on one aspect of Molière's originality in *L'École des maris*, namely the evocation of contemporary manners and moral issues that would strike close to the bone of the first audiences:

The play begins with a methodical exposition of its subject and main themes [...] The Argument, Between The Two brothers, concerns the right and wrong ways to behave in society. Ariste, the older brother, argues in favour of measuring and modifying one's behaviour in the light of the prevailing views and practice of the society to which one belongs. Sganarelle, the younger, believes that one should consult only one's own inclinations [...] From the opening lines the spectator is plunged into a serious moral argument and, throughout the play, he or she will be invited to follow, through the words, deeds and events, the ramifications of this argument.[6]

Molière's originality, however, lies less in the evocation of contemporary manners and moral issues than in his artful blending of such an evocation with structures derived from farce. Calder's description privileges serious moral argument over comic structures. If we put dramaturgy first, we will arrive at a better appreciation of Ariste's words, as well as of Molière's play as a whole.

This approach has been anticipated by two other critics, who correctly identify the role of the *raisonneur* as dramaturgically crucial in allowing Molière to create his new blend of comedy. Lawrence acknowledges that 'Ariste's presence makes the play more than a farce' and Forestier sees the relationship in this play between Sganarelle and Ariste, the figure from farce and the *raisonneur*, as the source

---

[5] Lionel Gossman, *Men and Masks: A Study of Molière* (Baltimore: Johns Hopkins University Press, 1963), p. 243; Noël Peacock, 'The Comic Role of the *Raisonneur* in Molière's Theatre', *Modern Language Review*, 76 (1981), 298–310, p. 307; Richard Fargher, 'Molière and his Reasoners' in *Studies in French Literature presented to H. W. Lawton*, ed. J. C. Ireson and others (Manchester University Press, 1968), pp. 105–20 (p. 107); Alvin Eustis, *Molière as Ironic Contemplator* (The Hague, Paris: Mouton, 1973), p. 186.

[6] Andrew Calder, *Molière: The Theory and Practice of Comedy* (London: The Athlone Press, 1993), pp. 31–2.

of its originality and the catalyst for Molière's subsequent output: 'C'est [...] avec [Sganarelle] que Molière inaugure sa technique qui consiste à mettre en exergue son ridicule en le confrontant dès le début de la pièce du personnage du raisonneur.'[7] *L'École des maris* is a farce in which the foolish man, Sganarelle, thinks he can keep his intended, Isabelle, locked away, the better to preserve her innocence; she, however, by a series of tricks and subterfuges carried out under his very nose, manages to escape his clutches and marry the desirable Valère, leaving Sganarelle angry and bewildered.[8] It is a three-act play, and this farcical structure occupies essentially the second and third acts. Sganarelle would be simply the stereotypical authority figure of farce, who is successfully and comically tricked, but for the introduction of Ariste and his own contrasting relationship with the youthful Léonor, whom he does not lock away but allows to pursue interests appropriate to her age. Ariste's opposition to Sganarelle's treatment of Isabelle and his dialogues on the matter with Sganarelle have the effect of giving topicality to a familiar farcical structure, and inviting spectators to see it in a new and moral (though emphatically not moralistic) perspective. In dramaturgical terms, Molière achieves this by preceding the farcical structure with scenes involving Sganarelle and Ariste and their respective wards (essentially 1. 1–2) and by ingeniously making use of Léonor and Ariste for the denouement of the farcical structure (essentially 3. 5–9).

The following analyses of Ariste's role show how Molière uses him simultaneously to introduce a morally topical dimension to the farcical plot and to promote audience laughter. To quote a few lines from his role and assert that they show him to be the repository of wisdom is to ignore the broader dramaturgical function of the role; similarly, to quote a few different lines and suggest that they depict a comic Ariste is to fail to appreciate Molière's original blend

---

[7] Francis L. Lawrence, 'The *Raisonneur* in Molière', *L'Esprit Créateur*, 6 (1966), 156–66, p. 161; Georges Forestier, *Molière en toutes lettres* (Paris: Bordas, 1990), p. 154.

[8] *L'École des maris* thus combines the tricks against a husband (in this case, would-be-husband) of French farce with the scheming young lovers scenario typical of the commedia dell'arte. See Bernadette Rey-Flaud, *Molière et la farce* (Geneva: Droz, 1996) and Roger Guichemerre, 'Positions critiques et nouvelles perspectives: Molière et la farce' in his *Visages du théâtre au XVIIᵉ siècle* (Paris: Klincksieck, 1994), pp. 147–63.

of farce and topicality, which relies on Ariste's sophisticated appeal to the fashionable audiences of 1661 the better to poke fun at the unfashionable and wayward Sganarelle. This new blend came to be the hallmark of Molière's comedies, ensuring both success and controversy.

ARISTE AND SGANARELLE (1. 1)

If we believe that 'the play begins with a methodical exposition of its subject and main themes' (Calder, p. 31), we fail to appreciate the dramatic complexity of the opening scene and the techniques by which Molière seeks to engage and amuse his spectators. We make the same mistake if we think of the opening scene as a debate about fashion.[9] Molière shows two brothers in mid-discussion, but its original focus is never made clear, and the focus of their discussion in the scene itself keeps shifting. The dramatic momentum derives from the way in which the brothers tease each other, both of them trying to score points. The comic momentum comes from the presentation of Sganarelle as doggedly determined to be old-fashioned, different from the crowd and proud of it. He can only appear so comically dogged, however, because he is shown in conversation with the fashionable Ariste and they are made to react against each other.

Ironically, Sganarelle's opening speech aims politely to close down the discussion that the two brothers have been having: 'Mon frère, s'il vous plaît, ne nous discourons pas tant' (1), and his tone is conciliatory: 'que chacun de nous vive comme il l'entend' (2). It is vital to Molière that he present his foolish protagonist as able to engage in polite conversation with his brother, because it is through a mixture of politeness and folly that he makes his audiences laugh at characters who in one sense derive from the purely theatrical tradition of farce and in another have an uncanny resemblance to people in the real world with whom the audience would have been familiar. Having established Sganarelle's politeness, Molière introduces the

---

[9] See Larry F. Norman, *The Public Mirror: Molière and the Social Commerce of Depiction* (Chicago: University of Chicago Press, 1999), p. 163, n. 7.

tone of teasing and point-scoring that will characterize the brothers' exchange, as Sganarelle invokes what will prove to be a running joke about Ariste's age: 'Bien que sur moi des ans vous ayez l'avantage / Et soyez assez vieux pour devoir être sage […]' (3–4). This subordinate clause is followed by a main clause which reveals the comic Sganarelle: an assertion that he will not listen to his brother and will do as he pleases (5–8). This is comic as an early sign of Sganarelle's refusal to listen and to learn; it is also comic for striking a discordant note after his initial attempt to close the conversation in a politely conciliatory way, for it shows him wanting to have the last word.

Those who try too hard to have the last word often find that their interlocutor replies, and that is what Ariste does here. To appreciate the force of his reply, it is important to sense the thrust of Sganarelle's first speech. He had wanted to close down the discussion by agreeing that he and his brother should each adopt their own different lifestyles. But he had tried to have the last word by asserting his great satisfaction with his own: '[Je] me trouve fort bien de ma façon de vivre' (8). Ariste's brief reply ('Mais chacun la condamne' (9)) is certainly provocative in that it reopens the discussion, but it is not egotistical, as Sganarelle had been; Ariste presents Sganarelle with overwhelming evidence that the latter's lifestyle is aberrant. If the audience has not yet worked out that its sympathies are meant to lie with Ariste rather than Sganarelle, the following rapid exchange makes this abundantly clear. Sganarelle responds not by engaging with Ariste's claim, but by dismissing it with an insult, calling his brother a fool, along with anyone else who would condemn his way of life. Ariste responds with calm urbanity and wit: 'Grand merci: le compliment est doux' (10).

Ariste's 'chacun la condamne' proves to be the driving force behind the rest of this encounter, as it prompts Sganarelle to ask what exactly his critics have to say about him. What Molière sets up here is an exchange of portraits. Ariste will paint the portrait of Sganarelle, in response to which Sganarelle will paint the portrait of his critics. But the audience reaction to each will be very different. Sganarelle asks to hear his portrait, but makes it plain to the audience that he wants to hear it only in order to disbelieve it. He says he wants to hear it 'puisqu'il faut tout entendre' (11), but the driving force here is simply curiosity, as he has already told Ariste that he has no intention of learning any lessons (6), and his description of his critics as 'ces beaux censeurs' establishes the ironical perspective in which he will view their strictures.

Ariste delivers the portrait of Sganarelle in a quatrain, which crisply sums up his brother's main character weakness and gives a specific example of it: he is severely unsociable; even his dress marks him out as an alien in society. Ariste insists that Sganarelle's mood makes him flee 'toutes les douceurs de la société' (14), a sure way of making the spectators take Ariste's side in this exchange, since the audience of 1661, by the mere fact of going to the theatre, was showing its own desire to take pleasure in sociability.

Sganarelle shows a comic inability to see the full force of the criticism by latching on to the specific instance of dress, and responds not so much by defending his own attire, but by mocking the fashionable attire of his alleged critics and turning the attack into a personal one against his own brother. Molière may well want audiences to laugh at the objects of Sganarelle's satire by persuading us momentarily to see them through Sganarelle's eyes and through his comically phrased language: the lengthy enumeration of fashion features, the alliterative mockery with which he refers to waistcoats as 'ces petits pourpoints sous les bras se perdant' (29), the derogatory rhyming association of 'petits chapeaux' and 'débiles cerveaux' (25–6), the comic image of legs enslaved by accessories of ribbon and lace worn above the knee and described by Ariste as 'grands canons' (35–6), or the one that equates ribbon-strewn shoes with pigeons' feet (33–4). Whereas Ariste's portrait of Sganarelle had essentially avoided the caricaturing and distorting devices of the satirist, Sganarelle has ample recourse to them. It may be that in the original performances Sganarelle's satire was bolstered by his pointing at fashionable features in Ariste's attire and in that of members of the audience. The comedy none the less redounds on Sganarelle, as the more features he chooses to criticize, the more he marks himself out as different from the fashionable crowd in the audience and the more he justifies Ariste's criticism of his lack of sociability. The climax of his satire is a personalized attack on Ariste himself: 'Et je vous vois porter les sottises qu'on porte' (40).

Ariste's reply, which deserves to be quoted in full, is one which modern critics typically invoke as an instance of *raisonneur* discourse, but without adequate contextualization. For Defaux it is Ariste's distillation of Aristotelian wisdom for the age of the 'honnête homme', his 'profession de foi bien connue' (p. 98); for Gossman, however, it is precisely the contents of this speech that he finds not very elevating (p. 243), a view shared by Eustis who claims that Ariste's opinion, expressed in this speech, that 'one should run with the crowd is not traditionally that of the sage' (p. 185). Eustis further thinks that Ariste is made to appear comic in this speech by opining that one should avoid excess in dress, while 'at sixty he is dressed in the height of fashion' (p. 185):

> Toujours au plus grand nombre on doit s'accommoder,
> Et jamais il ne faut se faire regarder.
> L'un et l'autre excès choque, et tout homme bien sage
> Doit faire des habits ainsi que du langage,
> N'y rien trop affecter, et sans empressement
> Suivre ce que l'usage y fait de changement.
> Mon sentiment n'est pas qu'on prenne la méthode
> De ceux qu'on voit toujours renchérir sur la mode,
> Et qui dans ses excès, dont ils sont amoureux,
> Seraient fâchés qu'un autre eût été plus loin qu'eux;
> Mais je tiens qu'il est mal, sur quoi que l'on se fonde,
> De fuir obstinément ce que suit tout le monde,
> Et qu'il vaut mieux souffrir d'être au nombre des fous,
> Que du sage parti se voir seul contre tous.
>
> (41–54)

To see Ariste as a laughable character on the basis that his view 'is not traditionally that of the sage' is misguided. In promoting explicitly the avoidance of excess and implicitly the search for a golden mean, Ariste is appealing to an ethical ideal that derives from Aristotle and that was not at all about easy compromises: perhaps the phonetic overlap in their names is not accidental. Audiences would have found Ariste's views unexceptionably wise. Moreover, in encouraging Sganarelle to follow the crowd, Ariste is echoing a commonly held view, which is also one that Montaigne expresses at the climax of the *Essais*: 'Les plus belles vies sont, à mon gré, celles qui se rangent au modèle commun et humain, avec ordre, mais sans miracle et sans extravagance.'[10] Nor is there any evidence to support Eustis' claim of a comic discrepancy

---

[10] Montaigne, *Essais*, 3 vols., ed. Pierre Villey and V.-L. Saulnier (Paris: Presses Universitaires de France, 1965), III, p. 1116 (bk III, ch. 13).

between Ariste's views about avoiding excess and his dress at the height of fashion. We know that Ariste is not yet sixty (as Eustis claims), because Sganarelle later refers to him as 'presque sexagénaire' (240). We know that he is not wearing the fashionable blond wig that Sganarelle evokes in his satirical portrait (27), because Sganarelle himself refers to Ariste's black wig (56). The only other evidence we have for Ariste's attire is Sganarelle's attacking claim that he wears 'les sottises qu'on porte' (40) and Ariste's own claim that he tries to observe fashion but without affectation.[11] Given that Sganarelle's claim is spoken at the end of his satirical portrait, characterized throughout by exaggeration, it is more likely that Ariste would have been dressed in unobtrusively fashionable clothes, and this would also have made Sganarelle's view more comic to the audience of 1661.

If Ariste's speech, however, is not in itself comic, this does not mean that his role is to teach the audience ethical wisdom. We need to attend to the dramaturgical context in which he makes this speech. McBride calls these two exchanges between Sganarelle and Ariste 'a moral banal [sic] debate on the excesses of fashion'.[12] But this remark leaves aside the dramatic context. The brothers are not debating fashion. Indeed they are not debating at all. Sganarelle wanted to know what critics say about him. Ariste replies that they object to his unsociability, and incidentally mentions that this can be seen in his dress. Sganarelle counterattacks by focusing exclusively on dress, and mocks the fashions that his critics follow and makes a personal attack on Ariste. In reply, Ariste is neither moral mouthpiece nor comic fool; he tries to defend himself against Sganarelle's criticism of his dress, but in such a way as to steer the discussion back to sociability. The first six lines of his reply make the general point that it is better not to draw attention to oneself by any show of excessive behaviour, and modes of dress as well as of language are given as instances. In steering the discussion back to sociability, he carefully

---

[11] See Stephen Varick Dock, *Costume and Fashion in the Plays of Jean-Baptiste Poquelin Molière: A Seventeenth-Century Perspective* (Geneva: Éditions Slatkine, 1992), p. 77. For Sganarelle's costume we have the evidence of the text, corroborated by Molière's *Inventaire après décès*, which tells us that in addition he wore an antiquated purse (*escarcelle*) (p. 76).

[12] Robert McBride, *The Sceptical Vision of Molière* (London: Macmillan, 1977), p. 141.

avoids the pronoun 'vous' so as not to antagonize Sganarelle, and he uses the rhetorical technique of showing sympathy with the views that his interlocutor has expressed: lines 47–50 reveal Ariste's own sensitivity to the absurdities of high fashion. What he finally offers as advice to Sganarelle, though still without the pronoun 'vous' and in undogmatic terms, is that it is not a good idea to 'fuir obstinément ce que suit tout le monde' (52). The word 'obstinément' is crucial here in determining Ariste's flexible approach to the topic, as distinct from Sganarelle's obstinate inflexibility. With an easy wit that is able to bring Aristotle's golden mean to bear on matters of fashion, Ariste concludes by returning to Sganarelle's earlier charge of folly and asserting a preference to be among the foolish majority than in wise isolation.

Ariste's speech has established the terms in which Sganarelle's folly can best stand out, and Molière capitalizes on this by making Sganarelle's reply reveal to what extent he resists the kind of sociability sketched out by his elder brother: 'Cela sent son vieillard, qui, pour en faire accroire, / Cache ses cheveux blancs d'une perruque noire' (55–6). This is not an aside; it is spoken very much for Ariste's hearing. But it is rude in addressing him in the third person. It is doubly insulting, in that it reverts to the running joke about Ariste's older years and uses his age as a way of accounting for views which Sganarelle clearly thinks too preposterous to be engaged with. Furthermore, he returns to the caricatural satire of dress the better to attack Ariste, with no acknowledgement of Ariste's attempt to change the topic to sociability, which is the nub of the issue and which Sganarelle himself had raised in his earlier question about his 'beaux censeurs'.

Whereas Sganarelle typically ignores the substance of his inter-locutor's speeches, Ariste responds directly to his younger brother's attack, while also trying to broaden the topic: he expresses puzzle-ment at the implied logic of Sganarelle's attack, that older people should not bother to turn themselves out presentably and maintain a cheerful disposition. But once again, Sganarelle is in no mood to engage with Ariste's argument, which he dismisses with a peremp-tory and uninterested 'Quoi qu'il en soit' (65), before asserting his determination not to change his wardrobe, to wear an old-fashioned hat, a 'bon pourpoint bien long et fermé' (69), 'haut-de-chausses fait justement pour ma cuisse' (71), and 'souliers où mes pieds ne sont point au supplice' (72). Blind to the folly of obstinate unfashionability and unsociability, Sganarelle does not realize that this enumeration is perceived by Ariste and the audience to be just as satirical as his earlier one against fashion.

At this point new characters arrive on stage, so the exchange between the two brothers ends, without the audience having been given any sense of a likely dramatic action. Without himself being subject to comic scrutiny and without any attempt to preach (he responded only to Sganarelle's questions and attacks), Ariste has enabled the audience to see the general nature of Sganarelle's folly, as well as one particular manifestation of it (his dress). The scene has whetted the audience's appetite for, and provided the context for an appreciation of, another particular manifestation of his folly, which will be revealed in the next scene and will provide the motivation for the dramatic action: he is so concerned to avoid future cuckoldry that the ward whom he intends to marry is to be kept away from other young people and their sociable ways.

ISABELLE'S EXCURSION (1. 2)

This scene is structurally complex, involving five characters, who converse in various configurations. The opening lines contain a dialogue between three young women, who turn out to be Isabelle (Sganarelle's ward), her sister Léonor (Ariste's ward) and Léonor's companion Lisette, and their interaction supposedly takes place outside the earshot of the two men. It is vital, however, for confirming the audience's perception of the two brothers and for establishing a context in which to interpret Sganarelle's obsession with the avoidance of cuckoldry. The women are young and fashionable and want to take the air on a lovely day. As Lisette points out, Léonor is fortunate indeed to be in the hands of the 'raisonnable' (80), whereas Isabelle lives in fear of her guardian, who normally will not let her out of his sight. Lisette's gloss on this man identifies him readily as Sganarelle, since she refers to his old-fashioned ruff: 'je l'envoirois au diable avec sa fraise' (83), and so confirms the audience's laughter at his dress-sense in the previous scene.

The main body of the scene begins with a practical demonstration of Sganarelle's fear of cuckoldry, before he articulates it as a matter of policy in his education of Isabelle, which in turn is held up to scrutiny by the other characters present, including Ariste. The demonstration of his fear comes in the shape of his suspicions about the women's behaviour and his flat refusal to let Isabelle go out with the other two. Ariste repeatedly intervenes in favour of Isabelle's excursion, but it is a measure of Sganarelle's obsession that he responds with a peremptory refusal:

ARISTE	Eh! laissez-les, mon frère, aller se divertir.
SGANARELLE	Je suis votre valet mon frère. (90–1)
ARISTE	Croyez-vous qu'elle est mal d'être avec Léonor?
SGANARELLE	Non pas; mais avec moi je la crois mieux encor. (93–4)

or with a rude, and in the first case insulting, interruption, before Ariste has even been able to make a point:

ARISTE	La jeunesse
	Veut …
SGANARELLE	La jeunesse est sotte, et parfois la vieillesse. (91–2)
ARISTE	Mais …
SGANARELLE	Mais ses actions de moi doivent dépendre. (95)
ARISTE	Il me semble …
SGANARELLE	Il me semble, et je le dis tout haut,
	Que sur un tel sujet c'est parler comme il faut. (109–10)

What is at stake here is not some abstract notion of educational method. It is whether or not Isabelle can go for a walk with her sister. Sganarelle's refusal to listen, his insults, and his abrupt assertions of his own will intensify the audience's laughter at him, and create a bond of sympathy between Ariste and the young women.

It is in this context that Sganarelle seeks to justify his opposition to the excursion with recourse to more general principles in a speech in which Molière locates the essence of his exposition, giving the audience the information they need to understand the development of the plot. With clarity and apparent reasonableness, Sganarelle explains how the father of Isabelle and Léonor, on his deathbed, entrusted them to the care of the two brothers and also offered them the option of marriage. It is important that this information is conveyed, but there is comedy in Sganarelle's careful setting out of the situation in the presence of characters on stage who are already familiar with it; and the comedy derives from the conclusion that Sganarelle draws: 'Selon vos volontés vous gouvernez la vôtre: / Laissez-moi, je vous prie, à mon gré régir l'autre' (107–8). In its neat formulation, this looks like a claim that Sganarelle is much accustomed to making. It may appear reasonable, taken in isolation, but when the audience remembers that Sganarelle is asserting his right to do as he pleases in order to prevent Isabelle from taking a walk, his explanation smacks of foolish tyranny rather than of sweet reasonableness.

He goes on, in satirical mode again, to spell out the difference between Ariste's alleged permissiveness (allowing Léonor to go out, dress fashionably, have a companion, and even talk to young men) and his own strict regime for Isabelle (staying indoors, dressed simply, and doing domestic chores). As in the first scene, Sganarelle unwittingly satirizes himself: he wants to make Ariste seem ridiculous; but the characters on stage make Sganarelle look ridiculous. The climax of this contrast is his frank admission of the reason for his treatment of his intended bride: 'Je ne veux point porter de cornes, si je puis' (126). If Isabelle is kept under constant surveillance and away from company, he can be sure that he will have a faithful wife.

All three women attempt to question Sganarelle's reasoning. Isabelle is promptly told to be quiet (129). Léonor does not have the opportunity to say very much. But Lisette explains wittily the obverse of Sganarelle's argument: women are most likely to be faithful if they are trusted, and most unlikely to be faithful if surrounded by constraints. She satirizes Sganarelle's regime as 'visions de fous' (153) and makes her general point more graphic by conjuring up her own likelihood of making a cuckold of such a husband: 'Et si par un mari je me voyais contrainte, / J'aurais fort grande pente à confirmer sa crainte' (159–60).

Instead of pondering this argument and considering its implications for his own situation, Sganarelle assumes that it is horrific for a woman to talk so brazenly of cuckoldry, and puts the whole blame on Ariste, whom he addresses sarcastically and incredulously: 'Voilà, beau précepteur, votre éducation, / Et vous souffrez cela sans nulle émotion' (161–2). Sganarelle may think that the evidence undermines Ariste, but the audience laughs all the more at Sganarelle. He does not stop to think, he is insensitive to Lisette's satirical tone, he does not even reply to Lisette herself, and he assumes, unreasonably, that Lisette's views are all to be laid at Ariste's door, when it is Léonor who is Ariste's ward. Finally, he lets Ariste speak at some length, with only one dismissive and insulting interruption ('Chansons que tout cela' (179)), which shows that even when he lets an interlocutor speak, Sganarelle is not listening properly.

Calder sees in Ariste the perfect sage: '[he] is seen to be sensible, fair-minded, modest and deeply respectful of the freedom of others, especially the freedom of the woman he hopes to marry; in fact he practises all the cardinal virtues' (p. 95). Eustis, however, believes that in this speech Molière has established in Ariste 'an ironic contrast, not a golden mean', a contrast that makes him too a comic target (p. 185). In dramaturgical terms, however, Molière wants to maximize the audience's laughter at Sganarelle, which he does by showing Ariste responding to all Sganarelle's attacks and by showing Sganarelle's deafness to the response. Molière is driving the scene to a climax in which Ariste will have so vigorously defended his permissive approach that Sganarelle can confidently anticipate his brother's being made a cuckold (234). Sganarelle's anticipation of this is vital for the audience's laughter throughout the play, when we see Isabelle scheming to outwit her guardian while he, unawares, remains confident of her loyalty: the dramatic ironies run all the more deeply for our clear perception of Sganarelle's confidence in his own safety and his brother's peril. His anticipation of Ariste's cuckoldry is particularly vital for his own comic downfall at the end of the play, when the very moment at which he hopes to triumph over a cuckolded brother proves to be the moment that he himself is allowed to see Isabelle's disloyalty. The confidence with which Sganarelle will ride for his fall is established at the end of this scene and it is brought about because Ariste is given the opportunity here to explain patiently his more indulgent method of bringing up Léonor, which Sganarelle can then joyously reject. To think that Ariste is subject to comic scrutiny is to undermine the force with which Molière seeks to portray Sganarelle's foolish confidence, and to see Ariste as a sage is to ignore the dramaturgical function which his speech here fulfils.

Ariste certainly has recourse to maxims, but they all are anchored in the specific charges that Sganarelle had made against him when justifying his own decision not to let Isabelle go out and when blaming him for Lisette's forthright views. The first part of his speech, before Sganarelle's rude interjection, is specifically a response to Sganarelle's outrage at Lisette's claims and to his blame of Ariste. He begins by aiming to defuse Sganarelle and encourages him to interpret Lisette's words as humorous and satirical rather than outrageous and immoral: 'Mon frère, son discours ne doit que faire rire' (163). Even as he says this, Ariste is helping the audience to see a major trait in the comic fool: a lack of humour. While distancing himself from her tone, the better to try to keep Sganarelle on side, Ariste tentatively introduces the idea that the substance of Lisette's speech merits attention: 'Elle a quelque raison en ce qu'elle veut dire' (164). He then restates clearly and in various formulations, but avoiding the humorous tone that had merely exasperated Sganarelle, the views that Lisette has already expressed. Those who see this speech as the one of a sage forget that Ariste is saying nothing here that the cheeky Lisette has not said; he is simply putting it in different terms in the hope that Sganarelle will listen and take note. The comic effect derives from the fact that Sganarelle never takes note, in whatever terms he is spoken to.

All Ariste's language is characterized by devices that seek to avoid alienating Sganarelle. He uses a maxim: 'Leur sexe aime à jouir d'un peu de liberté' (165), but the modifying expression 'un peu de' is all important, and gives the lie to Fargher, who finds Ariste comic because his views are 'alarmingly emancipated' (p. 108). His following maxim uses the same device: 'On le retient fort mal par tant d'austérité' (166); he is not questioning a degree of restraint, but recourse to excessive restraint. He makes clear what he means by excessive restraint: 'Et les soins défiants, les verrous et les grilles / Ne font pas la vertu des femmes ni des filles' (167–8). The specific imagery is not satirical or exaggerated. If Sganarelle were attentive, he would realize how closely tailored to his own situation it is. The starting point of this discussion was Sganarelle's objection to Isabelle's outing, and at the very beginning of the scene the women had commented precisely on how unusual it was that Sganarelle had not locked her inside the house that day (81–2). Although Ariste's exemplification of excessive restraint relates directly to Sganarelle's case, he does not use language that makes the link explicit, taking care to avoid second-person pronouns. Indeed in his following restatements of the same point, he uses the first-person plural and first-person singular pronouns so as not to appear aggressive or hectoring:

> C'est l'honneur qui les doit tenir dans le devoir,
> Non la sévérité que nous leur faisons voir.   (169–70)
>
> En vain sur tous ses pas nous prétendons régner.   (173)
>
> Et je ne tiendrais, moi, quelque soin qu'on se donne,
> Mon honneur guère sûr aux mains d'une personne
> A qui, dans les désirs qui pourraient l'assaillir,
> Il ne manquerait rien qu'un moyen de faillir.   (175–8)

These last four lines are the more modest restatement from the man's perspective of Lisette's concluding claim that she would be more tempted to cuckold a husband who tried to restrain her than one who trusted her. Just as Sganarelle spluttered with indignation on hearing her say it, he similarly interrupts scornfully on hearing Ariste make the same point. This pattern of interruption contributes to Molière's portrait of Sganarelle's supreme but misplaced confidence in his own policy. Eustis's gloss that 'Sganarelle starts to score points and Ariste seems to be the ridiculous character' (p. 185) ignores the care and cautiousness of Ariste's language and the rudeness and inattention that characterize Sganarelle's interjections (179, 209).

In response, Ariste avoids contradicting Sganarelle: 'Soit' (179); and he leaves aside his carefully phrased generalizations in order to speak specifically about his own treatment of Léonor. It is important to bear in mind that this is not an abstract debate about the treament of women. It is a disagreement about whether or not Isabelle should be allowed to go out with her sister Léonor. In the course of it, Sganarelle, in order to justify his objection, has attacked the permissiveness of Ariste's handling of his ward. Lisette and then Ariste argue against the imposition of constraints, but now Ariste defends himself against Sganarelle's specific charge against him. Without boasting, he presents his upbringing of Léonor as successful; and those who see his account as simply the comic opposite of Sganarelle's have not paid sufficient attention to his phrasing. It is true that he believes in kindness and indulgence, but when he says 'Des moindres libertés je n'ai point fait des crimes' (184), the word 'moindres' and the phrase 'fait des crimes' are crucial, since these words, far from implying irresponsible indulgence, suggest that there are some liberties that Ariste would have blamed in Léonor, but that he did not reprimand her for minor liberties in a disproportionate way. He admits that he has let her have her way, but points out that he has never had any cause to regret it (185–6). In conceding that he positively encouraged her sociability, he appeals to the educational value of the 'école du monde' (191). He lets her spend money on fashionable clothes, but is sure to win the approval of Molière's fashionable audience when he points out that this is not a matter of rash extravagance in a wealthy family. Again his wording is subtly persuasive, referring to the wealth 'dans nos familles' (195), and so encouraging Sganarelle to imitate his generosity. His final point responds with great subtlety to the final point that Sganarelle himself had made (125–8), namely that the root of all Sganarelle's concerns is his fear of cuckoldry. Ariste explains that Isabelle can see all he has to offer her, but that if she chooses to marry someone else, that will be preferable to an enforced marriage to him. There is no mention in these lines (197–208) of Sganarelle and his protective constraints, but Ariste's attitude should strike the audience and the female characters on stage as the obvious response to Sganarelle's fear of cuckoldry. The conclusion that Sganarelle could draw, namely that he could treat Isabelle kindly and not force her to marry him if she does not wish to do so, is emphatically not the conclusion that he does draw. He simply responds with yet another satirical attack against Ariste: 'Hé! qu'il est douceureux! c'est tout sucre et tout miel' (209). Ariste's reply is unapologetic and he attributes his policy to his particular humour.

Molière needs to end the scene on a climax which will reinforce the image of Sganarelle's foolish confidence in his own ability to avoid cuckoldry and highlight his certainty that Ariste will not be able to do so. He needs also to respond to the dramatic situation with which the scene began: Isabelle's attempt to go out. Molière combines both these considerations in the scene's climax by leading up to it with a further, but differently focused and differently conducted, exchange between the two brothers.

Sganarelle, who has been consistently deaf or dismissive when faced with the views of others, engages now, for the first time, with Ariste's views, arguing that indulgence is unwise because it must be difficult to withdraw it after marriage. Molière gives the exchange the shape of what McBride has called a 'rythme de ballet',[13] but which might more properly be viewed as a crescendo of paroxystic incredulity. Sganarelle becomes increasingly incredulous at the professed attitude of Ariste as future husband. Ariste refutes the very premise of Sganarelle's argument: he sees no need to cease being indulgent in marriage. Molière constructs their subsequent exchange as a rhetorical gradation of questions, posed by Sganarelle, and brief answers, given by Ariste. Each question focuses on the kind of indulgence that Ariste would tolerate in marriage: from fashion, balls, and the reception of young men, Sganarelle leads up to 'Et votre femme entendre les fleurettes?' (227) and then 'Et vous verrez ces visites muguettes / D'un œil à témoigner de n'en être point soûl?' (228–9). Ariste says that he would tolerate all these things. Sganarelle is finally driven to call his brother 'un vieux fou' (230), to send Isabelle back into the house 'pour n'ouïr point cette pratique infâme' (231), and gleefully to envisage Ariste's downfall: 'Que j'aurai de plaisir si l'on le fait cocu!' (234).

It does not much matter whether or not the audience believes that Ariste would behave as indulgently and imperturbably as he says in response to Sganarelle's prurient, obsessive, and ridiculous questions. His responses are emblematic of his overall position, which Molière allows him to restate: 'Je veux m'abandonner à la foi de ma femme' (232). What matters is that Sganarelle has asserted his views and exemplified them by sending Isabelle back indoors. During the rest of the play, the audience will watch the preparations for Sganarelle's downfall, of which he is blissfully unaware, as Isabelle arranges to flee and marry Valère. Molière intensifies our perception of his folly by making Ariste, Léonor, and Lisette all, once again, issue warnings that his behaviour is likely to have the opposite effect to the one that he intends. But Sganarelle thinks that the folly is theirs, dismisses them contemptuously, and prepares to take Isabelle to see his cabbage patch—the only excursion she is allowed. Ariste's interventions have all been geared towards softening the harsh treatment of Isabelle, whom Sganarelle forbids from going out with her sister, and, when the reasons for Sganarelle's severity become clear, towards making him

---

[13] Robert McBride, 'La Question du *raisonneur* dans les *écoles* de Molière', *Dix-septiéme siècle*, 113 (1976), 59–73, p. 64.

question his views on the avoidance of cuckoldry. These interventions do not make Ariste a comic figure, nor a spokesman for wisdom, since they are so specifically anchored in the dramatic fiction. They make him a dramatic agent, alongside Isabelle, Léonor and Lisette, in a mechanism calculated to heighten the audience's laughter at the folly of Sganarelle.

ARISTE AND THE DENOUEMENT (3. 5–9)

Readers of the play and audiences could be forgiven for thinking, during the last part of act 1 and the whole of act 2, that Ariste and his young ward Léonor had been introduced by Molière as merely expository characters, serving only to establish Sganarelle's folly. The play's dramatic action focuses exclusively on the attempts of Isabelle and Valère to communicate their love to each other, her attempt to escape marriage to Sganarelle by fleeing to Valère's house, and the unwitting assistance that Sganarelle affords them in bringing this to pass. Ariste and Léonor are not entirely forgotten, however. When Isabelle tricks Sganarelle into delivering a love letter to Valère by claiming that it is an importunate letter that she has received from Valère and that she wants to return unopened the better to deter him, Sganarelle is only too happy to help and reflects on the superiority of his upbringing of Isabelle over Ariste's treatment of Léonor:

> Je voudrais bien savoir, en voyant tout ceci,
> Si celle de mon frère en useroit ainsi.
> Ma foi! les filles sont ce que l'on les fait être.
>
> (509–11)

The irony is manifestly at Sganarelle's expense.

Act 3 begins with Isabelle's most daring plan yet, which is to take advantage of the evening gloom to escape unnoticed to Valère's house. Unfortunately, she runs into Sganarelle and has to think of a new trick that will both exculpate her and ensure that she can still make her escape. Molière so engineers this trick as to reintroduce Ariste and Léonor. But their reintroduction is not simply a mechanical way of bringing back characters who had almost been forgotten. Molière skilfully weaves them so tightly into the denouement that at the very moment that Sganarelle thinks he has triumphed over Valère and demonstrated the loyalty of Isabelle and the treachery of Ariste's Léonor, they are all present on stage to witness the complete collapse of his own plans and acknowledge that he has been the fool all along.

In order to capitalize on the build-up to this climax, Molière exploits some deep-running comic ironies. Isabelle claims falsely that Léonor is secretly in love with Valère, that she is in Sganarelle's house, dressed as Isabelle, so that Valère, when he turns up, will think he is talking to the woman he loves. Unhappy with such mysteries, Sganarelle is persuaded to let the fake Isabelle leave. Of course, it is the real Isabelle who leaves and under Sganarelle's very nose enters Valère's house. To compound the situation, Sganarelle asks the passing Commissaire and Notaire to enter the house and marry the couple in order to protect the lady's honour. He is perhaps less interested in the lady's honour than in the brilliant triumph he can enjoy over his brother: 'Je vais le réjouir, cet homme sans colère' (939). So Molière offers the audience the prospect of an imminent resolution to the plot, with Sganarelle teasing his brother relentlessly, confident that the dramatic ironies are operating against Ariste, while the audience knows that their target is Sganarelle himself and that the more he teases, the greater the defeat he is preparing for himself.

It is important to realize that, when Ariste comes outdoors in response to Sganarelle's call, he is in complete ignorance of Isabelle's plotting. So his confusion before Sganarelle's teasing questions can make him look the victim of Sganarelle's irony. But what Sganarelle thinks of as his superior knowledge, the audience knows to be inferior knowledge. Paradoxically, therefore, the man who thinks he knows everything, knows nothing; and the man who thinks he knows nothing, knows everything he needs to know. Sganarelle enjoys teasing his brother, just as the audience enjoys the folly of it. He deploys sarcastic insults: 'beau directeur, suranné damoiseau' (941). He promises news, but deliberately delays its delivery (942, 943, 944). Mockingly, he quotes back to Ariste his earlier advice about winning over a woman by kindness rather than constraint (949–54). He describes Léonor offensively as 'la rusée' (955). And he is so wrapped up in the situation he thinks he has brought about that he speaks unintelligibly: 'L'une fuit ce galant, et l'autre le poursuit' (962). None of this makes any sense to Ariste, and his expressions of puzzlement and requests for enlightenment, met with ever more teasing, serve only to intensify laughter at Sganarelle, because the audience knows that Ariste is safe in his ignorance.

Finally, Sganarelle explains clearly that Léonor is in Valère's arms and not at the ball where Ariste thought she had gone. Ariste is incredulous, and Peacock thinks this makes him comic: 'Ariste's dispassionate air is soon disturbed by Sganarelle's news that Léonor has slipped from his indulgent grasp' (p. 307); and he quotes Ariste's 'Cessons de railler, je vous prie' (967) in support. What it is important to realize, however, is that Ariste's repeated expressions of incredulity focus not on the possibility that Léonor might be in love with another man, but on the possibility that she might have lied to him by telling him that she was going to a ball if she was in fact going elsewhere. Molière is at pains to spell this out. The two brothers' very different educational approaches also have very different aims. Sganarelle wants a wife who will not make a cuckold of him; Ariste wants a young woman who will trust him and tell him honestly if she wishes to marry another man. His insistence that he would not object to her marrying someone else, but that it is quite out of character for her to tell lies, tallies with the audience's perception of their relationship in act 1 and should, therefore, give Sganarelle pause for thought. But he simply mocks Ariste's 'raisonnements' (993), showing his own insensitivity and blindness.

For the next stage in preparing Sganarelle's downfall, Molière brings the Commissaire and the Notaire back on stage, asking for the signatures of witnesses to the wedding. Sganarelle's teasing of Ariste is extended further, since Ariste, still incredulous, seeks confirmation that the bride is indeed Léonor. But Sganarelle, thinking that such a question can only upset the plan (because Valère thinks he is marrying Isabelle), repeatedly closes down all lines of inquiry that would lead to the truth. To Sganarelle, Ariste appears to be in a weak position. But Ariste's questions, which Sganarelle suppresses, are the very ones that, if answered, could save Sganarelle from defeat. His determination not to have them answered makes him look all the more foolish. Quite unawares, he is himself the agent of Isabelle's marriage to Valère. When Ariste signs the deed, saying 'je n'y comprends rien' (1038) and Sganarelle replies reassuringly that 'Vous serez éclairci' (1038), their

exchange could serve as an emblem for the dramatic ironies that have
provided the denouement with its momentum.

Ever inventive, Molière prolongs the ironies and momentum, even
as Léonor and Lisette arrive on stage talking about the ball which they
have just left. The dramatist creates stage business whereby Sganarelle
takes Ariste aside to gloat over what he thinks is the marriage of
Valère and Léonor; and this exchange so preoccupies them both that
they do not notice the young women arrive. When they do become
aware of them, they assume wrongly that they have come from
Valère's house and Ariste expresses his disappointment with Léonor's
'procédé' (1062), an abstract accusation which means nothing to her.
Both of them are the innocent victims of Sganarelle's own confusion,
which is dispelled by the appearance from Valère's house of Valère
himself, Isabelle, and the legal officers and by the polite explanation
that Isabelle gives of the strategy that she has had recourse to in order
to avoid marrying a man to whom she was not suited.

No stage directions or direct speech indicate Sganarelle's immediate
reaction to the explanations of Isabelle and Valère. But there is an
implicit stage direction for Sganarelle in the reaction of Ariste:

> Mon frère, doucement il faut boire la chose:
> D'une telle action vos procédés sont cause;
> Et je vois votre sort malheureux à ce point,
> Que, vous sachant dupé, l'on ne vous plaindra point.
>
> (1091–4)

Fargher sees a comic Ariste here: 'he perpetually thrusts advice on
his brother' (p. 108). This is to fail to recognize that this moment
is the apex of Molière's comedy and the climax of the laughter he
has so carefully directed at Sganarelle. Sganarelle is speechless at the
revelation that Isabelle has just married Valère, a wedding that he
directly brought about and to which he has so willingly added his
approving signature. But he is more than speechless; he is angry
and makes as if to assault Valère. This is the implication of Ariste's
intervention, made in order to restrain Sganarelle ('tout doucement
il faut boire la chose'). Ariste's comment on the causes of Sganarelle's
downfall might at first look as if he is telling him 'I told you so.' But it
needs to be set in context. First, it is related logically to Ariste's restraint
of Sganarelle: it is no good attacking someone else, when you brought

this about yourself. Secondly, it is the first of a series of polyphonic comments reflecting on the causes of Sganarelle's downfall, with which Molière ends his play. Ariste's own comment can be read as doubly correct: Sganarelle is the cause of Isabelle's marriage in the sense that he has mistreated her all along, but also in the sense that he has guided her steps, provided the notary and signed the deed. Léonor, however, is keen to distance herself from the attribution of blame: 'je sais bien qu'au moins je ne le puis blâmer' (1098). Valère's valet thinks him fortunate that the marriage has prevented Sganarelle marrying her himself and becoming a real cuckold. Sganarelle, when he recovers his tongue, thinks his misfortune can be attributed to the untrustworthiness of the female sex: 'Malheureux qui se fie à femme après cela' (1106). Lisette, on the other hand, interprets the episode as a lesson for all tyrannical husbands. The diversity and incompatibility of these lessons, so rapidly drawn, are sufficient indication, if one were necessary, that Molière does not want audiences to draw simple and clear lessons from watching his comedies, though the varied reactions might invite audiences to reflect for themselves on the implications of what they have seen.

Ariste has almost the last word: 'Allons tous chez moi. Venez, Seigneur Valère. / Nous tâcherons demain d'apaiser sa colère' (1111–12). In these lines Fargher sees yet more comedy at Ariste's expense, concluding that he 'will continue to preach after the curtain has fallen' (p. 108). The effect of these lines, however, is surely to demonstrate Ariste's generosity in inviting the young people, and especially the newly wed couple, to enjoy hospitality in his house. The lines also imply that Sganarelle is fuming with anger, aside from the happy crowd. Ariste's suggestion that he and others (Valère, and perhaps Isabelle) will try to reconcile Sganarelle to what has happened the next day does not target laughter at Ariste. On the contrary, Ariste's concern for Sganarelle and his desire to reincorporate him into the society with which he is momentarily out of sorts is Molière's way of ensuring that his play maintains the new blend of farce and contemporary realism with which it started. Without Ariste's expression of concern (and indeed Léonor's refusal to blame him), Sganarelle could easily at the end of the play have metamorphosed into the simple trickster tricked found in countless farces. He is certainly that, but his interactions with the fashionable Ariste draw him closer to the real world of the original audiences. Hence the specially powerful impact of Molière's comedy.

Ariste is the first of a series of male characters in Molière's plays who try to save the comic fools from the consequences of their folly.[14] If *L'École des maris* has not enjoyed the posthumous success of some of the later plays in which these characters appear, it might be, in part, because Molière has not fully integrated Ariste into the dramatic action. When he speaks to Sganarelle in act 1, for all the wit and laughter that Molière extracts from their encounter, their engagements might strike audiences as lacking the same degree of dynamism that similar engagements will demonstrate in later plays. This is because, in 1. 1, Molière has not established a problem in the dramatic action that can be appreciated by the audience as the grounding for Sganarelle's and Ariste's disagreements; and though there is such a grounding in 1. 2, which is Ariste's objection to Sganarelle's refusal to let Isabelle go out with Léonor, it is an episodic problem. When the dramatic action proper gets under way, Ariste is absent and is only effectively incorporated into it in the final act. In later plays Molière makes the role of the *raisonneur* even more dramatically compelling and more structurally central by associating it with the crux of the dramatic action.

It could be argued, however, that the introduction of Ariste and the nature of his engagement with Sganarelle are major factors explaining the reputation that Molière was rapidly acquiring as the French Terence. Molière's debt to Terence's *Adelphi* has been called into question by Bourqui on the grounds that the dramaturgical structures of the two plays are very different.[15] But if the specific borrowings of Molière from Terence are much less significant than they were once thought to be, his relationship to Terence's play is

---

[14] Robert McBride suggests that the role of Le Parent in *Sganarelle*, first peformed a year before *L'École des maris*, could be seen as a prototype of the *raisonneur*. Le Parent speaks 11 lines in scene 12, warning the foolish Sganarelle not to jump to conclusions too hastily, but has otherwise no role in the action. See McBride's 'Le Raisonneur comme déclencheur de l'action comique chez Molière' in *Œuvres de Molière*, ed. N. Akiyama, Tokyo: J. P. Rinsen, 2002, vol. 9, pp. 421–50.

[15] Claude Bourqui, *Les Sources de Molière: répertoire critique des sources littéraires et dramatiques* (Paris: SEDES, 1999): 'En fait, les similitudes avec l'*École des maris* sont pratiquement inexistantes: une lointaine parenté du sujet [...] quelques lignes de la première scène de la pièce' (p. 59).

none the less instructive. Terence's two brothers disagree as to the leniency or severity with which the two sons should be treated, and the dramatic action revolves around the attitude of the older men in the face of the youths' amorous escapades. Terence treats both protagonists with more or less equal weight (in quantitative terms), even if the audience's sympathies are more likely to be with the more lenient of the two. Molière's play focuses much more prominently on the more severe of the two brothers, who is clearly the foolish protagonist, and on the attempts by his ward to escape his clutches by pursuing the young man she loves. So it might appear that French farce rather than Terentian elegance is what most matters to Molière. What is Terentian, in *L'École des maris*, however, is the grounding of a dramatic action in a moral issue. Micio's attempts to reason with Demea in the *Adelphi* are paralleled by Ariste's engagements with Sganarelle. But the combination of farcical structures and moral issues is peculiar to Molière and its success accounts for the reappearance of the *raisonneur* in subsequent plays.

3

L'*École des femmes*: the *raisonneur* as friend
and counsellor

Voulez-vous qu'en ami je vous ouvre mon cœur?[1]

In *L'École des femmes* (1662), Chrysalde is the friend of the protagonist
Arnolphe, who is obsessed by a fear of cuckoldry. He appears three
times in the play, twice with Arnolphe, and once with virtually the
whole cast for the denouement. In the course of his conversations
with Arnolphe, he seems to offer a lesson in stoicism, to express views
on the ideal educational attainment of a wife, and to sing the praises
of cuckoldry.

CHRYSALDE AND THE CRITICS

Finding strong support in what they see as the obviously absurd
praise of cuckoldry, some critics have no hesitation in seeing
Chrysalde as a comic character. In his allegedly excessive praise
of cuckoldry, 'Chrysalde becomes the fool', according to Fargher.[2]
Eustis thinks him every bit as absurd as Arnolphe.[3] Peacock questions the approach that takes the *raisonneur* as the mouthpiece of

---

[1] Chrysalde, *L'École des femmes* (5).
[2] Richard Fargher, 'Molière and his Reasoners' in *Studies in French Literature
presented to H. W. Lawton*, ed. J. C. Ireson and others (Manchester University Press,
1968), pp. 105–20, p. 108.
[3] Alvin Eustis, *Molière as Ironic Contemplator* (The Hague, Paris: Mouton, 1973),
p. 187.

seventeenth-century *honnêteté*, saying that 'it is extremely unlikely that any audience in the seventeenth century, or for that matter the twentieth century, would identify itself with, for example, Chrysalde's praise of cuckoldry'.[4] He believes that Chrysalde's blindness to his own weakness contributes to the comedy: by this he means that 'in his unremitting attack' on Arnolphe, 'his own vulnerability is only too apparent' (p. 306). He thinks he becomes 'intoxicated with his own part' in 4. 8 (p. 305), and finds comic effect in the fact that 'Chrysalde's perorations' in 1. 1 and 4. 8 'are unheeded', a comic disproportion between effort and achievement (p. 307).

If Chrysalde means everything he says, and particularly about cuckoldry, in deadly earnest, he would probably strike any audience as a fool. But some critics recognize that Chrysalde's discourse can be ironic. Peacock himself seems to recognize this when he says that Chrysalde 'deliberately provokes and taunts Arnolphe with his eulogy of cuckoldry' (p. 301). Lawrence sees provocation in Chrysalde's words too, and calls this encounter a 'session of malicious baiting'.[5] McBride sees Chrysalde as a 'spectateur ironique du personnage principal' and prefers the appellation 'comédien-raisonneur'.[6] Dandrey is the most eloquent proponent of Chrysalde's irony, situating his praise of cuckoldry within the long tradition of paradoxical eulogy.[7] He sees Chrysalde's recourse to irony as part of his overall strategy of speaking with lucid logic.

But critics have taken Chrysalde more seriously too. Nurse identifies the humanist pedigree in some of Chrysalde's claims.[8] He finds that in 1. 1 'Chrysalde is not guilty of irony or deliberate provocation' (p. 70), and that in 4. 8 he 'goes out of his way to avoid a dogmatic or provocative tone' (p. 71). He finds in him a defender

---

[4] Noël Peacock, 'The Comic Role of the *Raisonneur* in Molière's Theatre', *Modern Language Review*, 76 (1981), 298–310, p. 298.

[5] Francis L. Lawrence, 'The *Raisonneur* in Molière', *L'Esprit Créateur*, 6 (1966), 156–66, p. 160.

[6] Robert McBride, 'La Question du *raisonneur* dans les *écoles* de Molière', *Dix-septième siècle*, 113 (1976), 59–73, p. 72.

[7] Patrick Dandrey, *Molière ou l'esthétique du ridicule* (Paris: Klincksieck, 1992), pp. 193–8.

[8] Peter H. Nurse, *Molière and the Comic Spirit* (Geneva: Droz, 1991).

of 'an enlightened liberal education as the proper basis for *honnêteté* in a woman' (p. 70). He points out that 'Chrysalde's defence of philosophical detachment, or *ataraxia*, has been essentially stoic', but that 'he adopts a more Epicurean note when he suggests that cuckoldry might even have its pleasures' (p. 71). Chrysalde's stoical arguments about marriage and cuckoldry are echoes of those used 'seriously' by Pantagruel to Panurge in Rabelais's *Tiers Livre* (ch. 10): 'N'estez vous asceuré de votre vouloir? Le poinct principal y gist: tout le reste est fortuit, et dependent des fatales dispositions du Ciel.'[9] Nurse reminds us too how Montaigne promotes a philosophy of resignation in the context of problems of marital fidelity: 'Confessons le vray: il n'en est guere d'entre nous qui ne craingne plus la honte qui luy vient des vices de sa femme que des siens.'[10] Nurse concludes that, in the light of these antecedents, it is unlikely that 'Chrysalde's arguments are meant to be laughed at' (p. 74). But he does not go on to conclude that these are Molière's own arguments or that they constitute the didactic message of the play. Nurse admits that Chrysalde's stoical arguments have a dramatic function: they heighten for the audience the comic incongruity between Arnolphe's confidence in his plan and his complete inability to make it work (p. 75). Defaux, however, relishes the humanist intertexts of Chrysalde's discourse, and when he acknowledges the irony of his praise of cuckoldry, he none the less insists that the essential message of the *raisonneur* is a serious one: 'l'ironie très apparente de la tirade [...], si elle module la pensée et la rend quelque peu difficile à saisir, n'en altère cependant en rien le bon sens et le sérieux fondamental'.[11]

Ridiculous fool, witty ironist, learned humanist: all these views will reappear in the following discussion of Chrysalde's role and be reassessed in the light of the dramaturgical and comic structures into which he is integrated.

---

[9] François Rabelais, *Œuvres complètes*, ed. Guy Demerson and Michel Renaud (Paris: Seuil, 1995), p. 580.

[10] Montaigne, *Essais*, ed. Pierre Villey and V.-L. Saulnier, 3 vols. (Paris: Presses Universitaires de France, 1965), III, p. 860 (bk III, ch. 5).

[11] Gérard Defaux, *Molière ou les métamorphoses du comique: de la comédie morale au triomphe de la folie* (Lexington: French Forum, 1980; 2nd edn, Paris: Klincksieck, 1992), p. 103.

CHANCE MEETING AND SPONTANEOUS
ADVICE (1. 1)

The opening scene of *L'École des femmes* is a conversation between Arnolphe, first played by Molière, and Chrysalde, first played by L'Espy. What is said has necessarily at this point in the play to fulfil an expository function, conveying information to the audience about Arnolphe and his bizarre marriage plans. In order to make this plausible Molière has created the fiction that Arnolphe has been out of town, that he has just returned with the intention of marrying Agnès the next day, and that he has, we are led to assume, come across his friend Chrysalde outdoors (they are talking in a public place) and just told him of the marriage project that he has hitherto kept secret. How Molière conceives of Chrysalde's role and what he makes Chrysalde say is determined by the dramatist's need to create a situation in which Arnolphe will reveal, for the audience's benefit, his own unusual approach to marriage in general and to his own marriage in particular.

If I stress the opening context of this scene, it is because not all critics pay sufficient attention to the fictional situations that Molière creates and in which he makes his characters speak. Nurse, for instance, says that Chrysalde 'has come as a friend, in private, to warn Arnolphe against committing an irrevocable mistake' (p. 70). But this is completely to misconstrue the situation and to risk consequent misconstructions of the characters' speeches. Nurse's description makes Chrysalde look like the earnest giver of advice, who has deliberately sought out Arnolphe to counsel him. But the opening line of the play, spoken by Chrysalde ('Vous venez, dites-vous, pour lui donner la main?' (1)), makes it clear that he has not sought out Arnolphe in private to advise him; he has just met him, he has just heard the news of his intended marriage and he responds spontaneously to it. This gives quite a different colouring to Chrysalde's discourse.

If we look at how the scene is constructed, at its dramatic dynamic, it becomes hard to see Chrysalde's role as that of spokesman for stoicism or *honnêteté*, though there are certainly arguments derived

from stoicism and *honnêteté* in the views he advances. It is equally
hard, however, to turn him into a comic character in his own right.
Molière makes Chrysalde speak plausibly as Arnolphe's friend in
response first of all to the news that Arnolphe intends to marry. And
Molière is at pains to establish friendly relationship and friendly advice
as the parameters of their conversation at the start of the scene, and
to remind us of this throughout. The reader of the play knows of their
friendly relationship even before the opening line, since Chrysalde is
described as 'ami d'Arnolphe' in the list of characters. What Chrysalde
says to Arnolphe and how he says it must be interpreted within the
framework of one friend responding to the surprising news of another.
For the audience that does not have the benefit of the list of characters,
Molière makes Arnolphe repeatedly use the word 'ami' so as firmly to
establish the nature of their relationship (9, 73, 151). Chrysalde too
establishes a context of intimacy for their conversation. It is the news
of Arnolphe's imminent marriage that makes Chrysalde pause, look
around and offer to give advice to his friend:

> Nous sommes ici seuls; et l'on peut, ce me semble,
> Sans craindre d'être ouïs, y discourir ensemble:
> Voulez-vous qu'en ami je vous ouvre mon cœur?
>
> (3–5)

The view that Chrysalde then expresses up to line 72, with inter-
ruptions from Arnolphe, is straightforward. He does not preach
stoicism. He does not tell Arnolphe not to marry. He explains why
Arnolphe's marriage gives him cause for concern in his capacity as
his friend. Arnolphe is known as an outspoken critic of cuckolded
husbands. For Arnolphe to take on marriage is for him to take the
risk that his own criticisms of others might be made against himself.
Chrysalde's concern is plausible dramatically in that he is a friend
responding to Arnolphe's news; it is necessary dramatically since it
immediately informs the audience of one of Arnolphe's key characteristics, his obsession with cuckoldry; and it is dramatically fertile
since it allows Arnolphe to reply in a way that comically reveals
his detailed observation and cataloguing of all kinds of cuckolded
husbands.

It is interesting to see how Molière introduces Arnolphe's interruption at this point. Chrysalde is at pains to develop his concern

by stressing the very public pleasure that Arnolphe takes in exposing other men's misfortune. He has mocked a hundred husbands for their cuckoldry (16): 'Que vos plus grands plaisirs sont, partout où vous êtes, / De faire cent éclats des intrigues secrètes ...' (19–20). If Arnolphe felt that Chrysalde's concern was unreasonable or hyperbolic, he could reply with a denial. But Molière constructs Arnolphe's interruption at this point so as to confirm that Chrysalde's characterization of him is indeed correct and so as to make the audience laugh at Arnolphe's obsession. Arnolphe interrupts Chrysalde not to refute him, but to agree with the portrait that his friend has just sketched of him: 'Fort bien: est-il au monde une autre ville aussi / Où l'on ait des maris si patients qu'ici?' (21–2). Whereupon he recites a gleeful list of men's marital tribulations, simultaneously justifying and demonstrating the pleasures these give him.

This interruption informs the audience graphically of Arnolphe's obsession and allows the audience to laugh, laughter which is perhaps directed both at the targets of Arnolphe's satire (he makes the husbands appear foolish) and at Arnolphe's excessive obsession (he catalogues six different types of marital infidelity). But the interruption means that Chrysalde has not yet spelt out precisely for Arnolphe what his concern is. Molière engineers the opportunity for him to do this by making Arnolphe conclude, after his list of cuckolds, with the question: 'Enfin, ce sont partout des sujets de satire; / Et comme spectateur ne puis-je pas en rire?' (43–4). We might imagine how Molière could enliven his performance by gesturing at men in the audience, especially those close to him on stage, occupying the most expensive seats in the house.

Chrysalde completes the warning he had begun earlier and answers Arnolphe's question in a famous phrase which establishes the pattern of comic action for the rest of the play: 'Oui; mais qui rit d'autrui / Doit craindre qu'en revanche on rie aussi de lui' (45–46). The formulation is general, but the application is specifically to Arnolphe. It is worth noting that in the whole of this first long scene (199 lines), Arnolphe speaks most, with three speeches over ten lines long (25 lines, 21 lines, 32 lines), while Chrysalde makes only one speech longer than ten lines and it is this one in which he explains how Arnolphe's loud denunciations of cuckolds will put him at risk if he does indeed marry (27 lines).

For some critics Chrysalde's own weakness and risibility become evident in this speech. Eustis thinks (though there is no textual evidence to confirm this belief) that Chrysalde is himself a cuckold, and that his advice to Arnolphe to accept cuckoldry as a misfortune is given from a position of weakness (p. 186). Herzel sees a slightly different weakness in Chrysalde's position. He thinks that Chrysalde's stance of not mocking cuckolds in the way that Arnolphe does is adopted not out of charity but out of fear (pp. 568–9). Hence Peacock's argument that Chrysalde is blind to his own vulnerability when attacking Arnolphe (pp. 306–7). These critics can find Chrysalde's words risible because they are interpreting them as a general piece of disembodied advice. But his words can be interpreted differently if they are considered in their dramatic context: they are the logical completion of an expression of anxiety for his friend upon hearing news of the planned wedding; they respond to Arnolphe's earlier speech in lines 9–12; they need to dwell upon Chrysalde's anxiety for Arnolphe in order to motivate Arnolphe's next revelation, vital for the exposition, about the education of his intended bride.

Chrysalde succeeds in expressing his concern in a friendly way. As well as using the appellation 'cher compère' (65), he does not harangue Arnolphe, even less attack him; he builds his speech on an antithesis, speaking first about his own attitude (47–64), then about Arnolphe's (65–73). But it is not a sharp, conflictual antithesis. He makes it plain that he shares with Arnolphe a desire not to suffer in silence the whims of a flighty wife (53–4). The difference between them, which his antithesis brings out and which is the cause of his concern, is that whereas he, Chrysalde, does not shout about cuckoldry from the rooftops, Arnolphe does. And in consequence, should Chrysalde be cuckolded by his wife, society would be less likely to ridicule him in public, whereas Arnolphe would be a sitting target.

In its content and structure, Chrysalde's speech is a patient, non-aggressive expression of anxiety for a friend. It is also a response to Arnolphe's earlier claim that Chrysalde should not be worrying about Arnolphe's marriage: 'Peut-être que chez vous / Vous trouvez des sujets de craindre pour chez nous' (9–10). This is perhaps the evidence that causes Eustis to claim that Chrysalde is a cuckold. If so, he has certainly overinterpreted Arnolphe's line, and he has, to my mind, misinterpreted its tone. That Arnolphe should speak to

Chrysalde in such a provocative way is a further sign of the solidity of their friendship. Arnolphe is teasing, implying that Chrysalde should be more concerned about being cuckolded himself. In saying this, Arnolphe tells us more about his own supreme confidence in his ability to avoid cuckoldry than he does about the state of Chrysalde's marriage. From a dramaturgical point of view, Arnolphe's focus on Chrysalde here helps to motivate Chrysalde's response in which he argues that he has less fear of the consequences of being cuckolded than Arnolphe should have. Friendly and reciprocal wit with a competitive edge sets the tone of their conversation.

It is vital that Chrysalde should not only establish for the audience Arnolphe's obsession with cuckoldry, but also that he should express serious concern about the likely consequences of Arnolphe being cuckolded, since this will allow Molière to make Arnolphe reveal another key piece of information about himself that the audience needs to know before the plot can proceed. Arnolphe interrupts Chrysalde's expression of anxiety in order to eliminate it: Arnolphe's bride has been chosen and trained in such a way that she will be unable to cuckold him, since she is unworldy, uneducated. All she can do is pray, love her husband, sew and spin—traditional wifely pursuits. These things apart, she is stupid, certainly too stupid to commit adultery.

As Arnolphe gives details of his scheme, Chrysalde tries to comment on three occasions (81, 103, 106), but Arnolphe's immediate inter-ruptions convey confidence in his plan. Finally, however, Chrysalde makes a short speech suggesting its limitations (107–16). He raises two objections, the first in a subordinate clause, as if to acknowl-edge that this one will carry no weight with the cuckoldry-obsessed Arnolphe: it would be boring to spend one's life with a stupid woman (109–10). After this he makes an objection which strikes at the heart of Arnolphe's plan. He distinguishes between the clever woman, whom Arnolphe has said he is keen to avoid, and the stupid one (113–16). He argues against Arnolphe that a stupid wife might be more likely to be unfaithful since she would be morally ignorant of what she was doing, whereas a clever wife would first have to overcome the moral objection to infidelity. It is too solemn and untheatrical to claim, as Nurse does, that 'Chrysalde's contribution here is partly to defend an enlightened liberal education as the proper

basis for *honnêteté* in a woman' (p. 71). In the context of the dynamic
of the scene as a whole, it is clear that Chrysalde raises this objection
in order to make his friend pause before taking a step that could
so easily lead to his undoing. He is also, as in his earlier speech,
predicting for the audience a pattern of behaviour that the comic
action will trace. The uneducated Agnès will indeed unwittingly flirt
with Horace.

But Chrysalde's acutely observed and concisely expressed objection
to Arnolphe's scheme is also intended to allow Molière to show
the audience how comically blind and obstinate Arnolphe can be.
Arnolphe's reply retains the witty tone of their amicable conversation,
but he bluntly refuses to engage with Chrysalde's argument:

> A ce bel argument, à ce discours profond,
> Ce que Pantagruel à Panurge répond:
> Pressez-moi de me joindre à femme autre que sotte,
> Prêchez, patrocinez jusqu'à la Pentecôte;
> Vous serez ébahi, quand vous serez au bout,
> Que vous ne m'aurez rien persuadé du tout.
>
> (117–22)

Sarcastic praise for the quality of Chrysalde's argument, the authority
of Rabelais's comic fantasy, and a plethora of plosive alliteration
maintains the witty tone, but does nothing to demolish the force
of the very argument that anticipates Arnolphe's downfall. When
Chrysalde replies only 'Je ne vous dis plus mot' (123), the joke is on
Arnolphe. Fargher's gloss on 'Je ne vous dis plus mot' is puzzling:
'Chrysalde [...] talks mostly sense but insists on talking it, even when
he has promised to be silent' (p. 108). In fact Chrysalde says no
more on the topic in this scene. Arnolphe's pretence that Chrysalde
has been defeated in argument, when he has so patently triumphed,
highlights the folly of Arnolphe's confidence in his own views while
maintaining good relations with his obstinate friend. Chrysalde's 'Je
ne vous dis plus mot' anticipates the barrister who in court says 'No
more questions' when the witness has discredited himself. Arnolphe
does not realize, of course, that he has discredited himself.

After 'Je ne vous dis plus mot', Arnolphe does not need to, but in
fact does, explain why he is so confident in his choice of bride. And,
maintaining friendly relations, he invites Chrysalde to have supper

with him and his future bride that very evening. The implication is that if Arnolphe cannot persuade his friend with argument, Chrysalde can meet Agnès himself and assess her character and innocence. Molière is clearly keen to make the audience laugh at the overconfident and salacious Arnolphe by making him dwell on her innocence with the story of her asking 'Si les enfants qu'on fait se faisaient par l'oreille' (164). Dorante in *La Critique de l'École des femmes* explains how this story told by Arnolphe in support of his scheme directed audience laughter against him: 'Pour ce qui est des *enfants par l'oreille*, ils ne sont plaisants que par réflexion à Arnolphe; et l'auteur n'a pas mis cela pour être de soi un bon mot, mais seulement pour une chose qui caractérise l'homme, et peint d'autant mieux son extravagance' (sc. 6).

There is one further expository function that this scene has to fulfil. It needs to establish that Arnolphe has taken on a new and noble name. Molière does this by making Chrysalde reply to the story about Agnès's innocence with Arnolphe's old name: 'Je me réjouis fort, Seigneur Arnolphe ...' (165), which provokes a correction from Arnolphe. Chrysalde satirizes Arnolphe for preferring the inelegant 'Monsieur de la Souche', but agrees to oblige his friend in future. That Arnolphe should be known variously by his old name and his new name is essential to the unfolding of the plot and its dramatic ironies. The public revelation that one and the same man has two names plays a crucial part in the denouement, and the agent of that revelation will be Chrysalde.

The characters take their leave of each other, and each speaks an aside. Chrysalde's 'Ma foi, je le tiens fou de toutes les manières' (195) is clearly meant to secure the audience's assent, since Arnolphe has obstinately refused to take on board anything that Chrysalde has said. This view is confirmed by Arnolphe's aside:

> Il est un peu blessé sur certaines matières.
> Chose étrange de voir comme avec passion
> Un chacun est chaussé de son opinion!

> (196–8)

Fargher interprets Arnolphe's words as a serious attack on character weaknesses in Chrysalde, in particular on his 'obsessions and obstinacy' (p. 108). But that Arnolphe should think Chrysalde is besotted with his own views when all Chrysalde has done is to express spontaneous concern, to suggest a serious weakness in Arnolphe's plan, to mock him gently for his grand name change, and at every point to indulge his friend, says more about the occluded vision of Arnolphe than it does about Chrysalde.

CHRYSALDE'S SUPPER (4. 8)

Chrysalde does not reappear until 4. 8, when he turns up for the supper that Arnolphe had promised him and for the inspection of his supposedly naive bride Agnès. But there is no supper to be had, no inspection of Agnès, and the overall tone of their exchange is quite different from the play's opening scene. This is because, in between their meetings, Arnolphe has discovered the relationship between Agnès and Horace, and despite all his efforts has been unable to do anything about it. Incontrovertible evidence has therefore been provided to the audience and to Arnolphe that Chrysalde was right to argue that an innocent and ignorant young woman would flirt with a man without thinking she was doing anything wrong. Arnolphe has just had further evidence of the communication between the two young lovers and has heard from Horace (who thinks he is Monsieur de la Souche, not Arnolphe guardian of Agnès) that the young man intends, with the use of a ladder, to let himself into Agnès's bedroom that very evening.

Critical discussion of Chrysalde's speeches in this scene tends to overlook the dramatic context and to assume quite wrongly that the characters are debating known facts. But it is essential to take into account the very different states of mind and degrees of knowledge of the two interlocutors when assessing the particular contribution of Chrysalde. When he walks up to Arnolphe, the would-be-husband can have none of the confidence that he demonstrated during their earlier meeting. But Chrysalde knows nothing of what has happened. And this situation allows Molière comically to juxtapose their now very different registers of communication. So to Chrysalde's cheery 'Hé bien! souperons-nous avant la promenade?' (1216), Arnolphe replies gloomily 'Non, je jeûne ce soir' (1217). And so it goes on, until Chrysalde asks explicitly about his friend's change of tone and teases him with a possible reason: 'Serait-il point, compère, à votre passion / Arrivé quelque peu de tribulation?' (1222–3). If Arnolphe is verbally reticent, his facial expression speaks eloquently of his despair and Chrysalde comments on this: 'Je le jurerais presque à voir votre visage' (1224)—further evidence of Molière's highly physical performance in the role of Arnolphe.

In reply Arnolphe does not reveal the cause of his distress, but gestures towards it only indirectly:

> Quoi qu'il m'arrive, au moins aurai-je l'avantage
> De ne pas ressembler à de certaines gens
> Qui souffrent doucement l'approche des galants.
>
> (1225–7)

It is abundantly clear to the audience that Arnolphe is anxious about Horace's progress in seducing Agnès. This is because the audience has observed all the dramatic action since the beginning of the play. Chrysalde has not, and to him Arnolphe's words must be rather mysterious. To tell the truth directly to Chrysalde would be to admit that his friend's earlier anxieties had been justified and his own earlier confidence misplaced. Arnolphe's terseness and evasiveness are dramatically important. He had been voluble in their previous encounter, always interrupting Chrysalde and speaking at greater length, but his current reticence is a sign to the audience of his distress and his fear of humiliation. It is important too to realize that Arnolphe's indirect reference to his problem ('l'approche des galants' and the future tense 'aurai-je') cannot convey to Chrysalde his very real and very urgent anxieties. To Chrysalde, Arnolphe's words could indeed mean either that Agnès has already been unfaithful or that Arnolphe is now even more determined that she should not be. It is important to bear in mind these two possible meanings for Chrysalde when considering his reply, since he tries, at different stages, to respond to both. If we remember their jovial banter of 1. 1, it will seem entirely plausible that Chrysalde would not now want to hurt Arnolphe by pressing to find out exactly what lies behind his words, and that the concerned Chrysalde would fill the silence created by Arnolphe with consoling words for his friend. Accordingly he delivers a long speech the purpose of which is to ease Arnolphe's evident distress as best he can, given his ignorance of the full circumstances.

For Fargher (p. 108) and Peacock (p. 307), Chrysalde takes his views to such extremes in this scene that he becomes comic. Eustis elaborates, claiming that Chrysalde is 'aggressive' (p. 187) and that Molière makes fun of his views which are, he says, 'a parody of the famous *juste milieu*, which according to his lights is to keep silent and accept horns, without however encouraging one's wife to bestow them' (p. 187). Rather than laugh at Chrysalde for expressing absurd views, other critics comment on the biting irony that characterizes his words in this scene. 'Quelle taquinerie diabolique, mille fois plus mordante que celle de toute à l'heure! Au lieu de tendre une perche à son ami, voilà Chrysalde qui se fait l'apologue ardent du cocuage,' says McBride (p. 70). Dandrey too insists on the irony of Chrysalde's praise of cuckoldry and sums up Chrysalde's stance as a 'point de vue de blague supérieur' (p. 194). Defaux admits there is irony in the praise of cuckoldry but patiently explains the serious message of adopting the *juste milieu* (pp. 102–3). Only Defaux's approach, it seems to me, recognizes a change of tone in the course of the speech. A dramaturgical reading, however, taking the fictional context and the dynamics of the dialogue into account, shows up clearly all the different elements in Chrysalde's discourse which fulfil different functions. He is at all times attempting to communicate with his increasingly distressed friend, whom he wants to relieve, but to do so he variously cajoles, teases, reasons, amuses, comforts and advises.

Seizing on Arnolphe's preoccupation with 'l'approche des galants' (whether it has already happened or is only yet being envisaged by Arnolphe), he begins by trying to shake his interlocutor out of his obsession with cuckoldry. He is not here speaking in praise of cuckoldry or even of tolerance of cuckoldry. He is trying to make his obsessed friend look at cuckoldry in a different perspective, which might relieve him in his present and evident agony. His argument is that there are many other kinds of behaviour that might be considered worse than cuckoldry; so, by implication, things cannot be all bad. He is not standing ironically above the situation, but he speaks with a wit which he hopes might benefit his friend. Hence the hyperbolic enumeration: 'Etre avare, brutal, fourbe, méchant et lâche, / N'est rien, à votre avis, auprès de cette tache' (1232–3). His first strategy, then, is to engage intellectually with Arnolphe, to amuse him, to make him see things differently, to diminish the supreme importance in human affairs that he attaches to cuckoldry.

His next argument follows on from this and appeals to the stoical concepts of fate and ataraxia in order to loosen the stranglehold that cuckoldry has on Arnolphe. This argument seems to be based on the understanding that 'l'approche des galants' has not yet taken place, that it is merely a hypothesis. Chrysalde's words might therefore seem vain to the audience and to Arnolphe. But it is important to realize that he is trying his sensitive best with the very little that Arnolphe has said to him. If there is discomfiture, it is Arnolphe's since he has not told, and clearly does not wish to tell, Chrysalde exactly what has happened. Chrysalde's first point is that Arnolphe's self-esteem should not depend so singularly on a chance happening over which he has no control. This line of argument does not turn Chrysalde into a stoic philosopher, an ironic sage, or an indulgent fool. The language in which he expresses himself is primarily geared to persuading and comforting Arnolphe in circumstances that are not at all clear to Chrysalde:

> A le bien prendre au fond, pourquoi voulez-vous croire
> Que de ce cas fortuit dépende notre gloire,
> Et qu'une âme bien née ait à se reprocher
> L'injustice d'un mal qu'on ne peut empêcher?

> (1236–9)

He begins with the comforting and encouraging phrase 'A le bien prendre au fond'; he expresses himself in an incredulous question directed specifically at Arnolphe; he generalizes his focus to 'notre gloire' since 'votre gloire', if more accurate, would have been too aggressive; and he flatters his interlocutor by inviting Arnolphe to think of himself as a naturally worthy person, 'une âme bien née'.

In the next ten lines (1240–9) he reiterates this same stoic argument, but using different language the better to get through to Arnolphe. He develops a sustained antithesis between on the one hand the misery that Arnolphe's attitude can bring to any man, a life of constant trepidation at the thought of 'un monstre plein d'effroi' (1242) of the man's own creation, and on the other hand 'du cocuage / […] une plus douce image' (1245), which means not worrying about the possibility of cuckoldry since it is, he says comfortingly, a chance event. This speech does not amount to praise of cuckoldry. Chrysalde is saying that it is more agreeable to live without anxiety. There is comedy in his recommendation of stoic indifference to what might happen, but it is very much at Arnolphe's expense. The audience knows, but Chrysalde does not, that it is hard for Arnolphe to be indifferent, since what might happen is already happening.

Chrysalde makes a delicately imperceptible transition into his final line of argumentation, which deals precisely with the possibility that Arnolphe might already have been the victim of infidelity. He has so far dealt with the relative importance of cuckoldry (and tried to diminish it) and with the attitude to be adopted towards cuckoldry. He now turns to a man's possible reaction to becoming a victim of infidelity, and though he does not know it, this is of course what is most relevant to Arnolphe's immediate fears concerning the relationship of Horace and Agnès. Chrysalde's approach is to identify three different reactions, two of which are extreme and are, he says, to be avoided; the third is to be recommended. Summed up like this, his approach might seem to be structured like a discursive essay. In fact, his presentation of the three different reactions is governed by his need to address the specific interests, prejudices and concerns of Arnolphe as far as he can perceive them.

Looking downcast, Arnolphe has said that he will not be the kind of man to suffer rivals in silence (1226–7). This litotes can be taken to mean that Arnolphe will be outspoken in his condemnation of any rival and loud in his attempt to defeat him. This might remind us of the point that Chrysalde makes in 1. 1, that it is better for a potential cuckold not to draw attention to himself the better to diminish the public humiliation should he eventually become a cuckold (59–65). Concern for Arnolphe leads Chrysalde to make the same point again, though in a new context.

But before he does so, he first sketches and condemns the reaction of a group he identifies as indulgent husbands, who:

> De leurs femmes toujours vont citant les galants,
> En font partout l'éloge, et prônent leurs talents,
> Témoignent avec eux d'étroites sympathies,
> Sont de tous leurs cadeaux, de toutes leurs parties.
>
> (1254–7)

There is a reason why Chrysalde deals with this indulgent reaction first and gives a satirical sketch of the type. It is a rhetorical ploy. He knows already that it will secure Arnolphe's assent, since in 1. 1 Arnolphe too had spoken satirically against indulgent husbands (21–45).

He and Arnolphe can agree to condemn the indulgent reaction to cuckoldry. Having won him over with this first kind, Chrysalde moves on to the reaction which is at the opposite extreme and which is precisely the reaction that Arnolphe implies will be his own when he says he will not suffer in silence. It is the reaction of loud fury and Chrysalde gently condemns it:

> Si je n'approuve pas ces amis des galants,
> Je ne suis pas aussi pour ces gens turbulens
> Dont l'imprudent chagrin, qui tempête et qui gronde,
> Attire au bruit qu'il fait les yeux de tout le monde.
>
> (1262–6)

In condemning the furious reaction, Chrysalde is at pains to remind Arnolphe that he too is against indulgence, reminding him of their common ground. It is significant that Chrysalde does not spell out the dangers of reacting furiously, which might terrify Arnolphe. But the dangers are strongly implied: the louder the reaction, the more noticeable, and hence the more humiliating, the effect will be.

Chrysalde's third way, which he recommends, is that of the husband who is 'honnête' (1268) and 'prudent' (1269). The fact that Chrysalde does not spell out a specific course of action does not make it risible. He defines it as 'Entre ces deux partis', which means avoiding indulgence and avoiding public remonstrances. Chrysalde is specific, however, as to the advantages to the husband of adopting the third way: 'Et quand on le sait prendre, on n'a point à rougir / Du pis dont une femme avec nous puisse agir' (1270–1). So the husband will not feel public shame in the same way as he would if reacting angrily. And the fact of cuckoldry can, on that account, seem less dreadful. It is important to insist on Chrysalde's terms here: 'Quoi qu'on en puisse dire enfin, le cocuage / Sous des traits moins affreux aisément s'envisage' (1272–3). This is no praise of cuckoldry. It is an admission that cuckoldry is a dreadful thing for the husband. But it is expressed as persuasive consolation for Arnolphe. If he fears he has a rival (a matter which Chrysalde has

still sensitively not tackled head-on), he should know that there is
a way of responding that will make his situation less bleak than he
might envisage it to be. Translations of this couplet can considerably
falsify Chrysalde's subtly calculated terminology and argumentation,
like Maya Slater's: 'I tell you, cuckoldry—whatever people say— / Is
perfectly alright, it happens every day.'[12] Molière's Chrysalde says no
such thing.

His speech is a triumph of delicately constructed consolation and
encouragement to a mysteriously distressed and obsessive friend.
But the audience, which, unlike Chrysalde, has repeatedly witnessed the rootedness of Arnolphe's obsession and knows how
close to collapse his whole scheme is, will not be surprised to
find Arnolphe little consoled by what he has just heard. His reply
is brief, sarcastic and dismissive. He calls Chrysalde's speech a
'beau discours' (1276) and says it will have cuckolds queuing up
to join the confraternity. Eustis thinks that Arnolphe's rejoinder is
a 'dead hit' against Chrysalde (p. 187). But Arnolphe's response
tells us more about himself than it does about Chrysalde's speech.
It tells us that he has blatantly misinterpreted Chrysalde, who has
painstakingly condemned indulgence of cuckoldry. It suggests, therefore, that he had not been listening. This is more likely to make
Arnolphe look foolish and inflexible than it is Chrysalde. Arnolphe's
response is understandable, however, in the light of his preoccupation with the urgent threat from Horace that he has not revealed to
Chrysalde.

Chrysalde is quick to correct Arnolphe's misunderstanding: 'Je ne
dis pas cela, car c'est ce que je blâme' (1280). Fargher thinks that
Chrysalde has failed to understand Arnolphe's irony (p. 109). But
it is Arnolphe who has misunderstood Chrysalde's careful speech
(through inattention, one might infer) and it is Arnolphe who will
fail to understand Chrysalde's irony when he soon changes tone
and invites Arnolphe to contemplate the advantages of cuckoldry. In
the meantime Chrysalde reformulates his advice with a new image:
marriage is like a game of dice; chance determines what happens, but
men can play skilfully to make the best of a bad job (1281–5). It is

---

[12] Molière, *The Misanthrope, Tartuffe and other Plays*, tr. Maya Slater (Oxford
University Press, 2001), p. 51.

an image which Arnolphe dismisses in such a way as to make it clear that he is still obsessed with his own case of potential cuckoldry.

Chrysalde has of course tried to diminish Arnolphe's obsession with cuckoldry at the beginning of his long speech, but he tries once again now. And once again he uses humour to try to win over his friend, inviting him to consider it as preferable to be a cuckold than to have a fiercely virtuous, domineering wife, his hyperbolic language making such wives sound fearful: 'Ces dragons de vertu, ces honnêtes diablesses, / Se retranchant toujours sur leurs sages prouesses' (1296–7). It is vital to understand that Chrysalde is trying to cajole Arnolphe with his wit so that the climax of his speech will be interpreted as humorously ironic:

> Le cocuage n'est que ce que l'on le fait,
> Qu'on peut le souhaiter pour de certaines causes,
> Et qu'il a ses plaisirs comme les autres choses.

> (1303–5)

This praise of cuckoldry is a rhetorical strategy. It is not meant seriously. He is teasing his friend and thereby trying to win him over in a different way. These words are his witty conclusion to the nightmare scenario of the tyrannical wife. The thrust of Chrysalde's speech is towards making Arnolphe laugh with him and agree with him.

But Arnolphe reacts to Chrysalde's ironic praise of cuckoldry with comic horror and anger, disassociating himself from any such indulgence. Here, more than ever, context matters. The three lines quoted above are not an aphorism for all time, but a rhetorical ploy, which is now followed by yet another rhetorical ploy. Chrysalde tries one last time to calm Arnolphe and uses a new, and also light-hearted, argument: better men than Arnolphe have been cuckolded, so he would be in good company (1313–15). But this argument angers Arnolphe even more. He thinks he is being made fun of by Chrysalde ('Mais cette raillerie, en un mot, m'importune' (1317)) and terminates the conversation. Chrysalde presses no further, noting Arnolphe's anger and promising to find out the cause: 'Vous êtes en courroux. / Nous en saurons la cause' (1318–19).

This last point is important. Whereas Arnolphe clearly comes to feel that Chrysalde is mocking him with his repeated injunctions not to be obsessed with cuckoldry, Chrysalde is right to realize that something deeper lies beneath Arnolphe's anger. And it is characteristic of his friend to want to get to the bottom of it. If Chrysalde has succeeded in this scene only in increasing Arnolphe's distress, it is because Arnolphe has refused to say what is wrong, leaving it to Chrysalde to guess what propositions might bring Arnolphe comfort. Chrysalde simply cannot know, but the audience does, that, all along, Arnolphe's mind is on the ladder that could imminently take Horace to Agnès's bedroom to make a cuckold of him. Chrysalde has tried his best to respond patiently, encouragingly, wittily to his friend's distress, without, however, wanting to probe him too much with insensitive questions. The laughter is directed at Arnolphe, who is so doggedly obsessed with cuckoldry and so singlemindedly preoccupied with his own imminent but unavowed downfall.

CHRYSALDE AND THE DENOUEMENT (5. 7-9)

After his dismissal in act 4 by the angry, preoccupied and unforth-coming Arnolphe, Chrysalde reappears for a third and final time in the last three scenes of the play (5. 7-9). Most critics are happy to form a judgement of Chrysalde's role on the basis of his first two appearances and ignore his last. Peacock points out 'his verbal "pas de deux" with Oronte, a series of mock romantic couplets' (p. 301). If Nurse dismisses this reappearance as of 'little importance except to be present at the dénouement' (p. 70), McBride does at least, though rather grudgingly, acknowledge that he does have a dramatic function here: 'Si Chrysalde apparaît dans le dénouement, ce n'est que pour rattacher les nœuds de l'intrigue en expliquant qu'Agnès est la fille de sa sœur à lui, destinée d'avance à Horace' (p. 72).

   If he has so far appeared detached from the plot, speaking only to Arnolphe in his capacity as friend, the fantastic recognition scene, which brings about the marriage of Horace and Agnès, weaves Chrysalde into the very fabric of the action, in much the same way as Ariste becomes the agent of the denouement in the last act of *L'École des maris*. Without him there would be no denouement, and without him there would no friendly concern for an isolated Arnolphe. Chrysalde continues to act as Arnolphe's friend, but he has a new function. When we see him walk on stage in 5. 7, with the mysterious Enrique, it emerges that they are brothers-in-law and that, as Enrique is the long-lost father of Agnès, Chrysalde is her uncle. Chrysalde has grasped all this by the time he comes on stage, but the audience understands it only gradually. The change in his status inevitably, however, has important implications for whatever he says to Arnolphe. He is no longer a disinterested friend, but a friend who is closely related to the woman Arnolphe has fashioned to be his bride.

In this same scene, Arnolphe is reunited with his friend Oronte, Horace's father, and tells him that he knows why he has come. It is essential that we remember that Arnolphe does not know as much as he thinks he does; he knows only that Oronte wishes Horace to marry Enrique's daughter; he does not know that Enrique's daughter is Agnès. Too confident in his all too partial knowledge, he wastes no time in urging Oronte to enforce his parental authority and make his son marry the girl in question, just as in *L'École des maris* Sganarelle is keen to hasten the marriage of Valère to the woman he thinks wrongly is Léonor, when it is in reality his own intended Isabelle. Arnolphe thinks that he is thereby saving Agnès for himself. But Chrysalde knows otherwise, and has some difficulty in understanding why Arnolphe, who claims to know why Oronte has come, should want to hasten the marriage of Horace and Agnès. This complex situation accounts for Chrysalde's two fair-minded contributions at this point. The first is to advise against the arbitrary exercise of parental authority. In response to Arnolphe and about Horace, he says: 'Si son cœur a quelque répugnance, / Je tiens qu'on ne doit pas lui faire violence' (1684–5). On the surface he is arguing against Arnolphe, who wants to expedite the marriage, but in arguing for Horace's right not to marry someone he might not like, Chrysalde is to some extent safeguarding Arnolphe's position and frankly cannot understand why Arnolphe so resolutely takes up the cudgels again in favour of the exercise of parental authority. His puzzlement leads to this honest aside to Arnolphe:

> Je suis surpris, pour moi, du grand empressement
> Que vous nous faites voir pour cet engagement,
> Et ne puis deviner quel motif vous inspire …
>
> (1698–1700)

The misunderstanding arises precisely because of Arnolphe's hasty claim to know what is going on. It is a sign of his friendship with Arnolphe that Chrysalde, instead of blandly supporting his new-found family interests, should want to explore with Arnolphe the loss to him that this new state of affairs would entail. But the laughter is, as usual, directed at Arnolphe, who will not respond to his friend's overtures, who interrupts him to say with profoundly comic irony at his own expense: 'Je sais ce que je fais, et dis ce qu'il faut dire' (1701).

Incorporating Chrysalde in the dramatic action of the denouement is vital for one major dramatic reason. Molière needs to engineer the public revelation that Arnolphe and Monsieur de la Souche are one and the same man. Horace still thinks that Agnès's captor is a Monsieur de la Souche whom he has not met. The denouement clearly requires that he be disabused. Chrysalde is the agent who can most readily bring this about. The discussion about names in 1. 1, when Arnolphe reveals testily how important it is to him to be called by his new name, is what motivates the disillusionment of Horace in act 5. When Oronte addresses Arnolphe as 'seigneur Arnolphe' (1702), Chrysalde reminds him that he has already told him about Arnolphe's new name: 'Ce nom l'aigrit; / C'est Monsieur de la Souche, on vous l'a déjà dit' (170–3). We might imagine Chrysalde telling Oronte about the new name in a satirical manner, given the way he had teased Arnolphe about it in act 1. At all events, in publicizing the name he is only doing Arnolphe's bidding, making sure that his friend becomes known by his preferred name. The dramatic effect, however, is to make Horace exclaim in enlightened horror. When he was told that he was to marry Enrique's daughter, he was clearly not told that she was the woman in Arnolphe's care, otherwise his horror at this point would be tempered by delight.

For the denouement to be complete, however, Arnolphe himself needs to discover that Enrique's daughter is none other than Agnès. The discovery is engineered with such complexity that it gives the lie to Molière's alleged lack of interest in plot. It is Arnolphe's final and heaviest fall in the play. For as the restive Agnès is brought on stage by Alain and Georgette and as Arnolphe prepares triumphantly to take her away with him, he is faced by a puzzled Oronte, who cannot understand why Arnolphe wants to take away the very girl who is to marry Horace. Both Oronte and Chrysalde express their confusion over Arnolphe's behaviour. Both of them had clearly assumed, when Arnolphe said he knew why they were there, that he really did know they had come to marry off Horace and to reclaim Agnès. But they were assuming wrongly that Horace had been put in the picture and had explained things to Arnolphe. Oronte and Chrysalde had therefore wrongly thought that when Arnolphe was urging Oronte to expedite his son's marriage to Enrique's daughter that he was doing it *en connaissance de cause*. Oronte, who knows nothing of Arnolphe's own plans for Agnès, cannot now understand why Arnolphe had adopted such an attitude: 'Sur quoi votre discours était-il donc fondé?' (1738). But for Chrysalde everything now falls into place. Molière has so handled the revelation that it comes as a surprise to both Arnolphe and the audience and both need to hear an explanation, which is given in stychomythic rhyming couplets by Oronte and Chrysalde. Agnès is the illegitimate daughter of Enrique and Chrysalde's sister, whom Enrique had entrusted to a peasant woman as a baby, the very peasant woman from whom Arnolphe had acquired her.

Over and above the reunion of Enrique and Agnès, and the mutual delight of Agnès and Horace, two final contributions from Chrysalde dominate the ending of the play. First, it is appropriate that he should speak to his friend Arnolphe who is reeling from the news, and who then leaves speechless and angry. His words are both consoling and ironic. He begins by expressing sympathy for Arnolphe, entering into his feelings: 'Je devine à peu près quel est votre supplice' (1760). His words throughout the play have attempted to make Arnolphe minimize his anxieties, and that is his approach again here. Arnolphe may feel distressed, but the way things have turned out will at least have the advantage of preventing Arnolphe from being cuckolded. Chrysalde generalizes this observation: 'Si n'être point cocu vous semble un si grand bien, / Ne vous point marier en est le vrai moyen' (1762–3). This may seem flippant, but it is characteristic of the way in which Chrysalde has attempted to console Arnolphe with humour and wit. He may seem to be giving different advice from earlier in the play, but this is because his advice always responds to the situation as he sees it. Earlier Arnolphe was on the point of marrying within twenty-four hours. Now his bride has been taken away from him. So Chrysalde's advice is logical in the light of Arnolphe's fears and appropriate to the circumstances. If it none the less seems too wittily abrupt, it needs to be understood in the context of the play's comically brisk ending and Chrysalde's new role in the action. As well as expressing concern for his friend, Chrysalde now also speaks as the happy uncle rejoicing, with his new-found brother-in-law, in the marriage of his niece.

Horace's ensuing explanation to his father that all has worked out well since Agnès is the woman he has been in love with and wanted to marry all along is the vital and final part of the denouement, and Chrysalde's role is central here. What this information will certainly reveal to Chrysalde is that Arnolphe's anxieties in 4. 8 about 'l'approche des galants' were real, that Arnolphe really was on the point of becoming a cuckold. This is Chrysalde's moment of recognition. As everyone rejoices, he wants to rejoice with them, but he also wants to look to his friend, who has walked off stage. These two sentiments, that befit Chrysalde's dual role in the final act, find expression in the last three lines of the play:

> Allons dans la maison débrouiller ces mystères,
> Payer à notre ami ces soins officieux,
> Et rendre grâce au Ciel qui fait tout pour le mieux.
>
> (1777–9)

There may well be a note of irony in 'soins officieux', since Arnolphe's care for Agnès has been far from disinterested. But if there is, it does nothing to diminish the value of the phrase 'notre ami'. The happy tone prevails as the comedy celebrates the triumph of young love, but it is no tragic ending for Arnolphe. The ties of friendship that throughout the play may not prevent him from being ridiculous but certainly prevent him from being despicable are vigorously reasserted in these closing lines. Arnolphe will now have more friends.

Chrysalde is needed to bring the plot to a conclusion and to maintain a balance between rejoicing with the young couple and attending to Arnolphe. The role he plays at the end has been prepared by the invariably concerned, supportive, patient, witty, and teasing words he has spoken to Arnolphe on his two earlier appearances. Like Sganarelle without Ariste, Arnolphe without Chrysalde would have been an obsessive and tyrannical figure from farce. With the friendly attentions of Chrysalde, Arnolphe becomes that peculiarly moliéresque creation: 'ridicule en de certaines choses et honnête homme en d'autres' (Dorante, *La Critique de L'École des femmes*, scene 6). The depiction of Chrysalde's generous friendship owes something to a long tradition of discourse on friendship with its roots in Cicero's *De amicitia*. The influence of this discourse on Molière's conception of the *raisonneur* will be explored fully in connection with his depiction of the most patient and long-suffering friend in all his theatre, Philinte in *Le Misanthrope*.

4

Tartuffe: the raisonneur as brother-in-law and polemicist

De l'hymen de ma sœur touchez-lui quelque chose.[1]

Cléante in *Tartuffe* (first performed in 1664, extant version in 1669) has been considered both a lucid spokesman for reason and an interfering bore. These incompatible views are even more problematic than the disagreements over the two previous *raisonneurs* in view of three complicating factors peculiar to *Tartuffe*: the contemporary controversy to which the play originally gave rise; the successive rewritings of the play that Molière had to undertake in order to obtain permission for it to be performed in public; and the evolution of Cléante's role, in successive re-writings, such as it can be deduced from the partial evidence that remains.

CLÉANTE AND THE CRITICS

For Bray, seemingly happy to contradict his general claim that there are no *raisonneurs* in Molière's theatre, Cléante is 'un pur raisonneur': 'c'est le sage, un truchement de l'esprit qui animait le chœur dans la tragédie grecque'.[2] For once agreeing with Bray, Defaux and Dandrey admire Cléante's lucidity and his eloquent support for the 'milieu

---

[1] Damis to Cléante in *Tartuffe* (217).
[2] René Bray, *Molière: homme de théâtre* (Paris: Mercure de France, 1954), p. 31.

qu'il faut' and see in him not only a spokesman for the 'honnêteté' of his age, but for Molière too.[3] Moore, however, had already denied that Molière's own views could be found in Cléante's speeches, claiming that Molière makes Cléante express certain views of religious devotion simply because they are 'the artistic opposite of Tartuffe's exaggerated and false piety'.[4] Other critics are quick to find fault with Cléante and turn him into a ridiculous character in his own right. The list of alleged vices is long. Peacock finds him prolix, overly rhetorical and cowering.[5] Fargher thinks he is unimpressive, cowardly, and inept.[6] For Herzel, he is self-important, long-winded, 'a ridiculous meddling bore'.[7] Eustis is emphatic that 'Cléante is a comic figure.'[8]

The critical dichotomy between eloquent sage and foolish bore, to which discussions of Ariste and Chrysalde have accustomed us, is once again in evidence in the case of Cléante. But since critical views of Cléante are also coloured by the various modern attitudes to the controversy which *Tartuffe* provoked, it is important to understand Cléante's role in the context of this controversy. It will be helpful, therefore, at the beginning of this chapter, to rehearse the three key stages in the play's evolution between 1664 and 1669.

CONTROVERSY AND EVOLUTION

Tartuffe received its first performance, as a three-act play, before Louis XIV at Versailles on 12 May 1664 in the context of a royal festival

---

[3] Gérard Defaux, *Molière ou les métamorphoses du comique: de la comédie morale au triomphe de la folie* (Lexington: French Forum, 1980; 2nd edn, Paris: Klincksieck, 1992), p. 104; Patrick Dandrey, *Molière ou l'esthétique du ridicule* (Paris: Klincksieck, 1992), pp. 190–1.

[4] W. G. Moore, *Molière: A New Criticism* (Oxford: Clarendon Press, 1949), p. 74.

[5] Noël Peacock, 'The Comic Role of the *Raisonneur* in Molière's Theatre', *Modern Language Review*, 76 (1981), 298–310, pp. 305, 307.

[6] Richard Fargher, 'Molière and his Reasoners' in *Studies in French Literature presented to H. W. Lawton*, ed. J. C. Ireson and others (Manchester University Press, 1968), p. 109.

[7] Roger W. Herzel, 'The Function of the *Raisonneur* in Molière's Comedy', *Modern Language Notes*, 90 (1975), 564–75, pp. 569–70.

[8] Alvin Eustis, *Molière as Ironic Contemplator* (The Hague, Paris: Mouton, 1973), p. 190.

intended to inaugurate the royal palace and known as the 'Plaisirs de l'île enchantée.' Molière played a central role in the organization of the festival, performed another new play, *La Princesse d'Élide*, and revived two others, *Les Fâcheux* and *Le Mariage forcé*. Within days, and as a result of largely hidden pressures, the king declared a ban on public performances of *Tartuffe*. In *Le Roi glorieux au monde*, published in August 1664 by the priest Pierre Roullé, Louis is praised for his firm treatment of Molière, who is viciously attacked as 'le plus signalé impie et libertin qui fut jamais dans les siècles passés' (*OC*, I, 1143). If not suppressed, the play, Roullé claims, would have been likely to 'ruiner la Religion catholique, en blâmant et jouant sa plus religieuse et sainte pratique, qui est la conduite et direction des âmes et des familles par de sages guides et conducteurs pieux' (*OC*, I, 1143–4). Given controversy of such virulence, it is hardly surprising that modern critics disagree with each other. In the same month that Roullé's pamphlet appeared, Molière published a short reply addressed to the king in which he defends himself and his play against the charges. His play, he claims, attacks religious hypocrisy not religious devotion (*Premier Placet, OC*, I, 889–91). We cannot verify Roullé's claims or Molière's defence, because this three-act version did not survive.[9]

Extended to five acts, the play had a number of private performances in aristocratic houses, and was finally performed in public in Molière's Parisian theatre, the Palais-Royal, on 5 August 1667 with a new title, *L'Imposteur*, and a new name for the religious hypocrite, Panulphe. The king was in Flanders on a military campaign, but the reaction of the judicial authorities came swiftly. On 6 August Lamoignan, premier président du parlement de Paris, responsible for policing Paris during the king's absence, banned Molière from putting on further performances. The dramatist acted equally swiftly, sending two of

---

[9] There are two hypotheses about the content of the three-act version of *Tartuffe*. One is that it was composed essentially of what later became acts 1, 3, and 4 (see John Cairncross, *New Light on Molière* (Geneva: Droz, 1956), pp. 1–53); the other that the three acts were what later became acts 1–3. The second hypothesis is supported by a comment in La Grange's *Registre* to the effect that '[on a représenté] trois actes du Tartuffe qui estoient les trois premiers' (*Registre de La Grange 1659–1685*, ed. Bert Edward Young and Grace Philputt Young, 2 vols. (Paris: Droz, 1947), I, p. 67). Cairncross interprets La Grange's comment as not necessarily meaning what it most obviously appears to mean (pp. 17–21).

his actors with a petition to the king on 8 August. Molière's petition alludes to royal authority to perform the play, which, unfortunately for Molière, must have been oral rather than written, and to changes he has introduced since the first version, in particular dressing his religious hypocrite as man of the world rather than in minor clerical orders, which, it is implied, is how he had appeared previously (*Second Placet, OC*, I, 891–2). Though Molière's actors did not get to see the king, they brought back his answer, which was that he would have the play scrutinized, and then performed, on his return. In the meantime, Molière met with further opposition. To judicial censure was added religious censure. On 11 August the Archbishop of Paris issued an *Ordonnance* that threatened with excommunication anyone seeing or reading, in public or in private, 'une comédie très dangereuse, et qui est d'autant plus capable de nuire à la religion que, sous prétexte de condamner l'hypocrisie ou la fausse dévotion, elle donne lieu d'en accuser indifféremment tous ceux qui font profession de la plus solide piété' (*OC* I, 1145). This intervention made Molière's position seem even weaker than after the first ban, but it did not prevent him from putting on private performances for the broad-minded prince de Condé in March and September 1668. Although this version of the play has not survived, we have a strong sense of what it was like, as an anonymous account of the first performance, scene by scene, was published in 1667 under the title *Lettre sur la comédie de l'imposteur* (*OC*, I, 1147–80).[10] It was very substantially like the text of the play that was eventually published in 1669 as *Tartuffe ou l'imposteur*, but there are differences which allow us to see what further changes Molière made before finally securing the king's permission to perform his play in public.

This final permission came in early 1669, and on 5 February the play was performed at the Palais-Royal, the same day on which Molière presented a further petition to the king, thanking him for bringing the play back to life (*Troisième Placet, OC*, I, 893). The king saw a private performance on 21 February and the play was published in March with a preface in which Molière defends *Tartuffe* in particular

[10] See La Mothe Le Vayer, *Lettre sur la comédie de l'imposteur*, ed. Robert McBride (University of Durham Modern Languages Series, 1994). McBride argues for the authorship of La Mothe Le Vayer; see also his reconstruction of the 1667 version: Molière, *L'Imposteur de 1667 prédécesseur du Tartuffe*, ed. Robert McBride (University of Durham Modern Languages Series, 1999).

and the theatre more generally against his enemies. This is the version of the play which we read today, and the only extant version.

It is crucial to bear in mind this polemical context and the three-stage evolution of the text of Molière's play if we are to grasp the significance of Cléante's speeches and understand some of the critical controversies which they have provoked. Molière's paratextual material and the anonymous *Lettre sur la comédie de l'imposteur* advertise, or at least allow us to deduce, efforts that the dramatist made in the course of the text's evolution to neutralize his opponents. Cléante's role is central to these efforts. We cannot know if a Cléante character featured in the first version of *Tartuffe* in 1664;[11] but we know from the 1667 *Lettre* that, in the second version, Cléante was intended to appear as 'un véritable honnête homme' (*OC*, I, 1165) and the proponent of an 'excellente morale' (*OC*, I, 1161). By comparing the 1667 *Lettre* with the 1669 edition of the play, we can deduce that certain of his speeches were relocated or reattributed to enhance his character as a good man and his dramaturgical and polemical effectiveness.[12] Molière's preface to the 1669 edition is clear about his own conception of the role of Cléante. The dramatist's interventions in the polemic always assume that the problem he needs to address is the charge that his play attacks religion, and this is indeed the main charge as framed by Roullé and the Archbishop of Paris. His defence is always to insist that he is not attacking religion, only religious hypocrites. He is at pains to point out how he has attempted to make this clear in dramatic terms. On the one hand, he has endeavoured to make it constantly plain that Tartuffe is not a devout person (even less a man of the cloth) who behaves badly, but a conscious hypocrite who uses religion as a cloak for his criminal activities. On the other, he has conceived and (we may deduce from the evolutionary process) refined the role of Cléante so that he expresses a positive vision of religious devotion:

J'ai traité [ma comédie] avec toutes les précautions que me demandait la délicatesse de la matière et [...] j'ai mis tout l'art et tous les soins qu'il m'a

---

[11] 'Cléante le raisonneur—existait-il même?—avait sans doute une part bien moins étendue à la parole' (Claude Bourqui, *Polémiques et stratégies dans le Dom Juan de Molière* (Paris-Seattle-Tübingen: Biblio 17 PFSCL, 1992), p. 36).

[12] These changes are discussed in more detail below in the analyses of the text of the play.

été possible pour bien distinguer le personnage de l'hypocrite d'avec le vrai
dévot […]. [Tartuffe] ne fait fait pas une action qui […] ne fasse éclater [le
caractère] du véritable homme de bien que je lui oppose.

(1669 preface, *OC*, I, 884)

This lengthy polemic and these unambiguous statements by Molière
inevitably give Cléante a special position among Molière's *raisonneurs*.
The dramatist claims to have written Cléante's role in such a way
that he will strike audiences as a sincerely and conventionally devout
man of his times and in the hope that, with such a character, his play
might no longer be interpreted as attacking religion. In this special,
polemical context, Cléante is a mouthpiece for Molière, not in the
sense that he is expressing views on religion which Molière wants to
preach to his audiences, but in the sense that he is speaking words that
Molière hopes will constitute an adequate defence of his play against
his enemies' claims. This does not necessarily mean that Cléante's
role is thereby dramaturgically weakened. Indeed this chapter will
demonstrate that dramaturgical structures and comic effect remain
prominent in the elaboration of Cléante's speeches and interactions
with other characters.

Nor do Molière's clear interventions in the controversy mean that
Cléante's specifically polemical role can be taken for granted. As well
as disagreeing over whether Cléante should be interpreted comically
or seriously, critics also disagree on the adequacy with which he
fulfils this alleged polemical role. Most think that he does constitute
the adequate defender of the play that Molière says he sought to
make him. For Calder, he 'illustrates, through both the soundness
of his arguments and the modesty of his behaviour, how a good
and honest man should behave'.[13] Lawrence notes how often the
words of Cléante resemble those of Christ: distrust of ostentatious
devotion, forbearance before the sins of others, toleration of sinners
but not sin, opposition to Tartuffe's hypocrisy as Christ opposed the
Pharisees.[14] According to Scherer, 'Cléante ne possède pas seulement

---

[13] Andrew Calder, *Molière: The Theory and Practice of Comedy* (London: The
Athlone Press, 1993), p. 175.

[14] Francis L. Lawrence, 'The Norm in *Tartuffe*', *Revue de l'Université d'Ottawa*, 36
(1966), 698–702. Lawrence's views are summed up approvingly by William Jaynes in
'Critical Opinions of Cléante in *Tartuffe*', *Œuvres et Critiques*, 6 (1981), 91–7 (p. 95).

la sagesse humaine. Il est également un dévot [...] Il pratique en effet des vertus chrétiennes, et pas seulement en paroles. Ces vertus sont la modération, la charité, le pardon des injures.'[15]

For Parish, however, Cléante does not fulfil the role that Molière claims to have given him: 'If we look within *Tartuffe* for perspectives which would compensate to some extent for these [Tartuffe's] distortions of Christianity, we find them lacking. Cléante does not in any respect constitute the positive correlative of which Tartuffe is the deformation.'[16] Parish approaches the play through a nineteenth-century school edition by a Roman Catholic priest, the abbé Figuière, and shares the abbé's view that Cléante 'n'est pas dévot du tout, et n'entend rien à la dévotion'.[17] Parish's main argument against the adequacy of Cléante is that his alleged defence of true devotion is wordly and unchristian. Parish quotes a passage from François de Sales' *Introduction à la vie dévote* (first published in 1608 and much reprinted) that warns Christians against the strategies of the worldy who try to divert them from the true path: the worldly will say that 'il faut vivre au monde comme au monde, on peut bien faire son salut sans tant de mystères; et mille telles bagatelles' (Parish, p. 79).[18] He then quotes lines from the play that he alleges are characterized by this same insidious quality against which François de Sales warns: 'Qui ne saurait souffrir qu'une autre ait des plaisirs / Dont le penchant de l'âge a sevré leurs désirs' (139–40) and 'Ah! vous êtes dévot, et vous vous emportez!' (552). But these lines are spoken by Dorine, not by Cléante, whom Parish tries to tar with the same brush, though without quoting any evidence from Cléante's own speeches. Furthermore, Parish considers Cléante's (to his mind) inadequate defence of Christianity as central to what he sees as the play's biting satire of the Church (p. 87).[19]

[15] Jacques Scherer, *Structures de Tartuffe*, 2nd edn (Paris: SEDES, 1974), p. 95. See also Gérard Ferreyrolles, *Molière: Tartuffe* (Paris: Presses Universitaires de France, 1987), who also sees Cléante as the representative of true religion in the play (p. 98).

[16] Richard Parish, 'Tartuf(f)e ou l'imposture', *The Seventeenth Century*, 6 (1991), 73–88, p. 86.

[17] Molière, *Tartufe* [sic] *ou l'Imposteur*, ed. abbé Figuière, 2nd edn (Paris: Alliance des Maisons d'Édition Chrétienne, 1895), p. 63 (first published in 1882).

[18] Saint François de Sales, *L'Introduction à la vie dévote* in his *Œuvres*, ed. André Ravier and Roger Devos (Paris: Gallimard, 1969), p. 253 (IV.1).

[19] See also Jacqueline Plantié, 'Molière et François de Sales', *Revue d'histoire littéraire de la France*, 72 (1972), 902–27. Plantié argues (though Parish does not

This argument seems to me unconvincing. Biting satire has to be blatant and unambiguous. Nobody else, not even the abbé Figuière, who deleted supposedly offensive passages from Molière's play but did not delete any of Cléante's lines, and not even Molière's bitterest enemies in the seventeenth century, thought that the role of Cléante could be understood as contributing to an aggressive satire. None the less, to deter us from adopting Cléante's point of view, Parish warns us that to do so is 'at best intellectual laziness and at worst [...] intellectual dishonesty' (pp. 79–80).

If Parish is categorical in stating his view, Defaux is no less so in stating the opposite view, seeing in Cléante 'non seulement le porte-parole de l'honnêteté du siècle, mais encore—mais surtout—*indiscutablement* celui de Molière lui-même (my emphasis, p. 104). We might well be amused by this clash of contrary assertions: Parish versus Defaux. If so, we would be following in the footsteps of the anonymous author of the *Lettre sur la comédie de l'imposteur*, which ends with an evocation of the highly discrepant responses the play provoked at the time and tells us that his own position is to 'ne regarder toutes choses qui se passent dans le monde que comme les diverses scènes de la grande comédie qui se joue sur la terre entre les hommes' (*OC*, I, 1180). Bemused detachment might appear attractive today too, but it is not critically productive. The following analyses will assess Cléante's words in their dramatic context, and compare the results with the critical positions that have been adopted hitherto: sage or bore; adequate defender of the play's Christian allegiance or inadequate defender of true religion and contributor to an alleged satirical intention.

STRUCTURE OF ACT 1

Cléante is on stage for the whole of act 1. He is the brother-in-law of Orgon, the brother of Orgon's second wife Elmire, and the helpful step-uncle of Orgon's beleaguered children Damis and Mariane.

accept her findings) that 'Quand Molière fait parler Cléante, il lui prête exactement le point de vue de François de Sales' (p. 912).

Along with all the other major characters apart from Orgon and Tartuffe, he contributes to the exposition, which first offers a vision of all the main roles before introducing the problem that sparks the dramatic action. The first scene is generally much admired as both a lively and a comic way of sketching the polarized reactions of Mme Pernelle on the one hand, and other members of Orgon's family on the other, to the dubiously devout Tartuffe, who has established himself in the house and engaged in tyrannical censorship of their ways. The dramatic skill with which Molière has shaped the whole act, however, as opposed to the first scene, tends to go unappreciated, but it is important for understanding Molière's treatment of Cléante's role.

The first scene, which ends with Mme Pernelle's departure, exasperated at the family's refusal to admire their allegedly devout guest, focuses exclusively on Tartuffe and the different reactions to him. The audience is left in no doubt that it should side with the family against Mme Pernelle, played originally by a man in drag, rude, bossy and forever interrupting.[20] Most of the family leave the stage at the end of scene 1 to see Mme Pernelle out of the house, but Cléante and Dorine stay on stage to avoid further dispute. This device allows Molière to reveal yet more of the impact of Tartuffe in the household than was revealed in the first scene: in particular, we learn that Orgon is even more obsessed with him than Mme Pernelle is. This could not so easily be said in the first scene: dramaturgically, it would have diminished the intense focus on Tartuffe; and in terms of verisimilitude, it would have been problematic to have wife, children, and servant complaining to Orgon's mother about an obsession which she herself shares. It is all the more plausible that Dorine should describe Orgon's obsession for the benefit of Cléante, as he has, we are led to deduce, not visited the house since Orgon has introduced Tartuffe. So the extent of Orgon's obsession is genuine news to his brother-in-law.

When Elmire and the children, Mariane and Damis, return from having seen off Mme Pernelle, Molière is able to introduce the dramatic action, and Cléante is given a central role in it. Elmire reports that they have seen Orgon returning home, to which Cléante replies that he will stay just long enough to say hello (216). Damis

---

[20] See Richard Parish, 'Molière en travesti: Transvestite Acting in Molière', *Nottingham French Studies*, 33 (1994), 53–8.

seizes on this proposed meeting between Cléante and his father to ask his uncle to bring his influence to bear on Orgon in connection with an important matter:

> De l'hymen de ma sœur touchez-lui quelque chose.
> J'ai soupçon que Tartuffe à son effet s'oppose,
> Qu'il oblige mon père à des détours si grands;
> Et vous n'ignorez pas quel intérêt j'y prends.
>
> (217–20)

This speech is crucial if we are to make sense of the dramaturgical function of Cléante's interventions in the course of the play. Damis' interest, which the dramatic action will not develop, is in the sister of Valère, the young man to whom Orgon had promised to marry Mariane. Damis wants his sister to marry Valère so as to increase his own chances of marrying Valère's sister. Cléante is given the task of promoting the promised wedding despite the indeterminate obstacles that appear to have been put in its way since Tartuffe has made his appearance. Bray calls him 'un témoin de l'action, non un acteur' (p. 31), but this speech gives him a key role in initiating and pursuing the dramatic action.

Orgon enters at this point and Molière leaves him on stage with Cléante and Dorine. We might expect this to be the scene in which Cléante will broach with Orgon the delicate topic of Mariane's wedding to Valère, but it is essentially a scene between Orgon and Dorine, composed of a celebrated comic routine, in which Orgon asks how things have been in his absence, but repeatedly shows no interest in Dorine's account of his wife's illness only in her description of Tartuffe's rude health. Four times he diverts her onto Tartuffe ('Et Tartuffe?') and four times he exclaims sympathetically and admiringly 'Le pauvre homme!' This comic interaction is, however, no gratuitously placed interlude, in which Cléante's silent presence might be embarrassingly awkward. It is a vital preparation for the next and final scene of act 1, in which Cléante will speak alone to Orgon and attempt to intervene on Mariane's behalf. His observation of Orgon's encounter with Dorine has given Cléante the full measure of his brother-in-law's obsession with Tartuffe. It is in the light of this knowledge, the knowledge that he has acquired of Tartuffe during his visit (and summed up for the audience in 1. 1), and the desire to help his niece that he will tackle the rhetorical mission requested of him by Damis and so initiate the dramatic action proper when he speaks to Orgon in 1. 5.

CLÉANTE AND MME PERNELLE (1. 1)

Before looking in detail at the encounter with Orgon, we need to consider what impression the first four scenes of the play create of Cléante. Those critics keen to establish him as a comic figure insist on his risible performance before Mme Pernelle in scene 1. Fargher says that he is 'unimpressive' in this scene (p. 109), Eustis that 'he wilts before the fury of Mme Pernelle's invective and cowers behind the servant Dorine' (p. 190), and Peacock that 'Cléante's cowering behind Dorine to avoid further contact with Mme Pernelle (171–3) [...] contradict[s] the self-possessed, imperious tone adopted elsewhere' (p. 307). However, to believe that Cléante comes across at the beginning of the play as coweringly weak is to ignore both the evidence of the *Lettre sur la comédie de l'imposteur* and the comic structures at work in scene 1.

The *Lettre* makes it clear that in the 1667 version of the play Cléante was a powerful opponent of Mme Pernelle. In particular, he made three speeches that he no longer makes in the extant version of the scene: in response to Mme Pernelle's praise of Tartuffe, 'le frère de la bru commence déjà à faire voir quelle est la véritable dévotion, par rapport à celle de M. Panulphe' (*OC*, I, 1150), a speech which, in the 1669 version, is deferred until his meeting with Orgon in 1. 5; in response to Mme Pernelle's reference to the allegedly exemplary neighbour, Orante, who openly criticizes the family's wordly ways, 'le frère de la bru continue par un caractère sanglant qu'il fait de l'humeur des gens de cet âge, qui blâment tout ce qu'ils ne peuvent plus faire' (*OC*, I, 1150), a speech which is reattributed to Dorine in the 1669 version; and in response to Mme Pernelle's further defence of Tartuffe's strictures, Cléante gives six or seven examples of devotion to demonstrate what true virtue is, a speech which is also deferred, in the 1669 version, to his meeting with Orgon in 1. 5. Interestingly, the *Lettre*, sensitive to the polemical context of the

1667 performance, attributes a non-dramaturgical motive to the last of these three speeches, which listed truly pious individuals 'pour aller au-devant des jugements malicieux ou libertins qui voudraient induire de l'aventure qui fait le sujet de cette pièce qu'il n'y a point ou fort peu de véritables gens de bien, en témoignant par ce dénombrement que le nombre en est si grand en soi, voire très grand, si on le compare à celui des fieffés bigots' (*OC*, i, 1151). There can be no doubt, therefore, that in the 1667 version Cléante was a vigorous respondent to Mme Pernelle, making clear from the very beginning of the play that numerous models of true devotion exist, from which the play's religious hypocrite unmistakably diverges.

But when Molière reworks the first scene for the 1669 version, and diminishes Cléante's role in the process, does he thereby render the character's responses so weak as to be risible? We should first consider why he might have transferred two of these speeches to the major encounter of 1. 5. The main reason seems to me to be that this is where they are dramaturgically and polemically more convincing. Rather than address these speeches to Mme Pernelle, it is more plausible that Cléante should exert himself to speak against Tartuffe and to attempt to demonstrate Tartuffe's hypocrisy, only when he has a dramaturgically compelling reason to do so (to dislodge Orgon's obsession with the man so as to remove what seems to be the obstacle to Mariane's wedding to Valère) and when he has seen a fuller picture of Tartuffe's influence (which it is one of the functions of scenes 2–4 to provide). The reason his satire of aged prudes is reattributed to Dorine in the 1669 version is probably that the re-attribution promotes his character as a serious and sensitive individual, not wanting to speak ill of those who may be misguided but are not criminal. Such lines are more plausibly spoken by the generally forthright Dorine.

So what role do the post-1667 changes to scene 1 leave for Cléante? They ensure a sharper comic structure, in which laughter is directed at Mme Pernelle for her refusal to listen to others, for the freedom with which she criticizes others, for her praise of Tartuffe's religious and moral strictures (despite the evidence proffered by other characters that he is a hypocrite and even has designs on Orgon's wife), and for her confidence in tittle-tattle apparently criticizing the family's fashionable lifestyle. In this structure, Mme Pernelle's role inevitably dominates; Cléante's is bigger than Elmire's and Mariane's, marginally smaller than that of Damis, and all these four characters say less than the outspoken Dorine. Molière gives Cléante three interventions, two oral and one gestural, all three handled by the dramatist to make him appear a thoughtful person in contrast with whom Mme Pernelle's ill-considered bluster is all the more comic.

His first intervention comes at the climax of a routine, which begins when Mme Pernelle says that she is leaving because nobody listens to her advice. Each character tries to object, but Dorine and Damis are cut off after one word, Mariane after two, Elmire after three and Cléante after four, and they are interrupted so that Mme Pernelle can deliver personal abuse against each of them in turn. It is significant that Molière makes the characters intervene in this order. Cléante is the one who most bides his time, he is the one who gets to utter a few more words than the other characters, and in doing so shows elements of politeness and social skill, calling his interlocutor 'Madame', and introducing the concessive phrase 'après tout' (33). Whereas Mme Pernelle's responses to each of the previous characters have been simply damning, her account of Cléante is more measured. She concedes his qualities, before blaming his allegedly endless moralizing. But when she says 'Pour vous, Monsieur son frère, / Je vous estime fort, vous aime, et vous révère' (33–4), this can be performed either as a signal to the audience that Cléante has real qualities, which even the foolish Mme Pernelle cannot deny, or, much more probably, as an ironically polite opening remark that is immediately belied by what follows. Her criticism ('Sans cesse vous prêchez des maximes de vivre / Qui par d'honnêtes gens ne se doivent point suivre' (37–8)) tells the audience more about her own absurdity than about Cléante, since the conversational mode she has so far demonstrated is such as to make us believe that she would never give anybody the verbal space in which to speak at length in her presence. Moreover, her specific charge that he teaches immoral maxims needs to be appreciated in the context of her just having announced that she is leaving because 'Dans toutes mes leçons j'y suis contrariée' (10). What the audience learns from these exchanges is that Mme Pernelle is the character who tries to preach endlessly and that she meets any opposition with a put-down and a charge of immorality.

Cléante's second intervention comes after Mme Pernelle has tried to bolster her support for Tartuffe's moral criticisms of the family with reference to their comings and goings and numerous social calls. Whereas Dorine intervenes to attack the gossips, Cléante does so to defend members of his family, and he uses reason rather than satire. He argues that gossips are a fact of life and that, if one's social activities are innocent, one should go on pursuing them without regard to what gossips may be saying. In framing this argument, he is keen not simply to oppose Mme Pernelle, but to persuade her not to attend to the rumours she hears, and to trust instead in the innocence of her family. Twice he tries to engage her attention with rhetorical questions: 'Hé! voulez-vous, Madame, empêcher qu'on ne cause?' (93) and 'Croiriez-vous obliger tout le monde à se taire?' (98). These questions apart, he avoids the use of the second-person form, preferring the more inclusive 'on' form, or the first-person plural, which is how he tries to win her over in his summary conclusion:

> A tous les sots caquets n'ayons donc nul égard;
> Efforçons-nous de vivre avec toute innocence,
> Et laissons aux causeurs une pleine licence.
>
> (100–3)

Mme Pernelle does not reply until Dorine has delivered her satirical portrait of Daphné, suspected of spreading the gossip that has reached the grandmother's ears. Her reply can be interpreted as a response to both Cléante and Dorine: 'Tous ces raisonnements ne font rien à l'affaire' (117). The summary dismissal of Cléante's argument, without any attempt to engage with it, signals the obstinacy of Mme Pernelle, not the weakness of Cléante.

His third and final intervention needs to be interpreted from an implicit stage direction contained in the final speech of Mme Pernelle before she sweeps out, frustrated, boxing the ears of her servant. Condemning her family's sociability once again, Mme Pernelle claims that too much conversation can turn the heads of sensible people. To support this claim, Molière gives her recourse to an etymological argument that she has heard from (presumably) a preacher:

> Et comme l'autre jour un docteur dit fort bien,
> C'est véritablement la tour de Babylone,
> Car chacun y babille, et tout du long de l'aune.
>
> (160–2)

Crucially, these lines, containing Mme Pernelle's double confusion ('Babylone' for 'Babel', and 'babiller' as deriving from 'Babylone') cause Cléante to grin, and Mme Pernelle notices: 'Voilà-t-il pas Monsieur qui ricane déjà!' (164). It is unclear why he reacts like this, though it is known that the face of the original actor, La Thorillière, wore a constant smile.[21] Is he amused by the preacher's etymological joke? Is he amused by the apparent seriousness with which Mme Pernelle refers to patently false etymology to criticize their social engagements? Is he more generally amused by the preposterousness with which her attack continues its relentless course? What is clear is that Cléante's amusement is shared by the audience. Like all Molière's fools, Mme Pernelle takes herself so seriously that she cannot tolerate being laughed at. This gives Molière the ending for his opening scene: Cléante's grin precipitates her departure.

PREPARATION FOR MISSION (1. 2–4)

It is unfair to claim that Cléante cowers behind Dorine at this point in not going to see Mme Pernelle out of the house. It is plausible that the old woman's daughter-in-law and grandchildren should accompany her to the door, and not implausible that Dorine and Cléante, without any direct relationship to her, should stay behind. Cléante's words to Dorine about his staying behind 'De peur qu'elle ne vînt encor me quereller' (172) are playful rather than fearful, and are a comment on Mme Pernelle's all-pervasive aggression, prompted most recently by his grin. His observation of the old woman's extraordinary obsession with Tartuffe motivates Dorine's description of Orgon's even greater obsession, which in turn lends credibility to Damis' request in scene 3 that Cléante tackle Orgon on the subject of Mariane's wedding because 'J'ai soupçon que Tartuffe à son effet s'oppose' (218). Damis' decision to make this request specifically of Cléante is corroborative evidence for the audience of the good sense of Cléante's character that was established in the first scene. And when Orgon comes on

---

[21] Roger W. Herzel, *The Original Casting of Molière's Plays* (Ann Arbor, Michigan: UMI Research Press, 1981), pp. 54, 79.

stage in scene 4, we see Cléante's ready sociability spring into action as he greets his brother-in-law: 'Je sortais, et j'ai joie à vous voir de retour. / La campagne à présent n'est pas beaucoup fleurie' (224–5). Cléante has just been given a mission and a problem, but he does not broach it immediately; he speaks to Orgon on his own terms about his return from the countryside. Orgon's response, which is to ask Cléante to wait until he has inquired about Tartuffe's well-being, demonstrates the precision, to both Cléante and the audience, of the obsession that Dorine has described in scene 2, and has the effect of modifying Cléante's rhetorical approach to Orgon when he is left alone with him at the beginning of scene 5.

CLÉANTE AND ORGON (1. 5)

This is one of the most problematic scenes in the play from the point of view of Molière's treatment of both religion and the *raisonneur*. What the audience has been led to expect of this scene is an encounter in which Cléante will show skill in broaching the topic of Mariane's wedding and sounding out what obstacle the presence of Tartuffe might represent, while Orgon will continue to demonstrate the degree of distraction and obsession that we have already seen. Read in a dramaturgical perspective, the structure of the scene and Orgon's and Cléante's speeches in it can be seen to intensify the folly of Orgon in the audience's eyes and establish the nature of (if not yet the precise reason for) the obstacle to Mariane's wedding to Valère. Read in the context of the polemic surrounding the play, Cléante's speeches can also be seen as the dramatist's sop to his enemies, a suggestion that truly devout people outnumber the hypocrites and a claim that the two can be readily distinguished; so the Church need not fear that the play would encourage audiences to be suspicious of the truly devout. Molière's skill is to make the polemical function operate within the context of the dramaturgical function of the speeches, and not in clumsy juxtaposition to it.

Cléante has had sufficient indication that Tartuffe might have something to do with the delay to Mariane's wedding and sufficient demonstration of Orgon's infatuation with Tartuffe. So in his opening speech of scene 5 he approaches his mission from the angle of Tartuffe, pointing out to Orgon that Dorine has been laughing at him for his preoccupation with his house guest, and corroborating her reaction with his own, which he expresses firmly but politely, and without Dorine's mockery: 'Je vous dirai tout franc que c'est avec justice' (261). He begins a sentence which is about the consequences of Orgon's attitude to Tartuffe and which the audience can deduce will climax in a question as to whether this is the cause of Mariane's problems. But Orgon shares with Molière's other fools a tendency to interrupt, which he does twice (266, 270), preventing Cléante from opening the subject that he has been charged to raise and from probing Orgon on his admiration for Tartuffe.

At the first hint that Tartuffe's qualities might be in question, Orgon gushes enthusiastically about him. The linguistic devices in which Molière makes Orgon express himself are all designed to prompt laughter at his expense for his undiscriminating approval of Tartuffe: *précieux* hyperbole ('vous seriez charmé de le connaître, / Et vos ravissements ne prendraient point de fin' (270–1)), aphasia ('C'est un homme ... qui, ... ha! un homme ... un homme enfin' (272)), perverse miscontextualization of Christ's words in Luke's Gospel (14: 26), due either to Tartuffe's erratic teaching or to Orgon's wild misinterpretation of his teaching ('je verrais mourir frère, enfants, mère et femme, / Que je m'en soucierais autant que de cela' (278–9)).

Cléante interjects one line at this point before Orgon's praise of Tartuffe continues: 'Les sentiments humains, mon frère, que voilà!' (280). Howarth thinks this line very bold on Molière's part, on the grounds that Cléante does not say ' "What a travesty of Christian doctrine!", but "What a travesty of human feeling!" ', so bold in fact that, for Howarth, the line 'can certainly be construed in its context as putting forward, by implication, a humanist alternative to the harsh inhumanity of the Christian precept'.[22] But what Cléante's line does is the opposite of this. It signals to the audience his awareness of Orgon's enthusiastically confused distortion of the Christian message and invites us to laugh at the man who is so admiring of Tartuffe that he trips himself up in this grotesque way. Cléante expresses himself

---

[22] W. D. Howarth, *Molière: A Playwright and his Audience* (Cambridge University Press, 1982), pp. 202–3.

ironically, and is in effect reassuring audiences that Orgon has failed
to express the real humanity of the Christian message. But all this is
done deftly and without preaching, since the focus is on laughter at
Orgon's folly. If Cléante does not say 'What a travesty of Christian
doctrine!', that is because for a character to use the word 'chrétien'
in a sarcastic exclamation in so controversial a comedy could well
have brought Molière more trouble rather than less.[23] When he tells
us in his preface that he wrote his play with all the precautions that
the delicate subject matter required, the precautions include precisely
such lexical niceties.

As if he has not heard Cléante's interjection, Orgon's praise of
Tartuffe continues in a long speech narrating their initial meetings
in church and the impact he has had on the household. In order to
understand Cléante's subsequent response, we need to attend to the
details of Orgon's admiration for Tartuffe. First, he is impressed by
his displays of religious devotion in church, though Molière makes
it crystal clear that Orgon is the gullible and unwitting victim of a
confidence trick:

> Chaque jour à l'église il venait, d'un air doux,
> Tout vis-à-vis de moi se mettre à deux genoux.
> Il attirait les yeux de l'assemblée entière
> Par l'ardeur dont au Ciel il poussait sa prière;
> Il faisait des soupirs, de grands élancements,
> Et baisait humblement la terre à tous moments.
>
> (283–8)

Tartuffe puts on a performance especially for his victim ('Tout vis-à-
vis de moi'). It is an extraordinary performance, characterized by
ostentation: when Orgon tells us that Tartuffe kissed the ground 'à tous
moments', he uses hyperbole to convey the extent of his admiration,
but the same hyperbole signals to the audience the excessive nature
of Tartuffe's performance. Orgon alone is entranced by it; the rest
of the congregation stares at him. How does Tartuffe know that his
strategy is working on Orgon? Because Orgon is ready to give him a

---

[23] Cléante uses the word 'chrétien' literally, positively, and non-sarcastically in
4. 1: 'N'est-il pas d'un chrétien de pardonner l'offense [...] ?' (1193). It is the only
occurrence of the word in the play.

significant amount of money at the end of each service. The second
feature of Tartuffe's behaviour that has impressed him, since he has
been welcomed into Orgon's home, is his extreme scrupulousness in
correcting the behaviour of others. Here again, Molière uses double-
edged hyperbole to signal Orgon's ill-judged admiration: 'Il s'impute
à péché la moindre bagatelle' (306). Orgon's contentment with the
general impact of this on his home ('depuis ce temps-là tout semble
y prospérer' (300)) is, for the audience, so transparently at odds with
the discontent that his family has expressed in 1. 1.

All Orgon's efforts have been intended to stifle the incipient
criticism of Tartuffe that Cléante was broaching at the start of the
scene as a way of turning to the question of Mariane's wedding. What
Orgon's enthusiastic display has just revealed to Cléante, however,
is that there is no point mentioning the wedding until he has first
tackled Orgon properly on the matter of Tartuffe and attempted
to make him see his error of judgement. Cléante's first strategy
misfires, but it misfires in such a way as to create further laughter
at Orgon's expense. Cléante thinks, as the audience too is surely
meant to think, that Orgon's speech so obviously reveals Tartuffe's
hypocritical performance that he tries to laugh it off, and adopts a
playfully teasing tone:

> Parbleu! vous êtes fou, mon frère, que je crois.
> Avec de tels discours vous moquez-vous de moi?
> Et que prétendez-vous que tout ce badinage? ...
>
> (311–13)

But Orgon's further interruption and serious response to Cléante
demonstrate the rootedness of his folly, since Cléante's sceptical lines
suggest to Orgon that his brother-in-law is a libertine. Given the comic
momentum of the scene so far, this accusation has to be interpreted
as yet another hyperbole on Orgon's part, another obvious error of
judgement.

In the face of Orgon's comic, but deadly earnest, accusation Cléante
has to adopt a different approach, defending himself against the
charge of libertinage, while trying to make Orgon see that Tartuffe's
behaviour is not that of a sincerely pious person, but of someone
pretending to be pious so that he can take advantage of Orgon. It
is true that Cléante has not yet seen Tartuffe, but the accounts that

he has heard, and most flagrantly Orgon's own account of Tartuffe's excessive displays of piety, leave him (and the audience) in no doubt. To achieve his purpose, Cléante makes a long speech, which is interrupted, though not deflected, by a disbelieving interjection from Orgon. It is this speech that has most divided critics in their assessment of Cléante. For Defaux, Cléante's words are so close in parts to views expressed in Molière's preface, the *placets* and the *Lettre sur la comédie de l'imposteur* that the character strikes us clearly as Molière's carefully constructed and eloquent denouncer of religious imposture (p. 104, 106–8). For Dandrey 'il s'efforce de rendre les choses les plus transparentes possible' (p. 190). Calder sees in Cléante the opposite of Tartuffe, someone whose 'sound dialectic is deployed most fully in the scene when he first discusses Tartuffe with Orgon' (p. 175). Guicharnaud, however, recognizes the polemical role that Cléante must play, but finds him 'ennuyeux, bavard et prétentieux', a criticism that lies at the root of subsequent readings which attempt to find him comic in this scene, or at the very least to find his speeches inadequate as a polemical defence.[24] He is seen to be variously boring, irrelevant, prolix, and platitudinous. Herzel sums up his view of the comic Cléante, who makes 'a longwinded and impertinent speech to provoke a silent display of comic impatience [...] and the laughter is at the expense of Cléante' (p. 569). Parish holds a similar view, but is particularly damning of Cléante's polemical role: 'his inadequate disclaimer is aggravated by the tedious prolixity of its expression [...] we, the audience, can be very easily taken in by Cléante (and, by extension, by Molière) if we too readily succumb to his platitudes' ('Tartuf(f)e', p. 87). So is Cléante eloquently lucid or boringly prolix?

Interpreting his speeches in a dramaturgical perspective sheds some light on the problem. It is unfair to criticize Cléante for making a spurious defence of true piety, since his dramatic role does not require him to defend piety. It requires him to shake Orgon's confidence in the dubious character of Tartuffe so as to prepare the way for a discussion of Mariane's wedding: this specific dramatic context is usually overlooked by critics. He has first of all to defend himself

---

[24] Jacques Guicharnaud, *Molière: une aventure théâtrale* (Paris: Gallimard, 1963), p. 37.

against Orgon's charge that he is a libertine, and this defence occupies the first part of his speech (318–25). It is a vigorously expressed defence, and needs to be, in view of Orgon's tenacious admiration for Tartuffe. He argues that it is unfair to call him a libertine just because he questions the motivation of Tartuffe's extraordinary display of devotion, as recounted by Orgon, and he protests his own religious conviction: 'Je sais comme je parle, et le Ciel voit mon cœur' (324).

This leads logically to the next part of his speech, in which he asserts that religious hypocrites do indeed exist and invites Orgon to agree with him that it is important not to confuse them with the truly devout. It might be the language that Cléante uses here that leads some critics to call him prolix or longwinded:

> Hé quoi, vous ne ferez nulle distinction
> Entre l'hypocrisie et la dévotion?
> Vous les voulez traiter d'un semblable langage,
> Et rendre même honneur au masque qu'au visage,
> Égaler l'artifice à la sincérité,
> Confondre l'apparence avec la vérité,
> Estimer le fantôme autant que la personne,
> Et la fausse monnaie à l'égal de la bonne?
>
>   (331–8)

The multiple antithetical metaphors for appearance and reality, underscored by the parallel syntactic constructions, are no doubt what lead Peacock to comment negatively on Cléante's 'heavily rhetorical structures' which 'contribute to the overall comic interest' (p. 305). But to judge Cléante's words as too rhetorical or prolix is to fail to appreciate the elegance of his accumulated metaphors and to forget the dramatic context in which he is speaking. He is trying to persuade not the audience, but Orgon in the first instance, that religious hypocrisy exists and should be treated differently from true devotion; and he has had ample evidence in this and the previous scene of Orgon's refusal to listen to anything other than praise of Tartuffe. So here he tries to make Orgon concede the general point (without mention of Tartuffe) and he spells out the point with great clarity—a clarity calculated to make an impact on his on-stage inter-locutor. The text does not tell us directly how the actor playing Orgon should behave at this point, but Orgon's lines eventually make clear his scorn for Cléante's views. The comedy resides in Orgon's obvious deafness to Cléante's patiently expressed and self-evidently correct view that one should seek to avoid being taken in by a hypocritical pretence.

In the final part of this speech, Cléante changes tone:

> Les hommes la plupart sont étrangement faits!
> Dans la juste mesure on ne les voit jamais;
> La raison a pour eux des bornes trop petites;
> En chaque caractère ils passent ses limites;
> Et la plus noble chose, ils la gâtent souvent
> Pour la vouloir outrer et pousser trop avant.
> Que cela vous soit dit en passant, mon beau-frère.
>
> (339–45)

McBride points out that 'taken in themselves [these words] are no more than platitudes about the golden mean'.[25] Defaux sees in them the kernel of Cléante's wisdom and 'le credo moral de la grande majorité de ses contemporains' (p. 104). Read in their dramatic context, however, these words function differently. Having earlier addressed Orgon directly in the second person and attempted to persuade him to accept the need to distinguish hypocrisy, Cléante ends by adopting a less challenging, more understanding, third-person mode of expression: when human beings see something good ('noble chose'), they can be too enthusiastic about it, without necessarily stopping to ask if they might be going too far. There is nothing 'preachy' about this.[26] He is not wagging a finger at Orgon and telling him to adopt the golden mean. He is sympathizing with what comes across as a common human foible so that Orgon should not feel too much under attack. And his closing line is knowingly humorous, acknowledging that he has been holding forth. He has aimed to suggest to Orgon, with no hostility, that he can question Tartuffe's credentials without any sacrifice of his religious convictions.

---

[25] Robert McBride, *The Sceptical Vision of Molière's Comedies* (London: Macmillan, 1977), p. 59.

[26] This is also the conclusion of the philosopher Olivier Bloch: 'Que Cléante dans *Tartuffe* énonce une morale de type aristotélicien ne tient pas, ou pas essentielle-ment, à un choix philosophique de Molière ou à son goût pour la juste mesure' (*Molière/Philosophie* (Paris: Albin Michel, 2000), p. 187).

Cléante's strategy fails, however, because Orgon does not engage with anything he has heard, but merely satirizes Cléante for his intelligent comments, calling him 'un docteur qu'on révère' (346), 'Un oracle, un Caton' (349). These comments should not be taken to undermine Cléante, but Orgon himself, because the audience knows that Cléante is right in his view of Tartuffe and that Orgon is wrong. Indeed Orgon's refusal to listen to his brother-in-law throughout this scene parallels the deafness of Sganarelle and Arnolphe. The more the fool shuts his ears, the more comic his downfall will be later in the play when he is made to see how wrong he has been.

Cléante politely sweeps aside Orgon's satirical description, and attempts once again to persuade him of the need to distinguish between true and false devotion. This time he goes further in that he demonstrates how it can be done, and without mentioning Tartuffe explicitly, which would be sure to antagonize Orgon, he makes it very plain how Orgon could apply certain principles so as to see through Tartuffe's mask of hypocrisy. It is only at the very end of his speech that Cléante draws this conclusion and directly makes the link to Tartuffe. Cléante resumes his persuasion of Orgon as follows: 'Mais, en un mot, je sais, pour toute ma science, / Du faux avec le vrai faire la différence' (353–4). Peacock finds him comic for asserting brevity ('en un mot') and proceeding to speak for some fifty lines (p. 305). There is a problem with this, however. Audiences laugh at an immediate stimulus. When Cléante says 'en un mot' the audience has no reason to find this funny, since it does not know how long Cléante's speech will be. Moreover, in context, 'en un mot' refers not to the whole of Cléante's speech, but to his undeniably pithy formulation of the main point ('Du faux avec le vrai faire la différence').

Cléante's speech is simply constructed and relies, even more than his previous speech, on emphatic restatement and multiple exemplification; again, this approach cannot be dismissed as prolix, since we need to bear in mind that it is intended to make a resistant Orgon question his attitude to Tartuffe so that Cléante might then be in a position to intervene on Mariane's behalf. He begins by protesting briefly his admiration for the truly pious (355–8), before expressing his disapproval of those who feign piety in order to advance their careers. Modern-day audiences need to remember the wealth and power associated with the Church in seventeenth-century France and the temptations that these could represent. He dwells on the kinds of behaviour typical of the charlatans in a passage that, far from being boring, has considerable potential for a performance enlivened by gesture. He notes how they deploy 'faux clins d'yeux' and 'élans affectés' (368), he describes them as 'brûlants et priants' (371), and claims that they assassinate their victims with 'un fer sacré' (380). His lines are entertainingly satirical for the audience and aim to be straightforwardly revelatory for Orgon.

In contrast, he then gives a portrait of the truly devout, and invites Orgon to consider unambiguous examples that are known to him: 'Regardez Ariston, regardez Périandre, / Oronte, Alcidamas, Polydore, Clitandre' (385–86). He characterizes their qualities in contradistinction to those of the hypocrites:

> On ne voit point en eux ce faste insupportable,
> Et leur dévotion est humaine, est traitable;
> Ils ne censurent point toutes nos actions:
> Ils trouvent trop d'orgueil dans ces corrections;
> Et laissant la fierté des paroles aux autres,
> C'est par leurs actions qu'ils reprennent les nôtres.
> L'apparence du mal a chez eux peu d'appui,
> Et leur âme est portée à juger bien d'autrui.
> Point de cabale en eux, point d'intrigues à suivre;
> On les voit, pour tous soins, se mêler de bien vivre;
> Jamais contre un pécheur ils n'ont d'acharnement;
> Ils attachent leur haine au péché seulement.
>
> (389–400)

Parish thinks that Cléante's 'recipe for *dévotion* is spiritually insubstantial' ('Tartuf(f)e', p. 86), but this perspective assumes that Cléante could be expected to teach Orgon and the audience what true piety is. It would have been presumptuous of Molière to think that a character in a comedy should do any such thing, and the attempt would certainly have incurred the displeasure of the religious authorities. It would also have been extremely undramatic. The polemical and the dramaturgical functions of Cléante's role coincide here. Molière's strategic defence does not require him to preach piety in the play, but to acknowledge that in the world depicted on stage, and by extension in the world off stage, there are many examples of truly pious people (even if they are not dramatis personae) and that there is much admiration for them. Cléante fulfils his polemical role at the same time as he fulfils the dramaturgical function of attempting to make Orgon see that Tartuffe is a hypocrite by suggesting that his behaviour is discrepant with that of those generally recognized as pious. Unlike the pious, Tartuffe criticizes constantly (as Orgon has already told us). The list of names creates the precise fictional context for Cléante's speech. He is speaking to Orgon about people they both know in the play-world. Unlike these individuals, Tartuffe makes a show of his devotion (as Orgon has so admiringly reported). Cléante's words concur with Church teaching. His admiration for humane and approachable devotion is not at odds with the advice of St Paul: 'Do not think of yourself more highly than you ought, but rather think of yourself with sober judgment' (Romans 12: 13). His observation that the pious hate the sin, not the sinner, tallies precisely with the words of Christ. The anonymous author of the *Lettre* makes it clear that in this scene Cléante's words (though probably fewer in 1667 than in 1669) were taken seriously, calling them 'des réflexions très solides sur les différences qui se rencontrent entre la véritable et la fausse vertu' (*OC*, I, 1153). If this remark makes Cléante's speeches sound a little too abstract, it has the advantage of recognizing their dramatically circumscribed nature: he is focusing precisely on how to distinguish true and false virtue; this is what Orgon needs to understand. He is emphatically not trying to teach us the nature of true devotion.

In philosophical terms, Cléante's argument can easily be criticized, and Gossman has led the way: 'Cléante knows there is a difference between true and false piety; what he distinguishes among the actual manifestations of piety, however, is not the true and the false; it is the obviously false and the possibly true.'[27] As a guidebook to detecting the religious hypocrite in the real world, Cléante's speeches are not infallible: a clever hypocrite might well be able to imitate the features of true piety. But a speech in a play is not a guidebook. Cléante adequately fulfils his polemical function of evoking examples of true piety, from which Tartuffe's hypocrisy is easily distinguishable. It was clearly thought adequate enough for Louis XIV to allow the

---

[27] Lionel Gossman, *Men and Masks: A Study of Molière* (Baltimore: Johns Hopkins University Press, 1963), p. 124.

1669 version to be performed. And Cléante fulfils his dramaturgical function, which is to persuade the audience that he has offered Orgon a sufficiently convincing way of seeing through Tartuffe's hypocrisy so that when Orgon rejects it, the laughter will be on Orgon, whom we see riding ever more confidently for a fall.

Those who want to find Cléante comic take comfort in Orgon's well-known response to this speech: 'Monsieur mon cher beau-frère, avez-vous tout dit?' (408). Peacock describes Cléante as 'crestfallen after his lofty, expansive argument [...] is laconically countered by Orgon's [line]' (p. 308). Orgon's question certainly verbalizes the impatience that we might imagine him demonstrating in gesture and facial expression throughout Cléante's speech. His impatience as well as his rudeness is also suggested in his movement towards the door. But when we laugh, we laugh at Orgon, who is so very obstinately deaf to advice that would save him from error, an error whose full gravity has yet to emerge. The *Lettre* comments appositely: 'Le bonhomme, pressé par les raisonnements de son beau-frère, auxquels il n'a rien à répondre, bien qu'il les croie mauvais, lui dit adieu brusquement, et le veut quitter sans autre réponse, ce qui est le procédé naturel des opiniâtres' (*OC*, I, 1154). This is telling confirmation of the effectiveness of Molière's repeated depiction of foolish protagonists who will not listen.

Far from being crestfallen, Cléante calls Orgon back with the intention of raising the matter of Mariane's wedding, for which he has so skilfully, but so unsuccessfully, been trying to prepare the ground. Fargher's comment that 'it is only after 85 lines of discourse that he finds the courage to make the point which Damis two scenes earlier had instructed him to make' (p. 109) entirely misunderstands the intention behind Cléante's previous speeches. And Cléante is not cowardly to raise the matter now; rather, he is showing a real determination to pursue his objective of helping Mariane, even though the strategies he has deployed so far have not borne fruit. This time his approach is direct and questioning. But to Cléante's ten probing questions and observations about Orgon's promise to marry Mariane to Valère and the reasons for his delay, Orgon gives the briefest and most evasive of replies before beating a hasty retreat. Cléante might appear to have achieved little, but he has revealed Orgon's potential for breaking his word to Valère and so ends the act with the conviction that there is a serious obstacle to Valère's wedding plans and with a determination to help further: 'Pour son amour je crains une disgrâce, / Et je dois l'avertir de tout ce qui se passe' (424–5). Cléante's dramaturgical contribution to the act has been to orchestrate the audience's laughter at Orgon's folly and to demonstrate the extent of its seeming ineradicability, so justifying the further measures that he himself will take and the exceptional measures to which Orgon's wife will resort.

CLÉANTE AND TARTUFFE (4. 1–3)

The audience has to assume that Cléante leaves the house to warn Valère and that this warning results in Valère's arrival in act 2. In the face of Orgon's now declared and stubborn determination to marry his daughter to Tartuffe (453–5), Dorine attempts to orchestrate the efforts of Valère and Mariane to stir up opposition to the father's plans. She sends Valère to drum up the support of his friends (the manoeuvre bears fruit in 5. 6). Meanwhile, she and Mariane will seek the help of Cléante and Elmire: 'Nous allons réveiller les efforts de son frère, / Et dans notre parti jeter la belle-mère' (813–14). Elmire is on the premises, so she is the first to help, and her efforts to persuade Tartuffe not to press ahead with the wedding are the focus of act 3. They result in his attempt to seduce Elmire, his exposure by Damis, the disbelief of Orgon, who furiously disinherits his son, gives his inheritance to Tartuffe, and declares his intention of marrying Tartuffe to Mariane that very day.

So when Cléante returns in response to this call for help, it is to a much aggravated situation. He is in mid-discussion with Tartuffe when act 4 starts, a discussion in which he will try to persuade him to reconcile father and son and to decline the inheritance that is rightly that of Damis. If this scene has received less critical comment than 1. 5, it has none the less been subject to very divergent interpretation. Calder thinks the dialogue demonstrates Cléante's superior reasoning: 'When he rebuts Tartuffe's sophistry at the beginning of act 4, his straight, pellucid and common-sense dialectic shows up the crookedness of Tartuffe's reasoning' (p. 176). But Eustis thinks just the opposite: 'he unmistakably comes off second-best' (p. 190). Considering the scene in a different perspective, Guicharnaud shows insensitivity to the dramatic form by claiming that the scene represents a pause in the dramatic action, a moment of stock-taking: 'une sorte de palier, de ferme tremplin—sur lequel l'action s'arrête un instant pour reprendre des forces et digérer ses acquisitions' (p. 113).

A dramaturgical perspective puts these divergent comments in a new light. Far from representing a pause in the dramatic action, the scene shows Cléante attempting to move the action forward from the crisis point that it has reached at the end of act 3. The fact that he fails to do so should not mean that the scene comes across as a dramatic pause, since every speech in the scene has the potential to drive the plot forward (or indeed to entrench the crisis). Moreover, in this encounter it is too simplistic to say that one character comes off better than the other, since the pleasure that Molière is offering his audience depends precisely on the confrontation of two well-matched rhetorical debaters, scoring points against each other by fair means (Cléante) or foul (Tartuffe). The comic effect resides in the incongruity between the audience's perception of a subtly balanced confrontation on the one hand, and on the other our awareness that one of the characters is right and the other is wrong. The audience can enjoy the display of clever argumentation serving to obfuscate, rather than to reveal, the truth.

Cléante's argumentational approach, as much as Tartuffe's, accounts for this delicate exercise in obfuscation, because Cléante (we are meant to deduce) has judged that it would be rhetorically more effective not to antagonize his interlocutor by accusing him of trying to seduce Elmire. Instead, he says he will assume that Damis' exposure of Tartuffe was unjust and that he was unfairly accused. The audience knows, and Cléante at the very least suspects, that Tartuffe is indeed guilty, but the rhetorical ploy of assuming his innocence plays into Tartuffe's hands because it allows him to argue on a basis of falsehood and pretence, in which skills he is well practised.

Peacock finds comedy in Cléante's claim that he will speak 'en deux mots' (1188), in the same way he did in his claim to speak 'en un mot' in 1. 5 (p. 305). Yet there are no dominating long speeches in this scene, but rather a more or less equally balanced sequence of exchanges between the two characters. If Cléante starts by assuming

Tartuffe's innocence of the alleged seduction, the audience will be keen to know on what front he is to tackle him. His initial argument and request are expressed clearly in a language that combines cajoling questions with the merest hint of a threat: if it is Christian to forgive, Tartuffe should pardon Damis and encourage his return to the household. Cléante is not at all hectoring. The nub of the argument is expressed in two rhetorical questions that appeal to the Christian sentiments that Tartuffe claims to profess:

> N'est-il pas d'un chrétien de pardonner l'offense,
> Et d'éteindre en son cœur tout désir de vengeance?
> Et devez-vous souffrir, pour votre démêlé,
> Que du logis d'un père un fils soit exilé?

> (1193–6)

Even when Cléante hints at a threat to Tartuffe, he does so in a seemingly helpful spirit. People are shocked by what has happened, so Tartuffe needs to act: 'Et si vous m'en croyez, vous pacifierez tout, / Et ne pousserez point les affaires à bout' (1199–200).

Tartuffe's reply distinguishes cleverly between the act of forgiving Damis in his heart and the possible consequence of supporting his return. For Cléante, the latter follows on naturally from the former. But not for Tartuffe. He claims that it is against the interests of heaven, because Damis' return would entail his own departure. His position might be imperilled by gossip to the effect that he was making his peace with Damis because he himself felt guilty. His reply is doubly clever, because after he has drawn his distinction, he does not explain the premises of the rest of his argumentation. If we had time in a performance to consider what they might be, they would look rather murky. Presumably he thinks that heaven's interests would not be served by his departure from the household, since that would deprive them of his Christian guidance; but that is a somewhat tainted argument since he has been instrumental in wrecking the relationship between father and son. And his view that people would think a reconciliation might imply his guilt carries no more weight than Cléante's report that people are discontented by the treatment of Damis; indeed, since Cléante's report is about what people are actually saying and Tartuffe's anxiety is about what people might say, the hypocrite's point could be judged to carry less weight.

None the less, his refusal to accept Cléante's advice and his failure to explicate the premises of his argument make it harder for Cléante to respond, and creates suspense for the audience as it tries to anticipate his response.

Cléante abandons his cajoling tone, and tells Tartuffe frankly that he thinks his arguments are strained ('excuses colorées', 'raisons [...] trop tirées' (1217–18)). He then tries to refute Tartuffe's skilfully ill-expressed arguments: if heaven's interests require that Damis be punished, heaven, not Tartuffe, should deal with that; he should not worry about what people might think of him, if forgiveness and reconciliation are the proper course. He then sums up his request once more: 'faisons toujours ce que le Ciel prescrit, / Et d'aucun autre soin ne nous brouillons l'esprit' (1227–8). This should not be thought of as tedious repetition on Cléante's part: he is putting his request a second time in the light of his refutation of Tartuffe's arguments.

Parish thinks that Tartuffe's four-line reply constitutes 'an astute distinguo':[28]

> Je vous ai déjà dit que mon cœur lui pardonne,
> Et c'est faire, Monsieur, ce que le Ciel ordonne;
> Mais après le scandale et l'affront d'aujourd'hui,
> Le Ciel n'ordonne pas que je vive avec lui.
>
> (1229–32)

Yet, far from making a subtle new distinction, this reply, as Tartuffe's opening phrase confirms, is a mere repetition, in summary form, of his previous speech. He does not even acknowledge, let alone respond to, Cléante's refutation of it, and it might well make the audience think that Cléante, in addition to occupying the moral high ground, has the intellectual edge over Tartuffe.

Tartuffe's refusal to engage further on the matter of forgiveness and reconciliation lead Cléante to tackle him on the inheritance. He puts to Tartuffe, in an aggressively worded question, that it is wrong to accept an inheritance bestowed on him by 'pur caprice' (1234). Tartuffe recovers his form and makes a reply that, in its

---

[28] Molière, *Le Tartuffe*, ed. Richard Parish (London: Bristol Classical Press, 1994), p. 100.

brilliant ingenuity, smacks of stereotypical views of Jesuit casuistry: he personally does not desire this wealth, but feels obliged to accept it lest it fall into criminal hands and be used for purposes other than Christian. The laughter of the audience is quite different here from the belly-laughs directed at Molière's foolish protagonists like Orgon. It is more intellectual, since it requires an appreciation of the skilful ironies by means of which Tartuffe seeks to defend his own greed and unchristian ambitions (it is only later in the play that his actual criminality becomes known). As before, Cléante is able to refute Tartuffe's argument, and he uses his own ironies in reply, telling Tartuffe not to be troubled by such 'délicates craintes' (1249). His refutation is that it is for the rightful heir, and nobody else, to worry about how the money is spent. He then sees the opportunity of bringing compellingly together this argument and his earlier one to make another appeal to Tartuffe. Parish accuses Cléante of merely repeating his earlier argument (p. 100), but Cléante does not repeat himself. He revises his earlier argument in the light of Tartuffe's own response to it so that it is even more compelling. He had previously suggested that Tartuffe should welcome Damis back into the house, and Tartuffe had replied that this was impossible; that he himself would have to leave if Damis returned. Cléante's revised argument takes up Tartuffe's point: if it is right that Damis should retain his rightful inheritance, and if Tartuffe cannot live under the same roof as Damis, it follows that Tartuffe should go.

When faced with Cléante's superior argumentation earlier in the scene, Tartuffe merely repeated his own position without modification. This time, he simply leaves the room, remembering a religious obligation he has to perform at half past three. Peacock insists that the audience laughs at the deflation of Cléante's reasoning and claims that he is left 'speechless' and 'frustrated' 'when interrupted in his increasingly zealous attempt to convert Tartuffe' (p. 307–8). Cléante's response to Tartuffe's abrupt departure is simply to say 'Ah!' (1269). This may imply frustration, as Peacock says; but equally it may be a knowing comment on the alleged, but evidently false, reason for Tartuffe's departure. Peacock is somewhat tendentious in suggesting that Cléante is attempting to convert Tartuffe. Cléante knows that Tartuffe is a hypocrite, and he is deliberately employing the religious arguments that Tartuffe claims to profess in the hope that these might force him to do (or embarrass him into doing) the right thing by Damis. In other words, his rhetorical strategy is to play to Tartuffe's mask. The scene that Molière has written is based on a comedy of considerable verbal sophistication and argumentational suspense. Cléante ultimately has the better arguments, but Tartuffe might take our breath away when he avoids answering them with his cheeky face-saving departure. Once again a defeated protagonist has nothing to reply except to cut short the debate.

Cléante remains on stage for the next two scenes, though he is not the focus of the action, which is rather Mariane's failed attempt to appeal to Orgon's paternal feelings and then Elmire's plan to make her husband see Tartuffe's true nature. In between Mariane and Elmire, Dorine and Cléante both start to speak, but both are immediately silenced by Orgon. So Cléante's role in the rest of this act is limited to supporting Elmire's scheme, to which Orgon reluctantly agrees, by going to fetch Tartuffe (1361).

RESTRAINT AND SUSPENSE (5. 1–7)

Cléante is on stage for the whole of act 5. Although his role is small in terms of the number of lines he speaks, it is significant in dramaturgical terms, since Orgon's family is in crisis and it is Cléante's restraining words that prevent Orgon and Damis from committing further acts of folly. Critics have paid relatively little attention to his role in this act. The *Lettre sur la comédie de l'imposteur*, however, sees his interventions as corroborating his already established position as a 'véritable honnête homme' (*OC*, I, 1165), whereas those who find him comic elsewhere continue to perceive comedy in his words here. Giving no evidence, Fargher asserts that 'his remarks in act 5 are pointless, inept, platitudinous' (p. 109).

Act 4 ended with an unexpected crisis. Elmire's exposure to Orgon of Tartuffe's licentiousness leads, dramatically, to Tartuffe's immediate claim to his newly conferred rights: Orgon's house belongs to Tartuffe, who now requires him to leave. Act 5 opens with the image of a frenetic Orgon, running around, whom Cléante has to calm down:

Il me semble
Que l'on doit commencer par consulter ensemble
Les choses qu'on peut faire en cet événement.

(1573–5)

Orgon reveals to Cléante that the crisis is even more serious, as he has entrusted to Tartuffe a strongbox containing documents belonging to his friend Argas, who had had to flee the royal authorities. Tartuffe is now therefore in a position to compromise Orgon politically. The *Lettre* sums up Cléante's reaction in favourable terms:

Le frère fait, dans ces perplexités, le personnage d'un véritable honnête homme, qui songe à réparer le mal arrivé et ne s'amuse point à le reprocher à ceux qui l'ont causé, comme font la plupart des gens, surtout quand par hasard ils ont prévu ce qu'ils voient. Il examine mûrement les choses et conclut [...] que c'est une affaire sans ressource.

(*OC*, I, 1165)

Orgon does not know what to do. Cléante sees the full danger, and offers advice: 'Le pousser est encor grande imprudence à vous, / Et vous deviez chercher quelque biais plus doux' (1599–600). To this suggestion that he act cautiously and handle Tartuffe with particular care, Orgon responds indirectly, and unhelpfully, expressing his outrage and frustration at Tartuffe's deceits. His own conclusion, characteristically ill-considered and extreme, is to be dismissive, henceforth, of 'tous les gens de bien', on the grounds that one person who had appeared to him to be good turned out not to be.

It could be Cléante's reaction to this outburst that leads Fargher to criticize him for speaking pointless platitudes. Parish calls Cléante's speech 'an extended didactic epilogue' (edition, p. 106). But the speech needs to be assessed in its dramatic context. Cléante is trying to urge a cautious course of action on Orgon, but Orgon is too preoccupied with Tartuffe's treachery to attend. So Cléante has necessarily to engage with Orgon on his own terms, and attempt to discourage him from thinking that all good people are bad. As Cléante patiently explains the obvious, the laughter is once again on the uncomprehending Orgon, who had earlier thought that every appearance of good signified true good and now wants to believe that every appearance of good signifies bad. Cléante's advice 'soyez pour cela dans le milieu qu'il faut' (1624) is the self-evidently correct position to occupy between Orgon's absurd extremes. We should not think that Cléante is attempting to give Orgon (even less the audience) a general lesson in Aristotelian ethics here; he is using the terminology of the 'juste milieu' to encourage Orgon to see a way forward out of his diametrically opposed and foolish views. Molière no doubt takes advantage of this speech to help his own polemical case, by allowing Cléante to assert once again the existence of true devotion in the world, but this is also highly relevant to his rhetorical approach to Orgon, who wants suddenly to think that no truly devout people exist.

Before Cléante can return to the topic of how best to handle Tartuffe, Molière makes dramatic capital by engineering two entrances in quick succession. Neither new arrival does anything to help Orgon in his crisis. Having heard the news, Damis returns, threatening to cut off Tartuffe's ears. So Cléante has to turn his attentions to the son and ward him away from violence. This is hardly inept. The comedy is surely of a crisis worsening, while Cléante does his level-best, faced with a foolish father and a firebrand son, to prevent further aggravation. But for Cléante's role, the play could easily turn into pure farce with one or other of them taking a stick to Tartuffe. Cléante, however, helps to ensure the particularly moliéresque blend of farce and realism.

Progress is further halted by the return of Orgon's mother, who simply refuses to believe in Tartuffe's treachery. Molière develops a comically ironical exchange in which Orgon attempts entirely in vain to persuade her that Tartuffe is not what he seems to be. Cléante stands aside, until, thinking of the urgency of the situation and the need to extricate the family from the crisis, he suggests that time is being wasted on Mme Pernelle, that Tartuffe has dangerous weapons in his hands, and that some kind of agreement needs to be made with him: 'Je voudrais, de bon cœur, qu'on pût entre vous deux/De quelque ombre de paix raccommoder les nœuds' (1711–12).

But it is too late. Molière intensifies the crisis even further. The first of Tartuffe's weapons, Orgon's inheritance, is deployed, as Monsieur Loyal arrives to dispossess Orgon. As Orgon, Damis and Dorine all threaten violence, Cléante's role is once again to avoid further aggravation by ensuring Loyal's prompt exit. Loyal's intervention has at least helped Orgon by disabusing Mme Pernelle on the score of Tartuffe. But as Cléante tries to focus on the next step ('Allons voir quel conseil on doit vous faire élire' (1822)), the crisis deepens yet further. Valère arrives with news from a friend that Tartuffe has delivered the compromising strongbox into the hands of the king and urges Orgon's prompt flight. Cléante's contribution is brief, but to the point, and he even interrupts in order to make it: 'Allez tôt: / Nous songerons, mon frère, à faire ce qu'il faut' (1859–60).

Yet again, and for the final time, Molière intensifies the crisis. Before Orgon can flee, Tartuffe and the king's officer walk on stage. Tartuffe faces the sarcastic comments of all members of the family (including Cléante) as he haughtily explains that his devoted service to the king will lead to Orgon's imminent arrest by the officer. Whereas others limit their reactions to sarcasm, Cléante attempts to use reason to cut Tartuffe down to size, and puts two questions to him: why did he not perform this service to the king until after Orgon had found him seducing his wife? and why did he agree to inherit the wealth of a man he thought guilty of a political crime? They are pertinent questions and they point pellucid logic at Tartuffe's self-serving hypocrisy. They also allow Molière to deploy a pattern of interaction that he has used in the encounter between Tartuffe and Cléante in 4. 1. As at the end of the earlier scene, Tartuffe reacts to Cléante's probing questions by not answering them: he now asks the officer to proceed to the arrest.

Criminal justice and poetic justice are meted out simultaneously, when the officer arrests Tartuffe rather than Orgon, since the king's powers of perception have identified in Tartuffe a well-known criminal, and his sense of gratitude for Orgon's own support for the monarchy has led him to forgive him for looking after Argas' documents. Orgon's response is to begin insulting Tartuffe, but once again Cléante interrupts him, urging him to moderate his reaction and suggesting that they should hope for Tartuffe's correction to the ways of virtue and that Orgon should go and thank the king for his kindness. If it is most obviously the king's intervention that brings about the happy ending, Cléante's advice is crucial too, since it deters Orgon from insulting Tartuffe and allows him to focus on expressing gratitude to the king and marrying his daughter to Valère. Cléante's every intervention throughout the act has been to prevent an assemblage of diverse characters plunging themselves from an aggravating crisis into a cataclysmic abyss. This is one of Molière's most suspenseful denouements, and Cléante's role in maintaining the suspense is vital. Without Cléante, the crisis would simply have worsened. With Cléante's strategically placed interventions, there is always hope of an amelioration. He is the instrument of dramatic suspense.

In the play as a whole, Cléante's role is particularly complex, because multiple. He certainly helps the audience to laugh all the more at the obstinate folly of Orgon by offering him clear and patient advice, which is decisively rejected. His urbane presence helps to situate Molière's play in that ambiguous world between farce and contemporary realism, which contributes so much to its comic power. The evidence of the *Lettre sur la comédie de l'imposteur* makes it clear that some of his speeches have been so framed by Molière as to provide an answer to the play's critics who thought that the existence of true piety was not adequately acknowledged: his speeches refer more than once to the truly devout. Molière engineers his encounter with Tartuffe to provide the comic pleasure of subtle verbal sparring, and the suspenseful denouement is predicated on his uniquely restraining presence. To sum him up as either a spokesman for wisdom, or a comic fool, or the hidden agent of an alleged anti-Christian satire is to read his words out of context, or to mis-read them altogether.

Like Ariste and Chrysalde before him, Cléante contributes to the comic effect by engaging with the foolish protagonist in ways that highlight the protagonist's folly. But more than Ariste and Chrysalde, Cléante plays an active role in the dramatic action, positively trying to help the young lovers Mariane and Valère. In the process, he is also enlisted by the dramatist to make a comedy about religion as unobjectionable as possible in the eyes of those who had the power to suppress it. Of all Molière's *raisonneurs* Cléante's role is unusually multivalent.

5

Le Misanthrope: the *raisonneur* as friend and rival

Vous vous moquez de moi, je ne vous quitte pas.[1]

In *Le Misanthrope* (1666) Philinte is the close friend of the eponymous protagonist Alceste, and, as the Greek root of his name implies, he can be considered, in some senses, as the opposite of Alceste: he approaches his fellow men with sympathy and prefers to accommodate himself to them despite all their failings. He himself invites us to consider their relationship as similar to that of the earlier coupling of Ariste and Sganarelle in *L'École des maris* (100). But before he can develop the similarities he sees between the two pairs, Alceste interrupts him to dismiss the parallel as uninteresting. It is certainly the case that the aristocratic world in which the friendship of Philinte and Alceste evolves is far removed from the bourgeois setting of the fraternal interaction of Ariste and Sganarelle.

PHILINTE AND HIS PREDECESSORS

Subsequent critics have tended to share Alceste's view of this parallel on the grounds that Alceste and Philinte enjoy a more complex relationship than that of their two predecessors: according to Mallinson, 'if Sganarelle and Ariste are clearly distinguished in their respective

---

[1] Philinte in *Le Misanthrope* (446).

folie and *sagesse*, the same is not true of Alceste and Philinte'.[2] If the relationship between Philinte and Alceste is indubitably more complex than that between Ariste and Sganarelle, and even that between Chrysalde and Arnolphe and that between Cléante and Orgon, it is due to two factors.

The first is the broader subject matter that sets the two characters in conflict. Ariste and Sganarelle disagree on how best to bring up their intended spouses, Sganarelle wanting to lock his indoors and Ariste willing to allow his full freedom to grow up in society. Alceste and Philinte, by contrast, disagree on the much broader subject of how to behave in society, Alceste claiming that people ought always to speak with the utmost sincerity, Philinte preferring to make accommodations with sincerity in order to ensure the smooth conduct of social relations. When we contrast these two pairs of characters, it is easy to see that the earlier two are set up in clear opposition to each other, whereas Philinte, if his views are different from Alceste's, is not so clearly the polar opposite of the protagonist. The opposite of Alceste's desire for absolute sincerity is the happy-go-lucky insincerity exhibited by Célimène, Acaste, Clitandre, and Oronte. This broader range of views on a broader subject inevitably makes the relationship between Alceste and Philinte more complex than that between Sganarelle and Ariste.

The other complicating factor is dramaturgical. The dramatic action in *L'École des maris* is geared to win the audience's sympathy for the young lovers Isabelle and Valère and thereby ensure our laughter at the foolish Sganarelle who tries to stand in their way. The same mechanism is at work in the cases of Arnolphe and Orgon, whose particular obsessions constitute obstacles to the love of Agnès and Mariane respectively. In all cases the so-called *raisonneur* character stands in clear opposition to the foolish protagonist, so channelling the audience's laughter at him. And in all cases the final outcome of the dramatic action, the marriage of the young lovers, sanctions this laughter.

In dramaturgical terms, *Le Misanthrope* is very different, and in ways that complicate the relationship of Alceste and Philinte. Alceste is not a protagonist whose obsession leads him actively to prevent

---

[2] Molière, *Le Misanthrope*, ed. Jonathan Mallinson (London: Bristol Classical Press, 1996), p. xxvi.

a marriage which the audience wants to take place. This fact *might* mean that the dramatic structure is less geared to provoking audience derision at the protagonist. The dramatic action that Alceste seeks to perform in the course of the play is to have a meeting with the flighty Célimène, with whom he is paradoxically obsessed, in the hope of discovering her real feelings for him. Since the protagonist is not actively trying to stand in the way of an outcome that the audience would think desirable, and since he is not actively trying to commit a major mistake, Philinte does not need to work so actively against these things. This fact might mean that the dramatic structure is less geared to making the audience feel that Philinte is pursuing a crusade with right on his side. These observations about Alceste and Philinte are not comments on the different ethical codes that they espouse; they are indications of likely audience response to this pair of characters, as compared to their predecessors, on the basis of the different dramaturgical structures at work in this play.

The complicating factors that pertain in the case of *Le Misanthrope* have inevitably had an impact on the theatrical and critical reception of the play. It is the play of Molière's which, even from the eighteenth century, has most readily lent itself to tragic interpretation.[3] It is easy to see how the subject matter (particularly Alceste's concern with sincerity), the dramaturgical structures that do not make his intentions as obviously wrong-headed as Sganarelle's, Arnolphe's and Orgon's are, and also the ending, when his offer to Célimène is rejected, can be so handled as to appeal to an audience's sympathy rather than laughter.

PHILINTE AND THE CRITICS

Modern critical voices allow for more ambiguity in the relationship of Alceste and Philinte than in the case of previous protagonists. Bourqui sums it up well:[4]

---

[3] On responses to the play in the eighteenth century, see Jonathan Mallinson, 'Vision comique, voix morale: la réception du *Misanthrope* au xviiie siècle', *Littératures classiques*, 27 (1996), 367–77.

[4] Molière, *Le Misanthrope*, ed. Claude Bourqui (Paris: Livre de Poche, 2000), pp. 21–2

Le public, qui attendait un misanthrope tout uniment ridicule, est dérouté, et tout autant la critique de la postérité, qui se demande depuis toujours qui a raison, Alceste ou Philinte? Et, de fait, Alceste a raison et a tort. Philinte a raison et a tort [...]. Philinte ou Alceste, Alceste ou Philinte. Tout dépend de l'angle de vision, c'est-à-dire des valeurs de référence du spectateur individuel.

Mallinson sees no prospect of deciding between them: 'The seemingly clear-cut opposition of *homme moral* and *homme social*, the *mélancolique* and the *phlegmatique* is subject to a shifting perspective; one is not able simply to take sides' (edition, p. xix).

Notwithstanding, the same critical voices that have become familiar in the case of previous *raisonneurs* can still be heard in the case of Philinte. Fargher thinks him 'a comic figure in his own right'.[5] Eustis thinks him supine, and that this 'makes him almost as ridiculous in his excessive caution as Alceste in his rahsness'.[6] Peacock charges him with pedantry and naivety.[7] Mallinson too thinks his words are susceptible to a comic reading on the alleged grounds that, like Alceste, he is inconsistent, utters questionable generalities and seeks regularly to affirm his authority (p. xviii).

Others, however, find more positive value in Philinte's words, though the views of these critics are more nuanced in the case of this character than they were in the case of the earlier *raisonneurs*. Forestier is most forthright in extolling Philinte's wisdom: 'les maximes de Philinte, si proches soient-elles de la tradition philosophique, expriment plus largement, mais très exactement, celles de l'honnête homme, héritier mondain de la sagesse humaniste'; and again: 'Toute la sagesse humaniste proclame que c'est Philinte qui a raison.'[8] Howarth too thinks that 'Philinte surely represents a very positive social ideal' and writes in opposition to the 'purely negative light' in which he believes this character has been cast for too long.[9]

---

[5] Richard Fargher, 'Molière and his Reasoners' in *Studies in French Literature presented to H. W. Lawton*, ed. J. C. Ireson and others (Manchester University Press, 1968), pp. 105–20, p. 106.

[6] Alvin Eustis, *Molière as Ironic Contemplator* (The Hague, Paris: Mouton, 1973), p. 188.

[7] Noël Peacock, 'The Comic Role of the *Raisonneur* in Molière's Theatre', *Modern Language Review*, 76 (1981), 298–310, pp. 305, 307.

[8] Georges Forestier, *Molière en toutes lettres* (Paris: Bordas, 1990), pp. 63, 148.

[9] W. D. Howarth, *Molière: A Playwright and his Audience* (Cambridge University Press, 1982), p. 67.

McBride and Defaux offer slightly nuanced versions of Philinte as a positive ideal.[10] As if responding to the unusual dramaturgical structures operating in this play and the ambiguities they seem to allow for, Defaux asserts that *Le Misanthrope* cannot be considered an entirely serious play with Alceste as a tragic hero, but neither can it be considered an entirely comic play with Philinte expressing the norm from which Alceste deviates (p. 162). Having made this claim, however, he goes on to speak highly of the ideals Philinte embodies and likens him to Cléante in *Tartuffe*: he is 'le parfait honnête homme, la preuve incarnée que Molière n'a jamais totalement douté de l'humanité'; 'comparable en tous points à celle de Cléante, sa lucidité ne lui permet pas [...] la moindre illusion' (p. 190). He also compares him to Ariste, as someone able to accept the ways and fashions of the world, but distinguishes him from the earlier *raisonneur* by acknowledging that 'ce monde dans lequel il accepte de vivre ne vaut rien' (p.195). This is essentially McBride's view of him too: 'Philinte is the most honest and the most lucid of all the characters in the play, because he recognizes the necessity of playing a role' (p. 158). 'It does not behove us to condemn him', he adds (p. 159). Seen in this perspective, Philinte embodies a kind of superior, ironic wisdom as compared to Molière's earliest *raisonneurs*. His words do not express an absolute truth, but a provisional truth that makes life in society possible, if not perfect. Both McBride (p. 117) and Defaux (p. 192) cite similarities between Philinte's views and those of the sceptic La Mothe Le Vayer who wrote a few years before the play was first performed.

Parish ingeniously insists on the comic perspective in the play, the laughter directed clearly at Alceste, without, however, requiring us to think that Philinte embodies an ideal that we should accept unquestioningly: 'L'adoption de Philinte comme point de repère permet en effet au spectateur de mieux identifier certains aspects du ridicule d'autrui; mais l'activité de signaler le ridicule n'implique aucunement celle de s'ériger en idéal.'[11] This view falls half-way between the comic and idealized interpretations of Philinte's role. For

[10] Robert McBride, *The Sceptical Vision of Molière* (London: Macmillan, 1977); Gérard Defaux, *Molière ou les métamorphoses du comique: de la comédie morale au triomphe de la folie*, Lexington: French Forum, 1980, 2nd edn, Paris: Klincksieck, 1992.

[11] Richard Parish, '*Le Misanthrope*: des raisonneurs aux rieurs', *French Studies*, 45 (1991), 17–35, p. 18.

Parish, Philinte speaks sufficient sense for the audience to laugh with him at Alceste's folly, but is not so perfect himself as to constitute an ideal which the audience might be supposed to admire.

A number of factors seem to account for the very varied assessments that critics have made of Philinte's role. One is the new dramaturgical structures operating in the play, which potentially make it less clear that the audience laughter is to be directed at a foolish protagonist and their sympathy at a helpful *raisonneur* figure. Another factor, as Bourqui's comments quoted above suggest, is that critics' perspectives on the ethical subject matter can be subjective: a specifically modern view of Philinte's apparent desire to conform, so as not to unsettle the society in which he lives, might look unattractive to us in the light of the history of Nazi Germany, for instance. By contrast, Forestier's favourable comment on Philinte's views is strictly historical. The ethical code of *honnêteté* in the mid-seventeenth century was an acceptable ideal, which Philinte espouses. A third factor is that, in making their assessments, critics tend to overlook (or take for granted) the dramaturgical structures that determine the ways in which Philinte and the other characters interact. These structures create specific contexts in which to assess the characters' words as the scenes progress. This is the perspective that the following analyses will adopt.

One critic not to have overlooked the dramaturgical structures in *Le Misanthrope* is Forestier, who recognizes the potential for ambiguity created by the absence of an opposition between foolish protagonist and young lovers, but sees that Molière has not, however, abandoned the relationship between foolish protagonist and *raisonneur* type: '[Alceste] n'en est pas moins désigné comme ridicule par la technique habituelle de Molière qui consiste à l'opposer au début de la pièce à un *raisonneur*' (p. 79). Indeed, this relationship is even more important in *Le Misanthrope* if Molière is to safeguard his characteristic type of laughter at a protagonist who is 'ridicule en de certaines choses et honnête homme en d'autres'. In the absence of a couple of young lovers over whom Alceste might have exercised authority, it falls more fully to Philinte both to point up the folly of Alceste and to lend him a degree of respectability by virtue of their friendly association. The similarity to previous relationships between fool and *raisonneur* is also indicated by the fact that Molière himself played Alceste and that

Philinte was played by La Grange, known for his social graces in both life and performance.[12]

DONNEAU DE VISÉ ON PHILINTE

Interestingly, approaching the play in general and this relationship in particular from a dramaturgical perspective is encouraged by the first known critical response to the play in the seventeenth century, Donneau de Visé's *Lettre écrite sur la comédie du Misanthrope*. Hostile to Molière during the controversy over *L'École des femmes*, Donneau de Visé subsequently became a firm admirer and his favourable account of *Le Misanthrope* was printed alongside the text of the play when Molière published it in 1667 (*OC*, II, 131–40). The *Lettre* is sensitive to the new effects on the audience created by this play, while also recognizing the importance of the continuing protagonist-*raisonneur* relationship. For Donneau de Visé, Philinte is an unambiguous character, so admirable that he is a model for the audience to learn from: 'L'ami du Misanthrope est si raisonnable que tout le monde devrait l'imiter: il n'est ni trop ni trop peu critique; et ne portant les choses dans l'un ni dans l'autre excès, sa conduite doit être approuvée de tout le monde' (*OC*, II, 140].

One of Molière's strokes of genius as a comic dramatist was to ensure that his ridiculous protagonists were never so completely ridiculous as to strike audiences as being simply the stock theatrical types of farces; his comedy is powerful because his fools have something of the real world about them. But Donneau de Visé finds more ambiguity in *Le Misanthrope* than in earlier plays with respect to the role of the protagonist. His comments on Alceste suggest that Molière has balanced the ingredients slightly differently for this character and that audiences will recognize in him more *honnêteté* than in Sganarelle, Arnolphe, or Orgon: 'Le Misanthrope, malgré sa folie [...] a le caractère d'un honnête homme, et beaucoup de fermeté [...] bien qu'il paraisse en quelque façon ridicule, il dit des choses fort justes' (p. 139).

---

[12] See Roger W. Herzel, ' "Much depends on the acting": The Original Cast of *Le Misanthrope*', *Publications of the Modern Language Association of America*, 95 (1980), 348–66, pp. 355–6.

It is this new balance of ingredients in the protagonist that explains Donneau de Visé's view of the play's effect on the audience. The play was constantly amusing, but the laughter was quieter, more inward: 'je crois qu'elles [des pièces comme celle-ci] divertissent davantage, qu'elles attachent, et qu'elles font continuellement rire dans l'âme' (p. 139). This famous observation needs to be treated with caution, however.

The phrase 'rire dans l'âme' is often evoked by critics, but it is important not to misinterpret it as implying that *Le Misanthrope* was somehow a more solemn play than Molière's others. Donneau de Visé is clear that the play is always amusing, that Alceste contains the characteristic traits of ridicule associated with Molière's earlier protagonists, and that Molière performed Alceste's misanthropy for comic effect: 'les chagrins, les dépits, les bizarreries, et les emporte-ments d'un misanthrope étant des choses qui font un grand jeu, ce caractère est un des plus brillants qu'on puisse produire sur la scène' (p. 132). Above all, Donneau de Visé comments specifically on the interaction between Alceste and Philinte as a comic mechanism: 'l'ami du Misanthrope, qui est un homme sage et prudent, fait voir dans son jour le caractère de ce ridicule [et] l'humeur du Misanthrope fait connaître la sagesse de son ami' (p. 132). The reason Alceste might appear to have a greater degree of *honnêteté* than his predecessors is that we do not see him trying to stand in the way of an obviously desirable marriage and that he utters some words that seem 'fort justes'. But the reason he appears ridiculous is that he expresses himself in inappropriate language in inappropriate contexts and it is Philinte's job to make that clear to the audience.

FRIENDSHIP (1. 1)

The first scene of the play is a long encounter between Alceste and Philinte. In dramaturgical terms, Molière needs to establish the focus of the dramatic action, namely Alceste's wish to have a private interview with Célimène to test her feelings for him. He needs to prepare for some complicating episodes, in particular Alceste's ongo-ing lawsuit, which will fail. And he needs to paint Alceste's peculiar folly: he sees insincerity and injustice in everything around him; he enjoys bemoaning these things, while claiming that he alone is decent enough to conduct himself with absolute sincerity. How is Molière to make the audience laugh at Alceste? By showing the extremity of his views in contrast to those of Philinte. Crucially, in this scene, Molière attends to his depiction of Philinte in a way that suggests he might be anticipating those subsequent critics who find Philinte's views too accommodating to an insincere society. Molière establishes Philinte as first and foremost an utterly loyal friend to the wayward Alceste. What Philinte says is important, but the fact that he speaks always as Alceste's friend is even more important, since his selfless friendship for an obviously difficult man ensures that the audience will share Philinte's perspective on the folly of Alceste and on the events of the play.[13]

Indeed, the first scene can be interpreted as a dramatization of friendship. The recognized authority on friendship, even in the seventeenth century, was the Roman philosopher and orator Cicero. His treatise *De amicitia* was well known and set the terms in which others spoke on the subject. One of the defining features of friendship for Cicero is the giving and receiving of advice. It must be given frankly and received patiently: 'Le propre de la vraye amitié c'est d'avertir ses amis de ce qu'ils doivent faire, c'est d'estre pareillement averti par eux; C'est de leur donner ces avis librement & sans aigreur, c'est la recevoir d'eux patiemment & sans repugnance.'[14] Philinte's status as Alceste's friend is made plain for both readers and audiences. Donneau de Visé's *Lettre* refers to him constantly as 'l'ami du misanthrope'; Molière's list of characters defines him as 'ami d'Alceste'; and the opening lines of the play explicitly advertise their friendship when Philinte says 'quoique amis enfin' (7). Throughout the scene Philinte behaves like a model friend, giving frank advice and receiving the

---

[13] On the importance of Philinte's friendship, see: René Jasinski, *Le Misanthrope de Molière* (Paris: Armand Colin, 1951): 'On ne saurait trouver plus parfait ami' (p. 196); Louis Jouvet, *Molière et la comédie classique* (Paris: Gallimard, 1965): 'toute la pièce repose sur cette amitié' (p. 13); D. F. Jones, 'Love and Friendship in *Le Misanthrope*', *Romance Notes*, 23 (1982–83), 164–9: 'a proper acknowledgement of the relationship between Philinte and Alceste is crucial to an understanding of *Le Misanthrope*' (p. 165).

[14] Cicero, *Dialogues de la vieillesse et de l'amitié* (Paris: La Veuve Jean Camusat, 1640), p. 166 (xxv. 91, according to the numerical divisions introduced into modern editions of the *De amicitia*).

advice given to him by Alceste with good humour. Molière makes his dramatization of the subject comic by showing Alceste unable to fulfil all the requirements of Ciceronian friendship. While he certainly gives advice, he gives it rudely; and he does not like hearing advice, let alone in a good-humoured and patient spirit. Alceste's failing as a friend is also established in the opening lines. When Philinte says they are friends, Alceste interrupts furiously: 'Moi, votre ami? Rayez cela de vos papiers.' (8). Alceste's evident inadequacies as a friend serve to highlight the extraordinary friendship demonstrated by Philinte. Why is Philinte so devoted? There is a hint of an answer when he says they are like the two brothers in *L'École des maris* and suggests that their brotherly relationship is due to their having been 'sous mêmes soins nourris' (99). Whatever this phrase might mean precisely, it suggests that they have been together since early childhood.

STRUCTURE OF 1. 1

Guicharnaud calls the first scene a 'long débat', a description which is unfair to the dramatic skill and liveliness with which Molière conveys the expository material.[15] The encounter, if long, is certainly not a long *debate*, since the dialogue has four distinct conversational focal points: 1 Philinte's allegedly excessive greeting of a man he barely knew; 2 contrasting attitudes to sociability; 3 Alceste's lawsuit; 4 Alceste's love for Célimène. The artfully informal transitions between them suggest more the nature of Philinte's friendship for Alceste than they do the structure of a debate.

The scene opens as Philinte wants to know what is wrong with Alceste, who tells him frankly that he is shocked by Philinte's cordiality with a man he hardly knew. This leads to the second focal point, introduced by Philinte, who raises the general point arising from Alceste's criticism of him in the spirit of wanting to moderate his friend's anger and make him see things in proportion: 'Mais, sérieusement, que voulez-vous qu'on fasse?' (34). Alceste says that people should not

---

[15] Jacques Guicharnaud, *Molière: une aventure théâtrale* (Paris: Gallimard, 1963), p. 353.

be treated with the same false familiarity but distinguished according to who they are and addressed with utter sincerity. This generally focused conversation allows Molière to prepare for Alceste's momentary downfall in 1. 2 when he finds it difficult to tell Oronte honestly and directly what he thinks about his sonnet. Philinte's doubts about Alceste's declared policy of complete sincerity lead Alceste to assert virulently his intolerance of all kinds of human misbehaviour.

Alceste's assertions are the stimulus for the third focal point, when Philinte tries again, gently, to moderate Alceste's ever-increasing anger: 'Ce chagrin philosophe est un peu trop sauvage' (97). This allows Alceste to defend his position by offering evidence of human evil: the man who is pursuing him in law. Alceste is so convinced that he has right on his side and yet so convinced that the process is corrupt that he anticipates the pleasure of losing his lawsuit. This development sets in train references to the trial throughout the play and prepares for the interruption of Alceste's climactic scene with Célimène in act 4 when he is required to deal with a crisis in the lawsuit and for news of his defeat in act 5.

Philinte shifts to the fourth focal point, again in a spirit of trying to help Alceste, by suggesting that his intransigeant view of human nature in connection with his lawsuit is at odds with his passion for the flirtatious society hostess Célimène. While acknowledging that matters of love are different from other things, Alceste explains that he has come to Célimène's house precisely to talk to her about his love and her apparent flirtations with other men. So in a scene of friendly conflict ranging in subject between on the one hand attitudes to adopt towards humankind and behaviour in society, and on the other the current preoccupations of Alceste, Molière has prepared the audience to laugh at Alceste's folly such as it will be exhibited in his encounters with Oronte and Célimène. But Molière could not have achieved this without the presence of Philinte.

PHILINTE'S GREETING (1. 1)

Everything about the opening, rapid exchanges between the two characters—lexis, implied tone of voice, implied gesture and movement—creates the impression that Alceste is an angry, exasperated, impatient man and Philinte his determined, concerned and good-humoured friend. Alceste interrupts (3, 8), uses imperatives (1, 3, 8), gestures Philinte away (3), uses the emphatic pronoun to assert his right to be angry ('Moi, je veux me fâcher' (5)) or to question his willingness to be Philinte's friend ('Moi, votre ami?'), before finally revealing that Philinte's behaviour has just made him forfeit Alceste's friendship, a forfeit expressed in hyperbolic terms: 'Je vous déclare net que je ne le suis plus [votre ami], / Et ne veux nulle place en des cœurs corrompus' (11–12). As Alceste disowns his friend, he stands up, an action which reinforces his language and makes it easier for him to move away from Philinte. The action is not evident in the text of the first edition of the play (1667), but there is a stage direction to this effect in the 1682 edition ('Alceste se levant brusquement' (8)). The first edition contains a frontispiece which depicts the moment just before Alceste rises: he looks agitated and uncomfortable on the edge of his seat.

The same illustration shows Philinte approaching his friend in a confident posture, both hands open and held out towards Alceste in a questioning but unthreatening gesture. His face registers a look of concern, but one that seems familiar and amused, in sharp contrast to Alceste's scowl. This visual representation of Philinte tallies with the linguistic evidence for his characterization at the start of the play. He asks questions (1, 2, 13). He speaks firmly, but politely, to his angry and unforthcoming friend, as suggested by his choice of the impersonal pronoun when he says: 'Mais on entend les gens, au moins, sans se fâcher' (4). He is willing to point out features of Alceste's aberrant behaviour, not to criticize them in their own right, but to indicate the obstacle they create for the free communication between friends: 'Dans vos brusques chagrins je ne puis vous comprendre, / Et quoique amis enfin, je suis tout des premiers ...' (6–7). To Alceste's disavowal of their friendship and his suggestion that Philinte has a 'cœur corrompu', the latter responds with an amused question: 'Je suis donc bien coupable, Alceste, à votre compte?' (13). This response might suggest to the audience that Philinte is used to dealing with such tantrums from Alceste. It certainly suggests skill in handling him. Instead of terminating relations, which is what Alceste was on the point of doing, Philinte's question gives Alceste the opportunity to pour out his anger and so reveal to Philinte and the audience what specific event has caused this display of hostility. By using Alceste's name, Philinte also shows that he is confident that their friendship is continuing.

In commenting on these opening exchanges, Mallinson paves the way for his view that the play is radically ambiguous in that, he says, the text gives moral authority neither to Alceste nor to Philinte, and so does not allow the audience to decide between them. To do this, Mallinson alleges similarities in their behaviour here: 'they each seek to affirm their own authority', 'both characters are clearly trying to teach the other how to behave', 'the balance is clear' (p. 70). It seems to me, on the other hand, that Molière does everything he can, in terms of language and implied movement and gesture, to create a sharp contrast, rather than a balance, between the characters. The calmly confident Philinte is trying to create a space in which his agitated friend can vent his spleen. Indeed Philinte is doing this precisely so that Alceste can criticize Philinte himself. The performance implied by these opening exchanges seems more likely to invite the audience to share Philinte's amused concern at Alceste's spluttering rage.

Encouraged to speak, Alceste resorts readily to further hyperbole, coupled with swearing and enumeration, when he recounts what has so shocked him—Philinte's familiar greeting of a man he barely knows:

> Morbleu! c'est une chose indigne, lâche, infâme,
> De s'abaisser ainsi jusqu'à trahir son âme;
> Et si, par un malheur, j'en avais fait autant,
> Je m'irais, de regret, pendre tout à l'instant.
>
> (25–8)

If Alceste's accusation of social hypocrisy were meant to carry any weight with the audience, Molière would be unlikely to have made him express it in such outrageously hyperbolic terms, the effect of which is to direct laughter at Alceste himself for the gaping disproportion between the crime on the one hand and the judgement and verdict on the other. In the face of this onslaught, Philinte retains his good humour and wit, twice repeating Alceste's verb 'pendre' in different forms, using the rhetorical technique known as polyptoton:

> Je ne vois pas, pour moi, que le cas soit pendable,
> Et je vous supplierai d'avoir pour agréable

Que je me fasse un peu grâce sur votre arrêt,
Et ne me pende pas pour cela, s'il vous plaît.

(29–32)

Parish thinks that the opening line of this speech is likely to prompt laughter at Philinte's expense, because he thinks it an example of 'casuistique pédantesque' (p. 19). But there is nothing casuistical or pedantic about Philinte's speech. Molière knows how to make fun of pedantry. A typical device by which he does this is to use overwrought syntax and to suggest semantic vacuity. He makes fun of casuistry in *Tartuffe*, and, through the character of his hypocrite, deploys ingenious argument in support of something that is obviously wrong (3. 3, 4. 1, 4. 5). Philinte has recourse to neither overwrought syntax nor ingenious argument. He simply laughs off Alceste's verdict of the death penalty for the absurd hyperbole that it is. He laughs it off ironically (hence the force of 'un peu' and 's'il vous plaît'), teasing Alceste for his inflamed reaction. Alceste's response acknowledges Philinte's jocular tone: 'Que la plaisanterie est de mauvaise grâce!' (33). But his dogged refusal to be amused suggests that Philinte needs to adopt a different strategy to bring his friend round.

ATTITUDES TO SOCIABILITY (1. 1)

Philinte's new strategy initiates the next stage in their discussion, successfully dislodging Alceste's furious obsession with this one episode and allowing both characters to address more generally their views on how to behave in society. Philinte marks the shift of perspective linguistically with the adverb 'sérieusement' and the open question: 'Mais, sérieusement, que voulez-vous qu'on fasse?' (34). In response, Alceste first, then Philinte state in summary form their differing views on how to conduct social relations. Alceste thinks one should speak to people with utter sincerity; Philinte that one should behave towards them with appropriate reciprocity. One thing to note about this short exchange of views is that it reveals Philinte's skill in suppressing (at least momentarily) Alceste's bluster and fury with his friend, and in re-establishing a degree of friendly discourse. More importantly, this summary exchange of contrasting views about social conduct might be thought to represent the nub of the intellectual issues raised by the play. And it might be thought to invite the audience to take a stance.

But we need to distinguish between consideration of these issues outside the confines of the theatre, where Molière and his audiences will have their personal and varied views, and consideration of them in the course of a performance. In the theatrical context, Molière has weighted his presentation of these two views so that we laugh at Alceste. This is evident even in the way they are expressed in summary form. Alceste is dogmatic, hyperbolic, unyielding: 'Je veux qu'on soit sincère, et qu'en homme d'honneur, / On ne lâche aucun mot qui ne parte du cœur' (35–6). By contrast, Philinte's view is more accommodating:

> Lorsqu'un homme vous vient embrasser avec joie,
> Il faut bien le payer de la même monnoie,
> Répondre, comme on peut, à ses empressements,
> Et rendre offre pour offre, et serments pour serments.
>
> (37–40)

Philinte's 'il faut bien' is much less assertive in impact than Alceste's 'je veux qu'on soit', not least because it is expressed impersonally. And his 'comme on peut' allows some scope for individual judgement and taste, whereas Alceste's 'aucun mot qui ne parte du cœur' allows no scope whatsoever for adapting oneself to the circumstances. This analysis does not mean that Molière personally thinks that Alceste is wrong and Philinte right in absolute terms (or that he wants to persuade the audience of this). But for the purposes of the comedy, and while we are in the theatre, he wants us to laugh at Alceste for the unbending way in which he holds and expresses his view; and this entails our sharing Philinte's perspective on him, which we can do because he is urbane and unaggressive in the way he holds his contrary view. Rigidity looks ridiculous when contrasted with flexibility.

This hint that Molière has so presented these differing views as to make us laugh at Alceste is confirmed by Alceste's long response to Philinte, and not least by his brusque, dogmatic, and personally offensive opening lines: 'Non, je ne puis souffrir cette lâche méthode / Qu'affectent la plupart de vos gens à la mode' (41–2). Alceste's vitriolic tirade against society's civilities reveals the root of his objection. It is not so much that he objects to even the slightest hypocrisies on principle. It is that civilities are accorded indiscriminately to those who deserve them *and* to those who do not, with the result that the deserving recipients receive no special treatment that would acknowledge their status. At bottom, we deduce that Alceste wants Philinte's attentions for himself and is slighted when he sees him accord them to someone else. The selfishness that lies at the heart of Alceste's professed admiration of sincerity could not be more nakedly expressed: 'Je veux qu'on me distingue; et pour le trancher net, / L'ami du genre humain n'est point du tout mon fait' (63–4). Even if we were tempted to admire his call for utter sincerity, the transparent selfishness that leads him to make it ensures that Alceste is the object of our laughter.

His selfishness is also transparent in the way in which he brings a discussion of general principle back to Philinte's alleged offence, away from which Philinte had attempted to steer him. Philinte tries once again to avoid discussion of his specific case and tries to make Alceste see that some accommodation with social politeness is necessary: 'Mais quand on est du monde, il faut bien que l'on rende / Quelques dehors civils que l'usage demande' (65–6). His use of 'on' acts both as a defence of his own behaviour and as a way of persuading Alceste to address the issue in broader terms. Philinte's language remains flexible and undogmatic compared to Alceste's. He is not insisting that his view is right. He asks only for Alceste to concede 'quelques dehors civils', thereby acknowledging Alceste's point that society's civilities may well be superficial. But this provokes Alceste to further dogmatic assertions against the use of vain compliments: 'Non, vous dis-je' (67), 'Je veux que l'on soit homme, et qu'en toute rencontre / Le fond de notre cœur dans nos discours se montre' (69).

Having at least persuaded Alceste to engage in argument with him, Philinte can now enjoy putting his friend's position to the test. It is important to realize that Philinte is not attempting to argue his own position, even less to impose it on Alceste. He is trying to persuade Alceste that *his* view, in practice, will not always work (and so, perhaps, defend his own behaviour, that Alceste has attacked, though any such defence remains implicit). He tries to get Alceste to admit that there are some circumstances in which speaking one's thoughts out loud would be a bad idea:

> Il est bien des endroits où la pleine franchise
> Deviendrait ridicule et serait peu permise;
> Et parfois, n'en déplaise à votre austère honneur,
> Il est bon de cacher ce qu'on a dans le cœur.
>
> (73–6)

The phrases 'bien des endroits' and 'parfois' make it clear that Philinte wants Alceste not to abandon his principle of sincerity, but to modify it on occasion. His tone remains friendly and teasing with the caricatural description of Alceste's honour as 'austère'. He then invites a response from Alceste by asking two general questions:

> Serait-il à propos et de la bienséance
> De dire à mille gens tout ce que d'eux on pense?
> Et quand on a quelqu'un qu'on hait ou qui déplaît,
> Lui doit-on déclarer la chose comme elle est?
>
> (77–80)

These are questions that invite the answer 'no'. They are meant to coax Alceste into modifying his intransigent stance. In the dramatist's perspective, they prepare the comic climax, in which Alceste answers in precisely the opposite way: 'Oui' (81). For someone who has been so voluble up to now, Alceste answers with exceptional brevity. The single word 'oui' alone conjures up his pig-headedness. Philinte pushes Alceste further by asking him two further questions about individuals known to them. Would he tell Émilie that she is mutton dressed as lamb? and Dorilas that he is a self-obsessed bore? Philinte wants Alceste to admit that it would be very difficult socially to speak to people in such terms, and the audience is surely meant to be amused by the absurdity of Alceste's position as revealed by Philinte's questioning scrutiny. Alceste himself replies simply that he sees no problem in speaking to Émilie and Dorilas as Philinte suggests. So when Philinte laughs at him ('Vous vous moquez' (87)), the audience laughs too, and the laughter is confirmed in the next scene when we see Alceste adopting all manner of indirect language to avoid telling Oronte forthrightly what he thinks of his sonnet.

Like Molière's other foolish protagonists, Alceste can see nothing humorous in his views, and he proceeds to reassert them in a far more extreme fashion than even Philinte had jokingly proposed. People are so thoroughly vice-ridden, he says, that he can no longer keep silent and will speak his mind to everybody:

> Je ne trouve partout que lâche flatterie,
> Qu'injustice, intérêt, trahison, fourberie;
> Je n'y puis plus tenir, j'enrage, et mon dessein
> Est de rompre en visière à tout le genre humain.
>
> (93–6)

His recourse once again to enumeration of vices and the hyperbolic imagery of the last line (along with his hesitations before Oronte) reveal this to be the spluttering and posturing that he knows he can permit himself in front of his patient and long-suffering friend: it is not a plan of action.

ALCESTE'S LAWSUIT (1. 1)

What Molière has done in Alceste's speech enumerating human vices is to prepare the ground for the third stage in the discussion between the two characters. Alceste is still, in theory, addressing the topic of the need to speak one's mind in society, but he makes his case for this by expressing his view that society is so multifariously vice-ridden that his only response to it is to attack it outright. Philinte's reply seizes on the broader topic that Alceste has unwittingly raised: no longer the use of civilities in human interaction, but a vision of humankind and the appropriate response to be made to it. Molière introduces the topic both to complete the picture of Alceste's deep-rooted misanthropy and to engineer, for the audience, the news of his lawsuit, which Alceste will adduce as evidence of his bleak view of humanity.

Philinte addresses first not Alceste's view of humanity, but the misanthrope's response to it. He tries to temper the violence of Alceste's reaction and does so frankly, but with gentle humour: 'Ce chagrin philosophe est un peu trop sauvage, / Je ris des noirs accès où je vous envisage' (97–8). The phrase 'un peu trop sauvage' is calculated to give Alceste pause for thought, but not to seem aggressive. Philinte is not saying that he disagrees with Alceste's reaction as such, but with the extremity of it. It is so extreme that Philinte is inclined to laugh at Alceste, so sanctioning the audience's laughter. This is the point at which he compares the two of them to Sganarelle and Ariste in *L'École des maris*. It would not be a flattering comparison to Alceste if Philinte were allowed to develop it, since Alceste would clearly be likened to the foolish Sganarelle who is distrustful of humanity. But, for spectators who know the earlier play, Philinte's metatheatrical utterance has the effect of inviting them to respond to the Alceste-Philinte interaction as they have done to that of Sganarelle-Ariste.

To Alceste's interruption saying that the topic should be dropped, Philinte responds firmly: 'Non: tout de bon, quittez toutes ces incartades' (102). Philinte's tone seems different here. The determined 'non' and the imperative, both more typical of Alceste, along with the pleading 'tout de bon' suggest that he abandoned the witty and teasing responses to Alceste's absurdities that have characterized his discourse so far and decided to say something that he wants Alceste to take seriously. He is asking Alceste to stop speaking with such violent bluster. The text does not tell us whether Philinte is impatient or urgent as he speaks this line. But it does allow him to give two reasons for making the request. The first, simply expressed, is that Alceste's rude criticisms of people will not have any salutary effect on them, so, by implication, he is wasting his energy: 'Le monde par vos soins ne se changera pas' (103). Mallinson thinks that the opening two lines of this speech undermine Philinte's moral authority: Philinte is inconsistent in telling Alceste that the world cannot be changed, while himself acting as if Alceste can be changed (p. xix). It is true that Philinte will go on to insist on the folly of trying to change the world (157–8), but in the current context he is claiming specifically that Alceste's peculiar method of being rude to people will not change them for the better. As we have seen Alceste's method in operation, it is hard to disagree with Philinte. Moreover, Philinte's envisaged 'correction' of Alceste is of quite a different order from Alceste's envisaged correction of the world. Alceste wants to reprimand people for their cowardice, injustice, self-interest, and treachery. In other words, Alceste wants to change human nature. Philinte's request 'quittez ces incartades' has much smaller ambitions: he does not want to change Alceste's nature, but to temper his public response to the foibles and weaknesses of other individuals.

The second reason for Philinte's request is particularly interesting for the interpretation of his character:

> Et puisque la franchise a pour vous tant d'appas,
> Je vous dirai tout franc que cette maladie,
> Partout où vous allez, donne la comédie.
>
> (103–6)

Mallinson thinks that these lines constitute yet another inconsistency on Philinte's part, which prevent the audience from adopting his perspective: Philinte criticizes Alceste's 'pleine franchise' (73), 'but he himself is capable of unsparing criticism' (p. xviii). There is, however, a considerable difference between the violence with which Alceste offers criticism and the wit with which Philinte does so here. Philinte knowingly refers to Alceste's desire for frankness by way of showing him what it is like to take some of his own medicine. But what Philinte's frankness reveals is not really unsparing criticism as such. He has already said that he finds Alceste's rages amusing, and says now that everyone else does too. It is, of course, a potentially wounding revelation. It is also a revelation that, yet again, sanctions the audience's laughter at Alceste. But why does Philinte give this reason for persuading Alceste to temper his behaviour? Because fear of public ridicule might prove to be a compelling argument. It is the argument used in the *Lettre sur la comédie de l'imposteur* to defend the potentially useful effects on an audience of that play (*OC*, i, 1177). And if Philinte speaks such a home truth to Alceste, it is because frankness is permitted, indeed sought, between real friends. Cicero said as much: 'Que nous prenions plaisir à les conseiller franchement & avec liberté. Que l'autorité de leurs salutaires persuasions soient sur nous absoluës. Que nous soyons bien aise de la voir employée, non seulement à nous donner ouvertement avis de ce que nous devons faire, mais mesmes à nous remonstrer avec severité, quand ils le jugeront à propos' (p. 119 (xiii.44)). So in alerting Alceste in this way, just as Chrysalde warns Arnolphe that 'Qui rit d'autrui / Doit craindre qu'en revanche on rie aussi de lui' (*L'École des femmes*, 45–6), Philinte is behaving like the perfect friend. He is not inconsistent, since he is warning Alceste against complete frankness with individuals who are *not* his friends.

It is a further measure of Alceste's inability to fulfil the contract of true friendship that he does not respond to Philinte's suggestion as Cicero would have expected. Far from agreeing with Philinte, Alceste rejoices that people find him funny, since this confirms his view that humankind is vicious and that he is right to hate it. Philinte tries to temper Alceste's general expression of hatred, but for Molière this is an opportunity to make Alceste express his misanthropy in the most hyperbolic terms, and so make Alceste seem even more comic: 'Tous les hommes me sont à tel point odieux, / Que je serais fâché d'être sage à leurs yeux' (111–12), 'je hais tous les hommes' (118). Philinte tries, in vain, to question the blanket coverage of Alceste's hatred (115–16), but this serves only to allow Alceste to explain how absolutely everyone arouses his disapproving fury. He hates all wicked men, of course; but he also hates everybody else for tolerating the wicked, instead of expressing hatred for them as he does.

The ideal illustration of wickedness and society's indulgence of it is Alceste's own legal case, now deftly introduced by Molière. Alceste describes the criminality of his opponent, who covers his deeds with a hypocritical veneer of respectability, adding that everybody who knows the man sees through the veneer. Alceste triumphantly reports this with characteristic enumeration and confident assertion: 'Nommez-le fourbe, infâme, et scélerat maudit, / Tout le monde en convient, et nul n'y contredit' (135–6). What most offends Alceste, however, is that everyone treats his enemy in person as if they did not see through his hypocrisy: 'Cependant, sa grimace est partout bienvenue: / On l'accueille, on lui rit, partout il s'insinue' (137–8). As we have only Alceste's version of events, Molière plays on the ambiguity whereby we cannot be sure if society is really guilty of tolerating his opponent's hypocrisy (as Alceste alleges) or rather if society is guilty of indulging Alceste by concurring with his doubtless enraged criticisms of the man in question as an outright scoundrel. The latter possibility, supported by the wording of lines 135–6, serves only to make Alceste look more comic for his self-obsession and skewed vision. Alceste remains comic at the climax of his speech: 'Et parfois il me prend des mouvements soudains / De fuir dans un désert l'approche des humains' (143–4). The comedy here resides in the fact that this conclusion is precisely opposite to the one he drew in lines 95–6, though the evidence on which it is based is the same.

The world is so wicked that he wants to tell everyone how wicked they are, he said in his earlier lines; but at the same time he wants to retreat into solitude. The inconsistent conclusions, both blusteringly expressed, prompt laughter at his ill-focused expressions of anger.

Philinte's reply has caused much ink to spill: sometimes he is held up as a spokesman for ethical comportment, sometimes derided as a pompous fool, as extreme in his own views as Alceste is in his. The dramaturgical perspective suggests a different approach to this speech, which needs to be understood specifically as a Philinte's friendly response to Alceste's previous speech. Philinte is clearly trying to soothe Alceste, who has finished his own speech with yet another paroxysm of anger:

> Mon Dieu, des mœurs du temps mettons-nous moins en peine,
> Et faisons un peu grâce à la nature humaine;
> Ne l'examinons point dans la grande rigueur,
> Et voyons ses défauts avec quelque douceur.
> Il faut, parmi le monde, une vertu traitable;
> A force de sagesse, on peut être blâmable;
> La parfaite raison fuit toute extrémité,
> Et veut que l'on soit sage avec sobriété.

> (145–52)

Moore is unimpressed by the principles to be found in this speech, which some critics have taken seriously as the play's message: 'La parfaite raison fuit toute extrémité' is a banal principle, he claims, and 'to insist that one should be "sage avec sobriété" is a piece of rather flat moralizing.'[16] For Moore, the dramatic value of this speech lies in the contrast it sets up with Alceste's: 'We should think of Molière, not as pillorying Alceste and therefore sharing the views of Philinte, but as imagining both elements in his contrasted pairs of characters' (p. 13). Moore's comments have had a powerful influence, but what exactly are their practical implications for the spectator in the theatre, who will react to Alceste as he speaks, and then to Philinte as he replies? Moore seems to think that spectators suspend their reactions until they are able to consider pairs of characters as abstract contrasts. His

---

[16] W. G. Moore, *Molière: A New Criticism* (Oxford: Clarendon Press, 1949), p. 116, p. 74.

comments, however, certainly lie at the root of those criticisms which find fault with Philinte. McBride, for instance, says that if one looks at these lines, 'one will see that [Philinte's] apparent moderation may well appear to be excessive moderation, which Molière calculatingly opposes to the full-blooded fixation of his other character' (p. 6–7). Against these approaches to Philinte's words is Forestier's insistence that these lines clearly represent not banal principles or excessive moderation but the wisdom of Montaigne and his seventeenth-century successors (pp. 61–2). Indeed Montaigne quotes St Paul's words, which Philinte clearly echoes: 'ne soyez pas plus sage qu'il ne faut, mais soyez sobrement sage'.[17] Mallinson acknowledges the respectability of Philinte's words, but implies that there are other ways in which his views here are undermined: 'Philinte may reflect familiar social attitudes, but this does not necessarily give him authority in the play's terms. Beneath his apparent wisdom, other comic possibilities are apparent. [...] Philinte has a very dogmatic, assertive attitude' (pp. 75–6).

None of these comments properly addresses the precise dramatic context in which Philinte speaks these lines. He is responding to a speech in which Alceste has expressed such outrage at the polite way members of their common circle treat his enemy, whose villainy they allegedly acknowledge, that he says he intends to retreat from society. Philinte's speech is not a disembodied assertion of an ethical position. It aims to temper Alceste's reaction to those members of society who are polite to his legal opponent, by suggesting how they might be excused. Linguistically, Philinte's speech shows every sign of wanting to avoid antagonizing Alceste further. He uses the inclusive 'nous' form to suggest that he is not speaking against Alceste: 'mettons-nous', 'faisons', 'examinons', 'voyons'. When he could say 'vous', he says 'on peut être blâmable'. He uses gentle modifiers to suggest that he is not opposing Alceste's position, but seeking to nuance it: 'moins en peine', 'un peu grâce', 'quelque douceur'. Given Alceste's repeated tendency to exaggerate and see things out of proportion, the audience might well wonder if Alceste's view of his legal opponent

---

[17] Montaigne, *Essais*, 3 vols., ed. Pierre Villey and V.-L. Saulnier (Paris: Presses Universitaires de France, 1965), I, p. 197 (bk I, ch. 30), quoting Romans 13: 3. The quotation was inscribed on the ceiling of Montaigne's library.

as an utter villain and of those who treat him politely as therefore
spineless is entirely objective. But Philinte does not question Alceste's
view. That would be too inflammatory. Instead, he questions only
Alceste's reaction. He does so by suggesting that, for society to operate
smoothly, people need to temper their expressions, and expectations,
of virtue and wisdom, and to understand people's failings rather than
rail constantly against them. When he says 'La parfaite raison fuit
toute extrémité', he is not asserting some sort of ethical golden mean
as an abstract argument; he is defending those members of society
whom Alceste has just attacked, suggesting that it is reasonable of
them not to treat Alceste's opponent rudely and aggressively for his
alleged want of virtue.

It is true that as well as defending members of society, Philinte
is also criticizing Alceste's hard-line stance, which is to want always
to point out to people their villainies. In suggesting that this is
madness, he refers to a sense of modern, as distinct from, ancient
custom, which is presumably meant to appeal to Molière's fashionable
audience:

> Cette grande roideur des vertus des vieux âges
> Heurte trop notre siècle et les communs usages;
> Elle veut aux mortels trop de perfection:
> Il faut fléchir au temps sans obstination;
> Et c'est une folie à nulle autre seconde
> De vouloir se mêler de corriger le monde.
>
> (153–8)

We need to be clear that these words should be interpreted not in
the abstract as an opposite ethical programme to that of Alceste, but
as Philinte's attempt to pacify his friend. He is not telling Alceste to
abandon the high aspirations for human conduct which he professes
to maintain; he is telling him that it is unreasonable to demand
openly of people that they behave perfectly. His use of the word
'folie' is a reminder of the argument he has already used, namely
that Alceste looks foolish when he expresses his inflexible views in
public.

None of this makes Philinte the opposite of Alceste, as some
critics maintain. He is sharing Alceste's views as far as he can, while
indicating where some modification of them would calm his friend's

temper and save him from public ridicule. He ends his speech by insisting on the common ground that they share as they contemplate human nature, while also suggesting the different attitude he adopts to it. He has not so far personalized his discussion, but his doing so now can be read as a friendly gesture:

> J'observe, comme vous, cent choses tous les jours,
> Qui pourraient mieux aller, prenant un autre cours;
> Mais quoi qu'à chaque pas je puisse voir paroître,
> En courroux, comme vous, on ne me voit point être;
> Je prends tout doucement les hommes comme ils sont,
> J'accoutume mon âme à souffrir ce qu'ils font;
> Et je crois qu'à la cour, de même qu'à la ville,
> Mon flegme est philosophe autant que votre bile.
>
> (159–66)

If Philinte has a lesson to teach Alceste, it is in this closing part of his speech rather than in the earlier part; but even here he does not adopt a didactic tone. It is true that his sudden recourse to the first-person singular here might encourage an actor to express in these lines the 'desire to pontificate' that Mallinson sees in them (p. 76). But it is possible to read them in a different way. After Philinte has attempted in general terms to defend those members of society whom Alceste has attacked and to suggest the folly of Alceste's public statements of outrage, he now explains how he responds to the bleak vision of humankind which, by implication, he shares with Alceste. In other words, he uses 'je' and 'vous' in order to make clear the personal and friendly import of his speech. Moreover, he does not use 'je' and 'vous' in opposition to each other. Philinte's linguistic usage is subtly calibrated so as not to irritate Alceste or to appear to be preaching to him. 'Je' and 'vous' are therefore set in parallel, not in opposition, when he insists on their common vision of human failure: 'J'observe, comme vous'. And in expressing this vision, he even adopts Alceste's tendency to hyperbole, which might have the effect of keeping his attention: 'cent choses tous les jours'. But in order to show Alceste a different way of responding to this vision, he does need to distinguish between them. To avoid a potentially conflictual opposition between 'je' and 'vous', he resorts to an ingenious arrangement of pronouns: 'En courroux, comme vous, on ne me voit point être.' Though this line certainly does distinguish between them—Alceste's anger, and Philinte's lack of it—it is possible to interpret Molière's phraseology as an indication that Philinte is trying very hard not to be conflictual. This would certainly fit with his approach throughout the scene so far, which has been to speak honestly to his friend, while also trying to temper Alceste's fury. These lines have been read as Philinte's attempt to teach Alceste a different way of responding to the world, as he sets himself up as an example. But Philinte at no point uses the language of instruction. He does not tell Alceste that he should be different. He does not criticize Alceste's anger. This observation leads me not to accept Mallinson's view that Philinte is attempting to establish himself as a 'figure of authority trying to outplay' Alceste (p. 76), thereby undermining himself in the eyes of the audience. My own reading of Philinte's language is that he is not trying to correct Alceste, but to calm him down.

Indeed the last line of Philinte's speech, 'Mon flegme est philosophe autant que votre bile', invoked by Fargher as evidence of Philinte's being as 'immoderate and excessive in his preaching of [sweet reasonableness]' (p. 105) as Alceste is in his immoderate rages, needs to be interpreted in the light of the previous three lines and as a response to Alceste's speech which had brought about this third section of the scene. In that speech (87–96) Alceste has expressed, in general terms, his view that the world is so corrupt that he has to shout aloud about it, and he has used the imagery of the humours, his own being black bile: 'Mes yeux sont trop blessés, et la cour et la ville / Ne m'offrent rien qu'objets à m'échauffer la bile' (89–90). The last four lines of Philinte's speech are a delayed response to Alceste's expression of his own position. Whereas Alceste is offended by what he sees, Philinte tries to accustom himself not to be offended: 'J'accoutume mon âme à souffrir ce qu'ils font' (164). It is important to realize that Philinte's position is not one of complacency. He is suggesting that it requires effort not to be irritated by the behaviour of people. Alceste has referrred to both court and town in order to evoke the ubiquity of villainy, and Philinte's reply repeats this phrase. It is easy to forget that the apparently resounding line with which Philinte's speech ends does not, in fact, stand syntactically by itself. It is a subordinate clause that is dependent on the much more tentative introductory phrase 'je crois que'. Moreover, it is a line which, while certainly drawing a distinction between the two men, is expressed, like so many of his other lines, in terms that are not antagonistic. Alceste's desire to tell people forthrightly about their vices may well be inspired by a high sense of virtue (Philinte is being generous here, as the audience knows Alceste's rages are also inspired by selfishness), but Philinte's position is no less virtuous since he recognizes vice but tries hard not to let it anger him. This is to spell out a distinction which Philinte's speech, peaceable in intention, glosses over by calling *both* their responses philosophical.

Philinte's speech explains; it does not preach. His language in no sense justifies Fargher's gloss that he is 'inexorable in his desire to reform Alceste' (p. 106). It is true that an actor could speak in a didactic tone, but Alceste's reply, interestingly, suggests that he has understood Philinte's speech precisely as an explanation of his friend's different reaction to the world's vice and not as a philosophical lesson. For Alceste does not say, 'I'm not going to take your advice'. In fact his reply is unusual for him, as it does not contain any first-person pronouns at all. He is sarcastic about Philinte's argument ('qui raisonne si bien' (167)), before expressing incredulity that Philinte can control his anger. The laughter is directed at Alceste, because he demonstrates his obsession with anger: 'Ce flegme pourra-t-il ne s'échauffer de rien?' (168), 'Verrez-vous tout cela sans vous mettre en courroux?' (172). And he reveals his failure to appreciate Philinte's position, caricaturing it as one of easy indifference rather than stoical control. Alceste's obsession leads him to think that vocalized anger alone is an adequate response to the world's evils. Interestingly, he also reveals further self-obsession in the examples he gives of bad behaviour. They are all clearly the actions of his own legal opponent: betrayal, scheming to do one down financially, spreading rumours.

Alceste's incredulous questions are insensitive to the subtlety of the position that Philinte has explained, and are phrased so as to push Philinte into assuming an extreme position. The first word of his reply 'Oui' might seem to adopt the viewpoint of easy indifference that Alceste wants to impose on him; and a critic like Eustis is quick to find Philinte ridiculous on the grounds that he is too cowardly and flegmatic (p. 188). But the rest of his reply constitutes a more complex response to Alceste:

> Oui, je vois ces défauts dont votre âme murmure
> Comme vices unis à l'humaine nature;
> Et mon esprit enfin n'est pas plus offensé
> De voir un homme fourbe, injuste, intéressé,
> Que de voir des vautours affamés de carnage,
> Des singes malfaisants, et des loups pleins de rage.
>
> (173–8)

First of all, there is a sense of humour and teasing in this reply, which might suggest it is not a full and literal statement of his position. In enumerating human vices, he partly echoes Alceste's own list in line 135. This could be a way of suggesting to Alceste how much in agreement they are; but it could also be gently satirical of his friend. In implying an equation between human vice and the behaviour of beasts (scavenging vultures, mischievous monkeys, rabid wolves), he could be trying to keep Alceste on side, since Alceste's vision of humankind is typically expressed in hyperbolic terms; but Philinte's hyperboles here are so graphic that they might well indicate a degree of amusement at the lengths he has to go to in order to persuade the misanthrope. At all events, Philinte's speech attempts vigorously to assert common ground between them ('Je vois ces défauts') and does not suggest that his response to vice is calm indifference. What he says is that human evil does not offend him more than evil of beasts. This does not mean that he is indifferent to human vice, but that he has set it in a broader perspective than Alceste, a perspective which justifies his attempt to temper any angry response he might have, as he explained at the end of his previous speech.

The comic effect derives from the fact that Philinte's patient, yet vigorous and humorous attempts to engage with Alceste are deflated by his friend's dogged inability to grasp the subtlety of any position which is not his own. So, Alceste's next reply is even more incredulous, and suggests that he has now begun to think that Philinte is attempting to urge him to adopt a new position. Alceste tries to project Philinte's approach onto the experience of his own lawsuit, and is so exasperated at the thought of having to control his anger that he becomes speechless, momentarily:

Je me verrais trahir, mettre en pièces, voler,
Sans que je sois ... Morbleu! je ne veux point parler
Tant ce raisonnement est plein d'impertinence.

(179–81)

Alceste also looks ridiculous alongside Philinte because whereas the latter does try to reason with his friend, Alceste can only posture and exclaim rudely.

Demonstrating simultaneously his wit and his desire to help his friend, Philinte seizes on Alceste's momentary silence to suggest that a more prolonged silence would be a good way forward in dealing with the lawsuit:

Ma foi! vous ferez bien de garder le silence.
Contre votre partie éclatez un peu moins,
Et donnez au procès une part de vos soins.

(182–4)

Mallinson comments oddly on this passage as 'a sudden change of direction [which] reflects on Philinte himself; he answers Alceste's criticism of him by changing the subject [to the specific point of Alceste's lawsuit]' (p. 77). But Philinte does not change the subject. Alceste himself has raised his lawsuit in both of his immediately preceding speeches. Initially Philinte answered him in general terms (173–8). Here he responds precisely to Alceste's evident concern with the lawsuit by giving helpful, if amusingly expressed, advice. Rather than make repeated imprecations against his opponent, which he has done in lines 123–40, 169–72, and 179–80, Alceste would be well advised to pause for thought about the best preparation for the lawsuit. In the stichomythic exchange that follows, which in the face of Alceste's repeated interruptions disintegrates into a more loosely constructed series of rapid exchanges, Philinte suggests simply that his friend should do what was normal practice at the time for all litigants: to press his case with the judges in advance of the hearing. Alceste's obstinate refusal to take practical action looks increasingly foolish. He hardly lets Philinte speak before asserting his preference for losing his case over taking preventive action now:

PHILINTE Mais ...
ALCESTE   J'aurai le plaisir de perdre mon procès.

PHILINTE Mais enfin …

ALCESTE Je verrai, dans cette plaiderie,
Si les hommes auront assez d'effronterie,
Seront assez méchants, scélérats et pervers,
Pour me faire injustice aux yeux de l'univers. (196–200)

In dramaturgical terms, Molière is doing here what he did in the earlier part of the scene when Alceste was insisting on always speaking the truth to people. Molière is making him ride for a fall. When he reports the loss of his lawsuit in 5. 1, it will be without any pleasure whatsoever, but with even more hyperbolic expressions of outrage. Philinte does not press further, but comments on Alceste with the frankness befitting a good friend: 'On se riroit de vous, Alceste, tout de bon, / Si l'on vous entendait parler de la façon' (203–4). There may be a hint of warning here, but Alceste has already shown that he is deaf to warnings about public ridicule. There is certainly a note of affection in the use of Alceste's name. There is also a reassuring suggestion of the complicity appropriate to a close friendship: Alceste's interactions with Philinte are envisaged as a private affair, in which Alceste is protected by his friend. Philinte's comment is, however, yet another signal to the audience that the proper response to Alceste is laughter.

ALCESTE'S LOVE FOR CÉLIMÈNE (1. 1)

Philinte now starts the fourth and final section of the scene, in which Molière needs to unveil the expository information that will initiate the dramatic action: Alceste's love for Célimène, which he intends to further by telling her what he thinks about the welcome she extends to other men in her home. It is also revealed that two other women are interested in Alceste: Arsinoé and Éliante. The sincere Éliante would be an ideal partner for him in Philinte's view; even Alceste agrees that reason should lead him to prefer Éliante, but he is in love with Célimène. Not only does this information pave the way for the sequence of interactions in the following acts, it completes, and complicates, the portrait of Molière's foolish protagonist. And it is Philinte who articulates this complexity for the audience.

In the face of Alceste's refusal to leave the moral high ground, which he insists so vociferously on occupying, Philinte attempts to identify a chink in Alceste's armour which, once revealed to him, will show him that he is not as intolerant of human failing as he claims to be. Why does Philinte make Alceste face up to his contradiction now? In addition to Molière's need to convey expository information, the new development in their encounter could be interpreted as Philinte's way of scoring a point against Alceste. But that would make him mean-spirited and ignore the recurrent evidence throughout the scene of his friendly disposition towards Alceste. Interpreted as friendly, Philinte's move might aim to make Alceste acknowledge his actual scope for flexibility and so revise his approach to his legal opponent and his lawsuit to give him a better chance of success. But this is not how Philinte directs the conversation. It is directed specifically towards the accomplishment of a different friendly aim, that of saving Alceste from a relationship with Célimène, to whom he is catastrophically ill-suited. Philinte does not actually tell Alceste to abandon Célimène. That would be too didactic for a friend so unaccustomed to taking advice. But he points out the discrepancy between Alceste's pretension to absolute moral rectitude and its absence in Célimène: 'Cette pleine droiture où vous vous renfermez, / La trouvez-vous ici dans ce que vous aimez?' (207–8). He tells him that Éliante is attracted to him and that she would be an ideal partner: 'Son cœur, qui vous estime, est solide et sincère, / Et ce choix plus conforme était mieux votre affaire' (245–6). He is frank about Célimène's 'humeur coquette' and 'esprit médisant' (219), and presses Alceste to say what he thinks of her transparent failings: 'Ne sont-ce plus défauts dans un objet si doux? / Ne les voyez-vous pas? ou les excusez-vous?' (223–4). And when Alceste, for once, admits his contradiction, acknowledges her failings, but claims he cannot stop loving her, Philinte presses him even further: 'Vous croyez être donc aimé d'elle?' (236).

It might be tempting to take Alceste seriously at this point. After all, not all Molière's foolish protagonists are prepared to admit to weakness, and Alceste has doggedly refused to do so until this point. But any sympathy for him needs to be tempered by his claim, odd in a lover, that he is the first to condemn Célimène's faults (228). Molière will show Alceste doing this in his encounters with Célimène and extract comedy from the ridicule of his querulous love: 'l'on n'a jamais vu un amour si grondeur', as Célimène puts it (528).

Philinte might have another purpose in this discussion, but one which the audience can only imagine retrospectively. It will emerge that Philinte himself feels affection for Éliante (4. 1) and that the two of them will agree to marry at the end of the play. When we consider these later parts of the play, it will be important to bear in mind this scene in which Philinte tries determinedly to make Alceste see the error of choosing Célimène and persuade him instead to prefer the more suitable Éliante. Given his own interest in Éliante, which he implies in lines 243–4, it may be that Philinte is sounding out Alceste to see whether there would be any hope for a partnership between himself and Éliante. But he is doing more than sound out Alceste. He is positively trying to persuade him of Éliante's desirability as a match and to deter him from pursuing Célimène ('Je crains fort pour vos feux' (249)). And in retrospect, such a gesture can be interpreted as yet another sign of his profound loyalty to Alceste. Cicero warns of the dangers that come in the way of friendships. Rivalry in love is a key one: 's'il arrive que cette amitié dure jusqu'à l'adolescence, il est malaisé [...] qu'elle ne se rompe [...] par la concurrence en la recherche des plaisirs illicites' (p. 121 (x.34)). If friendships survive such rivalries, it is because they are real and lasting, like Philinte's for Alceste.

If, in this part of the scene, Philinte dwells on Alceste's inconsistency, Mallinson finds an undermining inconsistency in Philinte too. When Alceste has admitted Célimène's foibles, he says he hopes he will be able to purge her soul of them (234), and Philinte replies: 'Si vous faites cela, vous ne ferez pas peu' (235). Mallinson comments: '[Philinte] may mock Alceste for believing he can change Célimène and yet he has implicitly sought to change Alceste in this scene' (p. 78). My own understanding of the interaction between the two characters in the first scene is different from this. Alceste is the one who has consistently spluttered his intention to reprimand people for their vices by shouting at them. Philinte is not guilty of a comparably vain hope of correcting Alceste's nature simply because he tries to persuade him to shout less about the world's evils. Throughout the scene Philinte is reacting to Alceste, looking to his best interests as a friend. Molière certainly entertains us with Philinte's displays of good humour, wit, and ready responses. But the comic focus is Alceste, whose spluttering and relentless anger has all the more opportunities to manifest itself in view of Philinte's patient attempts to engage him. We do not need to share Philinte's apparent efforts to cultivate stoic ataraxia in order to laugh with him at Alceste's folly. It seems to me that Molière's depiction of their friendly relationship ensures our adoption of Philinte's view of the foolish protagonist. In Ciceronian terms, Philinte is the ideal friend, all the more admirable for his friendship since its object, Alceste, is such a bad friend.

THE PERILS OF LITERARY CRITICISM (1. 2–3)

Alceste and Philinte are interrupted by the arrival of Oronte, who has come specially to see *them* in the absence of Célimène and her cousin Éliante on a shopping expedition. This long scene, followed by a short coda after Oronte's departure, generates comedy by creating a conflict between the vain Oronte and the misanthropic Alceste. Molière engineers a situation in which the concerns raised by Alceste in the first scene can be put to the test. Most obviously, this means Alceste's stated intention to speak with absolute frankness. When Oronte asks for an honest assessment of his sonnet, Alceste asks uncomfortably to be excused; when pressed, he speaks with casuistical indirectness, until he can no longer maintain this level of discourse and offers a devastatingly negative critique of the poem. The comedy lies first in the gap between Alceste's firm intentions and hesitant practice, and then in the gap between his polite hesitations and the offensive expression of his true views. The scene also plays comically on other concerns Alceste raised in the first scene. Alceste loves the flighty Célimène and thinks he is loved by her. He has come to tell her that he wants her all to himself. Oronte's arrival is comically timely, for everything about it suggests that he too has come to declare his love to Célimène and we are led to suspect that he has written the love sonnet for her. So we see Alceste facing one of the rivals he thought he could easily dispense with. Yet another concern of scene 1 which this encounter revives is Alceste's clashes with the law. When Oronte leaves the stage, furious and offended, at the end of the scene, Philinte warns Alceste 'pour être trop sincère, / Vous voilà sur les bras une fâcheuse affaire' (439–40). Philinte has correctly read Oronte's mood; Alceste will discover in 2. 6 that he is summoned before the Maréchaux to answer for his rude behaviour. The scene with Oronte therefore offers an insight into how Alceste might have come to have on his hands the major legal case that preoccupied him in the first scene. It follows from all this that, in scene 2, Philinte's own lines are few, but the scene as a whole has important implications for the interpretation of his role and his relationship with Alceste.

These implications start with Oronte's opening speech, which is addressed not to Philinte but to Alceste, and in which he asks to be Alceste's friend:

> J'ai monté pour vous dire, et d'un cœur véritable,
> Que j'ai conçu pour vous une estime incroyable,
> Et que, depuis longtemps, cette estime m'a mis
> Dans un ardent désir d'être de vos amis.
> Oui, mon cœur au mérite aime à rendre justice,
> Et je brûle qu'un nœud d'amitié nous unisse:
> Je crois qu'un ami chaud, et de ma qualité,
> N'est pas assurément pour être rejeté.
>
> (253–60)

In performance, Oronte's gushing protestations of friendship to Alceste are particularly comic because, according to an explicit stage direction (261), Alceste is looking deep in thought and not paying any attention to Oronte, who has to stir him into discourse: 'C'est à vous, s'il vous plaît, que ce discours s'adresse' (261). We can only guess what might have been the subject of Alceste's private thoughts (Oronte's rivalry, his social hypocrisy), but this momentary episode, coming at the end of the long scene between Alceste and Philinte, offers an alternative model of friendship to the one we have witnessed so far. Oronte's vocabulary foregrounds the theme of friendship: 'de vos amis', 'un nœud d'amitié', 'un ami chaud'. He has the supermarket approach to friendship: he notices someone whose friend he would like to be and thinks that by announcing this, he can simply acquire a new friend. The deal has to be struck by the would-be-friend, and Oronte invites Alceste to do this:

> Souffrez qu'à cœur ouvert, Monsieur, je vous embrasse,
> Et qu'en votre amitié je vous demande place.

> Touchez là, s'il vous plaît. Vous me la promettez.
> Votre amitié?
>
> (273–6)

But Alceste declines the gesture of friendship: 'l'amitié demande un plus plus de mystère' (278). Molière plays with two models of friendship: the ideal Ciceronian friendship based on frankness, understanding, and patience, on the one hand, and on the other, society friendships designed to oil the wheels of social intercourse. Molière ensures that the audience sees things through Philinte's eyes by presenting him as the model Ciceronian friend, even though he is also able to participate in purely social friendships. Alceste is a figure of ridicule not because of his principled objection to purely social friendships, because of his rude and ill-timed expression of this objection, and because of his failure to acknowledge explicitly the real friendship that Philinte maintains for him. Oronte is comic because his language suggests an excessive investment in such friendships. Throughout this strained exchange between Alceste and Oronte, Philinte remains silent. Molière provides no indication as to how the actor should behave; this should no doubt be determined by the evidence for his behaviour in the rest of the scene, though that evidence is problematic.

Oronte punctures the tension by politely agreeing to give their friendship time to develop. To foster it, he invites Alceste to give his honest opinion of a sonnet. Philinte's interventions, unsolicited, occur early in this sequence, praising Oronte's poem after every few lines: 'Je suis déjà charmé de ce petit morceau' (319), 'Ah! qu'en termes galants ces choses-là sont mises!' (325), 'La chute en est jolie, amoureuse, admirable' (333), 'Je n'ai jamais ouï de vers si bien tournés' (336), and before Oronte's incipient display of modesty, Philinte offers reassurance, 'Non, je ne flatte point' (338).

There are four ways of accounting for these interventions. The first is that Philinte is moved to express genuine admiration for Oronte's poem. This is the least plausible interpretation, since in dramaturgical terms there is no interest for Molière in indicating to the audience what Philinte might really think of the sonnet. The second takes its cue from the outraged asides of disagreement that Alceste utters to Philinte after each of his expressions of praise. It could be that Philinte 'cannot resist provoking Alceste', as Thomas believes.[18] Against this interpretation is the whole of the first scene which shows Philinte attempting to spare Alceste public ridicule. In view of that, it is unlikely that he would deliberately provoke him to express outrage in public, and certainly not in front of one of his rivals for Célimène. Alceste's fury is in fact spoken only to Philinte and not to Oronte, and when he does eventually give his frank opinion of the sonnet, it is the result of pressure from Oronte, not provocation from Philinte. A third explanation, McBride's, is that Philinte speaks words of approval because he is concerned 'with fulfilling the appropriate code of *bienséances* which will help to maintain both the harmony of society and his own *repos*' (p. 153). It is certainly the case that Philinte is prepared to engage in the conventions of sociability: this stance has emerged very clearly from the first scene. But it is unlikely that this is the only reason why Molière would give him these interventions in the sonnet scene. Molière's aim is not primarily to show Philinte behaving in a consistent way; it is to show the interaction between Philinte and the foolish Alceste. It seems to me, then, that the fourth interpretation of his interventions is the most convincing. Philinte intervenes in order to say those things that Oronte wants Alceste to say, because he wants to spare his friend social embarrassment and personal aggravation. He is acting as a protective friend. There is evidence for this interpretation in the coda to this scene immediately after Oronte's departure. Philinte starts to explain: 'J'ai bien vu qu'Oronte, afin d'être flatté ...' (441). Alceste's interruption does not allow him to complete the sentence, but it looks like the beginning of an explanation of how Philinte's polite approach would have saved Alceste the 'fâcheuse affaire' that his rude honesty has brought upon him. Philinte's interventions are intended to help Alceste and the fact that they do not succeed highlights all the more Alceste's incorrigible obsession with rudeness and aggression.

Philinte makes two further interventions in the scene. The first occurs after Alceste has demolished Oronte's sonnet and recited, in preference to it, an old-fashioned love song, followed by the approving critical comment: 'Voilà ce que peut dire un cœur vraiment

---

[18] Merlin Thomas, 'Philinte and Éliante' in *Molière: Stage and Study*, ed. W. D. Howarth and Merlin Thomas (Oxford: Clarendon Press, 1973), pp. 73–92, p. 80.

épris' (413). Philinte does not speak, but laughs, as Alceste's lines, addressed directly to him, make plain:

> Oui, Monsieur le rieur, malgré vos beaux esprits,
> J'estime plus cela que la pompe fleurie
> De tous ces faux brillants, où chacun se récrie.
>
> (414–16)

We know from the first scene that Philinte finds Alceste amusing, but we also know that he wants to prevent him from making a fool of himself in front of others. So why does Philinte laugh at him here in front of Oronte? It could be performed as an involuntary laugh at Alceste's outmoded poetic preferences, and it might be unnoticed by Oronte but for Alceste's foolishly drawing attention to it. Alternatively, it could be a laugh intended to be noticed by Oronte, a laugh of complicity at Alceste in the hope of reducing the growing tension between the fop and the misanthrope.

Certainly his final intervention in the scene is aimed explicitly at reducing tension. Indeed the implication is that the stichomythic exchange between Alceste and Oronte is becoming so heated that only Philinte's intervention prevents them from coming to blows. That is what is suggested by the stage direction '*se mettant entre-deux*' (435) and by his firm appeal addressed to both men equally: 'Eh! Messieurs, c'en est trop; laissez cela, de grâce' (435). This signals Oronte's departure on a note of bitterly sarcastic politeness, which is what prompts Philinte's expressions of anxiety in 1. 3. But Alceste, bad friend that he is, will not listen, keeps interrupting, determines to retreat from society ('Plus de société' (442)), and wants to leave alone ('ne suivez point mes pas' (445)). Philinte, good friend that he is, insists on accompanying him ('Vous vous moquez de moi, je ne vous quitte pas' (446)). And so the act ends as it began, with Alceste furiously trying to avoid the company of his sociable, and assiduously attentive friend.

PORTRAITS (2. 4–6)

Act 2 begins with Alceste's attempt to talk with comic firmness to Célimène, but he is interrupted by the arrival of her society friends.

Philinte is among them, and is present with them until the end of the act. He says very little, but what he does say, especially in the so-called *scène des portraits* (2. 4), has been interpreted as undermining his friend Alceste and therefore as undermining himself in the eyes of the audience. When assessing his words, it is important to bear in mind the highly complex dramatic context in which he is speaking. These are crowd scenes, and Philinte has to draw on all his resources of diplomacy to satisfy his very different audiences: Célimène, whose salon it is; Éliante, the sincere woman with whom it will emerge he is in love; Célimène's society friends, the two marquis Acaste and Clitandre, who are also Alceste's rivals for her affections; Alceste himself, whose bad behaviour inevitably manifests itself and which Philinte has somehow to manage in a friendly way; and, in the last scene of the act, the official who has come to summon a recalcitrant Alceste to the Maréchaux at the instigation of the wounded Oronte. If Philinte's speeches do not always seem transparent, this is an effect of Molière's skill as he shows him juggling different balls.

The first scripted indication of Philinte's involvement in the *scène des portraits* comes early on, but after Clitandre and Acaste have already established the pattern of naming individuals (the socially maladjusted Cléonte and the longwinded bore Damon) whose satirical portraits Célimène completes. Philinte does not speak at this point, but he is the exclusive audience for an aside spoken by Éliante: 'Ce début n'est pas mal; et contre le prochain / La conversation prend un assez bon train' (583–84). As Thomas says, this remark sets up 'a kind of collusion between them' (p. 82). Its importance for the interpretation of their contributions to the rest of the scene is vital, since, with its general irony, it establishes a distance between them and the *médisants*. The implication is that Éliante and Philinte agree that there is unkindness in speaking satirically, behind their backs, about close acquaintances. But it is also implied that the pair of them are used to hearing such conversations and accept them as part of salon life.

They are both silent as the portraits accumulate: Timante, who makes mountains out of molehills, the name-dropping Géralde, the yawningly tedious Bélise, Adraste, who is puffed up with pride. Throughout all these portraits, Molière's text offers no indication as to the behaviour of Alceste, Éliante or Philinte, though in the light of Éliante's earlier aside, there should probably be complicitous glances between her and Philinte. When Clitandre asks Célimène for her view of Cléon, Éliante joins in. What is interesting is that Célimène, breaking her satirical habit, sums up Cléon in a couplet that is entirely positive: he's a good host with a superb chef. It is at this point that Éliante speaks just one line to add that the food served is very delicious: 'Il prend soin d'y servir des mets fort délicats' (627). Éliante shows her willingness to participate in the social exchange of portraits, but only when they are not satirical, not spoken 'contre le prochain'. Éliante was, however, misled by Célimène's apparent change of tone, since it immediately turns out that Célimène was saying something nice about Cléon only to make her satire of him more compelling, by contrast. She takes up Éliante's word 'servir' and condemns him:

> Oui; mais je voudrais bien qu'il ne s'y servît pas:
> C'est un fort méchant plat que sa sotte personne,
> Et qui gâte, à mon goût, tous les repas qu'il donne.
>
> (628–30)

The audience will certainly feel that Cléon has been crushed, but will probably also feel that Éliante has been crushed for her naïvety in thinking that it was appropriate to paint a positive portrait.

It is at this very moment of Éliante's vulnerability that Philinte speaks his first lines in the scene. He takes the initiative, that has so far resided with Acaste and Clitandre, of introducing a new portrait and asking Célimène's view of Damis. Critics who argue that Molière undermines Philinte's authority in the play as well as Alceste's suggest that Philinte's motives in introducing the portrait of Damis could be 'very provocative' vis-à-vis Alceste (e.g. Mallinson, p. 93). Thomas says that the intervention implies a 'mischievous streak' in Philinte (p. 83). The reason for such an interpretation is that Célimène's portrait of Damis has allegedly close parallels with Alceste so that it functions simultaneously as a covert satire of him. In the light of this, Thomas says, 'it is hard to believe that Philinte's choice [of Damis] is accidental' (p. 83). It is true that there are obvious links between Damis and Alceste: he finds fault with what people write, he cannot bring himself to offer praise, and he thinks himself superior to everybody else. The audience may well recognize these links and the actor playing Alceste may well behave in ways that suggest self-recognition (though Molière gives no indications on this score). Certainly after two exclamations of praise for Célimène's talents as a portraitist, Alceste finally intervenes to condemn her, and his timing and tone may well be interpreted as a sign of his discomfort on seeing something of himself in Damis. But such recognitions are a game that Molière may be playing with the audience.

The dramatic logic of the scene militates against interpreting Philinte's choice of Damis as a mischievous way of making fun of Alceste. It is even hard to believe that Célimène can be aware of the points of contact that Alceste might recognize between himself and Damis. Her portrait, for instance, dwells on Damis' criticisms of contemporary writers, but she has no knowledge of Alceste's clash with Oronte over his sonnet. Moreover, the essence of Damis' portrait is quite different from Alceste. Damis' weakness is above all to think himself so great a wit that he becomes intolerable to others:

> et dans tous ses propos,
> On voit qu'il se travaille à dire de bons mots.
> Depuis que dans sa tête il s'est mis d'être habile,
> Rien ne touche son goût, tant il est difficile.
>
> (635–8)

Quite unlike Alceste, Damis wants to shine in society. So when he finds fault with what people write, it is because this, in his view, will enhance people's perceptions of his intelligence. And when he looks on people with condescension, he does so 'en pitié' (648), whereas Alceste does so with thunderous disapproval. If there are similarities between Célimène's portrait of Damis and Alceste, there are sufficient basic differences of character between Damis and Alceste to suggest that we should not think that Philinte has suggested this portrait to her in order to see Alceste under fire.

There are other compelling reasons for not interpreting Philinte's intervention as mischievous. First, his friendship for Alceste has led him to want to protect him from public ridicule. It would be quite at odds with his advice to Alceste in the opening scene if Philinte were now to be the agent who knowingly exposed him to such ridicule. And secondly, Philinte's intervention comes after Molière has built a complicitous relationship between him and Éliante based on a feeling that satirical portraits are unkind and after Éliante has tried to paint a positive portrait of Cléon and been crushed by Célimène for doing so. In its dramatic context, therefore, Philinte's intervention seems most likely to represent 'a desire to assist Éliante', as Mallinson puts it (p. 92), or at least to express solidarity with her feeling that portraits can also be positive ones. For the wording used by Philinte when he introduces Damis invites Célimène to comment on his positive qualities: 'On fait assez de cas de son oncle Damis' (631). Célimène appears to respond appropriately: 'Il est de mes amis' (632). And Philinte capitalizes on this shift towards positive portraiture, by insisting on Damis' qualities: 'Je le trouve honnête homme, et d'un air assez sage' (633). Célimène agrees, but, as with Cléon, goes on to deliver her damning assessment. It might be objected that Philinte's words about Damis, if positive, do in fact impel Célimène to criticize him, since they leave her room for manoeuvre ('assez de cas', 'assez sage'). But a nuanced portrait would, for him and Éliante, represent a step forward from the relentlessly negative portraits that have so far dominated, and a purely laudatory portrait would definitely have offended against the rules of the genre currently being practised and would also have offended Alceste, who, we know, sees all praise as hypocritical. Philinte's introduction of Damis is therefore probably best interpreted as well-timed and well-intentioned, and Célimène's refusal to play the new game that Philinte tries to establish can be seen as Molière's satirical jibe at her for her unshakeably relentless pursuit of salon pastimes.

Philinte makes two further interventions in this scene, each brief, each responding immediately to a contribution from Alceste. Having been completely silent until the two marquis praise Célimène's portrait of Damis, Alceste finally makes an outburst. In order to interpret Philinte's contribution, we need to be clear about the nature of Alceste's outburst. It is comic, not only for its display of anger, but for its choice of addressee. Alceste expresses outrage at the unsparing criticism of the portraits, but he addresses his words specifically to 'mes bons amis de cour', Acaste and Clitandre, not to Célimène. What he says he most particularly objects to is the hypocrisy they will demonstrate when they next greet effusively the individuals who have been attacked. In response, Clitandre is immediately defensive, suggesting that he should address his criticism to the portraitist herself. But Alceste insists that it is the two marquis who are at fault, because their praise for, and laughter at, Célimène's portraits serve to encourage her.

It is at this point that Philinte intervenes to ask why Alceste the misanthrope is so concerned about the victims of Célimène's satire: 'Mais pourquoi pour ces gens un intérêt si grand, / Vous qui condamneriez ce qu'en eux on reprend?' (667–8). With this question, according to Guicharnaud, 'Philinte prend le parti du groupe' (p. 412). McBride agrees, and elaborates: Philinte 'aligns himself automatically with the group against his friend [...]. By refusing implicitly to differentiate between Alceste's censoriousness and that of the group, Philinte performs the invaluable function of exploding the self-created myth of Alceste's superiority' (p. 155). Mallinson also agrees, but questions Philinte's motivation so as to make him too the victim of Molière's comedy: 'Philinte's observation serves to puncture [Alceste's] claims to moral superiority, yet it is another strange, dimly motivated statement. It suggests that Philinte may not have fully understood the specific nature of Alceste's objections, but it also reveals contradictions within his own character. Philinte had earlier criticized Célimène's 'esprit médisant' (219), but in her presence he takes a different line. He is as vulnerable to comic scrutiny as Alceste' (p. 94). To find Philinte comic for not criticizing Célimène here seems to me to disregard the specific contexts in which he speaks now and spoke earlier of her 'esprit médisant'. He did not take up position against Célimène's 'esprit médisant' earlier, but rather questioned Alceste about his attitude to it, with the aim of suggesting that she was an inappropriate partner for him. And in his current question to Alceste, he is not in any sense taking a line on Célimène's slanderous cast of mind. His contributions earlier in the scene would rather imply that he would like to temper her unsparing criticisms of people.

So why does he engage with Alceste here? Does he fail to understand what Alceste has said? Is he siding with the group against his friend? Philinte's predominant silence in the scene might suggest a reluctance to engage in the kind of satirical portrait that is being cultivated. His earlier intervention appears to be made as a gesture of support for Éliante and attempts to make the portrait-painting less negative. If he intervenes now, dramatic logic might suggest it is to help his friend

Alceste. But it is harder to help Alceste, because he has spectacularly broken the contract of polite conversation that the other characters, in their different ways, had all skilfully maintained. Alceste has set himself up in virulent opposition to two of Célimène's other guests. The audience (and Philinte) might anticipate a pattern of rapidly mounting conflict such as occurred between Alceste and Oronte in 1. 2. To believe simply that Philinte sides with the group against Alceste ignores the substantial evidence of his friendship with, and concern for, Alceste. On the other hand, it would be unreasonable to expect him simply to defend Alceste, not least because that would fan the flames of hostility. Philinte's instinct, as in the first scene when he was himself under attack from Alceste, is to restore conversational interaction. Philinte's question can be interpreted as a highly skilful way of attempting to do this. Alceste has attacked the two marquis for their encouragement of Célimène's satirical portraits. Whereas Mallinson thinks Philinte might not have understood Alceste, his question seems to me cleverly to divert attention away from the inflammatory situation involving the characters on stage and towards the objects of Célimène's satires. It is true that this is a diversion from Alceste's main point, but it is one which might moderate Alceste's immediate hostility. It looks as if Philinte is pointing to an inconsistency in Alceste's attitude—Alceste wants to condemn people's faults, but objects to Célimène's condemnatory portraits—but his question actually serves to take the heat out of the conflict between Alceste and the marquis; it maintains a social bond with Célimène and her guests by questioning Alceste's outburst against them; and, crucially, it points to common ground between them and Alceste. Molière shows Philinte attempting to walk on a tightrope. We might well be amused by the extremely awkward situations Molière creates for him, but we are likely to be impressed by the dexterity with which he deals with them.

Philinte's question is momentarily successful in defusing the tension between Alceste and the marquis, because it inspires Célimène to propose an answer, which is a portrait of Alceste as an 'esprit contrariant' (672). The result is laughter at Alceste from unspecified characters on stage and an assertion of martyr-like defiance from Alceste himself: 'Les rieurs sont pour vous, Madame, c'est tout dire / Et vous pouvez pousser contre moi la satire' (681–2). With Alceste in a newly vulnerable position as the object of Célimène's satire, Philinte intervenes again to address Alceste:

> Mais il est véritable aussi que votre esprit
> Se gendarme toujours contre tout ce qu'on dit,
> Et que, par un chagrin que lui-même il avoue,
> Il ne saurait souffrir qu'on blâme, ni qu'on loue.
>
> (683–6)

It looks very much as if Philinte has abandoned his friend to the ridicule inflicted on him by the society satirist, whose portrait he himself confirms. Certainly Mallinson says that Philinte is 'on the offensive' and calls this speech 'a provocative attack' (p. 94). But we need again to bear in mind Philinte's various audiences in making sense of this speech. He does not want to offend the hostess of the salon, so he appears to agree with her assessment of Alceste. On the other hand, in the light of his and Éliante's behaviour earlier in the scene, it is unlikely that he would want her to see him participate in a satirical attack on his friend. If we look closely at the speech, Philinte's words agree with Célimène in the first couplet before diverting attention to Alceste's specific inconsistency of objecting both to criticism and to praise of individuals, an inconsistency the accuracy of which is immediately confirmed by Alceste himself in a spluttering outburst insisting that he is right to object to 'Loueurs impertinents, ou censeurs téméraires' (690). It is true that Philinte's ideal of friendship would deter him from criticizing his friend in public. But he is not saying anything here which he has not already said to Alceste in private. And a possible reading of this speech is that yet again Philinte is making it in order to prevent a more dangerous topic being raised, which would be sure to make matters even worse for the whole group and for Alceste in particular. That topic is the real reason why Alceste makes his outburst against the two marquis. Mesnard is right to point out that Célimène is only partially right when she explains his intervention as being due to his spirit of contradiction.[19] The real reason that he makes his attack on the marquis (and not on Célimène) is that he is stung to jealousy by the

---

[19] Jean Mesnard, '*Le Misanthrope*: mise en question de l'art de plaire', *Revue d'histoire littéraire de la France*, 72 (1972), 863–89, p. 876.

sociable exchange of portraits that reveal happy relations between Célimène and his rivals. Alceste imputes moral motives to an attack that is inspired by jealous rage. It could be that Philinte has understood this and judges it safer to attack Alceste on more familiar ground in order to divert attention away from the more inflammatory conflict of amorous rivals in the very presence of the object of their desire.

The pattern established in the scene with Oronte was that Alceste was only too ready to let hostilities intensify. This is what happens again. Alceste himself brings up the question of the appropriate treatment of Célimène and disagrees with the polite flatteries of the marquis. As the four individuals caught up in this web of sexual jealousy all have their say, and the situation looks set to grow worse, Éliante makes her longest speech in the play (711–30), arguing elegantly that a lover will interpret as virtues what strike others as vices in the loved one. From the point of view of a modern director of the play, Thomas sees Éliante's speech as a problem: 'An awkward moment: the speech stops the action dead [...]. Poor Éliante! Why does she do it?' (p. 84). Like Philinte, she has different audiences in mind. It is a thematically relevant contribution to the argument about the perceived faults of the loved one. It is, in one sense, an argument against Alceste's assertion that the loved one's faults should not be indulged. But in view of Éliante's own amorous feelings for Alceste, her speech is also perhaps a covert communication to him that she finds attractive the faults that others have found in him. It is above all the making of the speech, rather than its content, that shows her concern for Alceste. It is precisely the fact that she makes such a controlled, authoritative and elegant speech, stopping the action dead, that reveals her desire to save Alceste from the increasingly hostile conflict into which he has thrown himself.

Of course, Alceste is a fool, and after the lifeline which Éliante has offered him, Molière makes him look even more foolish by giving him the following, absurdly assertive rejoinder: 'Et moi, je soutiens, moi...' (731). Célimène may be a comic character, but she is not a fool. She interrupts him, following Éliante's lead, and terminates the conversation: 'Brisons là ce discours, / Et dans la galerie allons faire deux tours' (731–2). The foolish Alceste, however, tries to initiate a new conflict with his rivals, asserting that he will not leave Célimène's house until they have done so. With supreme comic timing, Molière engineers the arrival of Célimène's servant, followed by an official, who insists that Alceste leave immediately with him to appear before the Maréchaux. Alceste has to lose face immediately in front of the two marquis, and the last scene of the act is predominantly, though in the presence of the assembled group, an interaction between Alceste, reluctant to leave, determined not to make any concession whatsoever to Oronte over his sonnet, and Philinte, his ever faithful friend, explaining calmly to the others, on his behalf, what has happened, and coaxing Alceste, urgently, but politely, to do what is required, lest he bring further aggravation upon himself: 'allons, disposez-vous ...' (759), 'Allons, venez' (767), 'Allons vous faire voir' (768). At the same time, he offers Alceste advice about how, in his own best interests, he should deal with the Maréchaux: 'd'un plus doux esprit' (764), 'Vous devez faire voir des sentiments traitables' (766). Such advice will intensify the comedy of Alceste's eventual, and predictably conflictual, meeting with the Maréchaux, as recounted by Philinte, when he next appears on stage in act 4. His unambiguous concern for Alceste in this closing scene of act 2 provides circumstantial evidence that his comments in the *scène des portraits* were most likely calculated to help, rather than to injure, his friend.

PHILINTE AND ÉLIANTE (4. 1)

When act 4 opens, Philinte is talking to Éliante. It is perhaps significant that he appears to have come to Célimène's house without Alceste and that he has probably arranged this private interview with Éliante. Alceste had returned to see Célimène at the end of the previous act, but had been waylaid by his admirer, Arsinoé, who has taken him to her own house to see a letter, which allegedly will prove Célimène's infidelity to him—a spiteful move on her part. The audience needs to remember Célimène's supposed infidelity during Philinte's scene with Éliante, since this adds a note of dramatic irony to their conversation.

Guicharnaud thinks the scene uninteresting. His only dramaturgical comment on it is that it provides a moment of respite for the audience: 'le spectateur est invité à se détendre un instant entre la

menace de l'acte précédent et l'entrée tumultueuse d'Alceste' (p. 439).
He explains the respite with reference to the characters of Philinte and
Éliante who, he clearly thinks, are colourless: 'Ils offrent l'image d'un
monde sans chaleur, sans passion' (p. 439). Others have seen more of
interest in this scene. Thomas calls it 'a scene of great subtlety' (p. 85).
Its dramatic interest lies in the fact that more is going on between the
two characters than appears on the surface; and its dramatic challenge
to the audience is to work out just how much more is going on.

The scene itself is a challenge to Molière, since he needs primarily to
show his audience that he is advancing the plot, while also, secondar-
ily and covertly, making preparations for his unusual denouement.
The plot is advanced in this scene by Philinte's account of Alceste's
appearance before the Maréchaux (so that thread in the action is tied)
and by the depiction of a growing complicity between Éliante and
Philinte. The denouement is prepared by the suggestion of an eventual liaison between Philinte and Éliante. Generic convention, nearly
always observed, requires comedies that focus on love interests to end
in marriage. The dominant focus of the action is on Alceste's pursuit
of Célimène and his conflicts with his rivals. But it is unthinkable that
Molière would end his play with the marriage of his foolish protagonist to a flirtatious coquette. Marriages at the end of comedies create
an illusion of order and happiness amidst the confusions, frustrations
and follies that otherwise inhabit the comic world. Alceste's marriage
could not fulfil this purpose. So Molière satisfies the generic require-
ment of a conventional marriage at the end of his dramaturgically
unconventional play by marrying Éliante to Philinte.

The seeds of their relationship have been sown throughout the
play. In the very first scene, when Philinte encourages Alceste to
think of Éliante rather than Célimène, he frankly admits his own
admiration for her: 'Pour moi, si je n'avais qu'à former des désirs,
/ La cousine Éliante aurait tous mes soupirs' (243–4). Act 2 shows
a collusion between them, and shows Philinte taking Éliante into
account as well as Alceste and Célimène's society friends, when he
formulates his interventions. The first scene of act 4 is the one in
which a possible liaison between them will come to the fore. But such
a thing is highly problematic in dramatic terms. How can two polite
and sensitive characters, whose limited interaction so far has been
based on a concern for the welfare of their friend Alceste, suddenly

turn to discussion of a possible love between the two of them? How can Éliante, whose serious affection for Alceste is known to him and others, appear to contemplate the prospect of marriage to another man without loss of audience sympathy? And, most problematically, how can Philinte, Alceste's so dependable friend, raise the question of marriage to a woman whom he knows to feel affection for Alceste and whom he himself has urged Alceste to consider marrying, without appearing underhand and treacherous?

Molière does not ignore these problems. He uses them to inform the writing of this scene, and to create subtle undercurrents that keep the audience guessing as to the true feelings that lie beneath the surface of the characters' words. When the scene starts, Philinte is in the middle of his account to Éliante of Alceste's appearance before the Maréchaux. It is a comic narrative dwelling on Alceste's intransigence and liberally exploiting direct speech in which the actor playing Philinte might satirically imitate the elocutionary excesses of Alceste. The comic climax is the casuistical resolution of the affair: Alceste will not concede that Oronte's sonnet was good, but Oronte will be happy with Alceste's statement that he very much wishes he had found the sonnet better. Philinte is clearly telling the story to entertain Éliante, and Molière is making him tell it to entertain the audience. As Mallinson says, however, over and above the telling of a story, 'something is happening between speaker and addressee' (p. 109).[20] But what? In view of the way the conversation develops, we can legitimately assume that Philinte is intending to sound out Éliante on her commitment to Alceste and to assess any chances he might have with her himself. This does not necessarily mean, however, that his story is calculated in advance to make Alceste look ridiculous in order to assert his own authority, as Mallinson thinks (p. 109). Such a reading would undermine his status as Alceste's friend, and is not entirely consonant with the full dramatic context of the speech. To judge by the frankness of their conversation in 1. 1, Philinte is not saying anything here about Alceste that he would not say to his face. His account of Alceste's behaviour certainly makes

---

[20] Quentin M. Hope expresses the same point differently ('Philinte is no anonymous messenger') in 'Philinte's *Récit* in *Le Misanthrope*', *Papers on French Seventeenth Century Literature*, 12 (1985), 511–24, p. 515.

him look ridiculous, but less so than Alceste's own behaviour in front of Philinte and Éliante during the *scène des portraits*. Moreover, in giving this account, Philinte is aware that Éliante appreciates Alceste's apparent failings, such being the strong implication of her long and decisive speech made towards the end of the portrait scene. In telling Éliante about Alceste's legal imbroglio, Philinte is benefiting from their known complicitous concern for their friend in order to enjoy a private interview with Éliante; he is probably not trying to do an injustice to Alceste.

Éliante replies specifically to the portrait of Alceste that Philinte has painted and, as Philinte might have been hoping, gives her considered view of their friend. Her view is interesting for audiences, and critics, in the light of the assessment of Alceste given in Donneau de Visé's *Lettre écrite sur la comédie du misanthrope*. She finds Alceste's desire for sincerity noble and heroic, a rare but admirable quality. But his behaviour is absurd: 'Dans ses façons d'agir, il est fort singulier' (1163). The friendship of Philinte and the admiration of Éliante save Alceste from being the fool of farce (in love with a woman who is simultaneously juggling other lovers) and invite the audience to consider the positive implications of Alceste's outlook, but the immediate impact of Alceste in performance is laughter, because what the audience sees and hears most insistently is his 'façons d'agir'. On the surface, the conversation develops as an expression of concern for Alceste's welfare. Philinte is anxious that Célimène might be an inappropriate object of his affections, though Éliante is more prepared to allow for the attraction of opposites. Philinte doubts that Célimène loves Alceste, and Éliante agrees that even Célimène probably does not know what her true feelings are. These doubts lead Philinte to think that there is trouble in store for Alceste, and to admit to Éliante that, in his view, Alceste would be better suited with her. On the surface, this discussion looks as if the characters are talking about Alceste, and certainly there is no reason to doubt their concern for him. Philinte refers to him as 'notre ami' and in positively promoting the idea of Célimène's unsuitability and Éliante's advantages, Philinte cannot be said to be treacherously looking to his own interests. And yet, it is Philinte who chooses to bring up the topic of Alceste's relationship with Célimène, which does not follow on automatically from his account of Alceste's visit to the Maréchaux. In doing so, Philinte

clearly wants to discuss relationships. And in admitting that he thinks
Éliante a better match for Alceste, he uses a phrase which, in its very
ambiguity, prepares the way for the revelation of his own feelings: 'Et
s'il avait mon cœur, à dire vérité, / Il tournerait ses vœux tout d'un
autre côté' (1187–8). 'S'il avait mon cœur' could be a throw-away
phrase, but in the context is probably not. It makes Éliante's response
to his suggestion a particularly delicate one. Should she respond simply
to his suggestion about a match between her and Alceste? or should she
also acknowledge the possible implications of 's'il avait mon cœur'?

The delicacy with which Éliante is called upon to speak might
account for Mallinson's comment on it, namely that her 'response
is quite impenetrable' (p. 111). Yet her speech *can* be understood,
because Philinte has understood it when he makes his reply. The
impression of confusion, uncertainty, hesitation that her words create
is caused, linguistically, by her recourse to *précieux* abstractions and
awkward syntax and, dramatically, by the complex intimacy of the
subject she has been required to address:

> Pour moi, je n'en fais point de façons, et je crois
> Qu'on doit, sur de tels points, être de bonne foi:
> Je ne m'oppose point à toute sa tendresse;
> Au contraire, mon cœur pour elle s'intéresse;
> Et si c'était qu'à moi la chose pût tenir,
> Moi-même à ce qu'il aime on me verrait l'unir.
> Mais si dans un tel choix, comme tout se peut faire,
> Son amour éprouvait quelque destin contraire,
> S'il fallait que d'un autre on couronnât les feux,
> Je pourrais me résoudre à recevoir ses vœux;
> Et le refus souffert, en pareille occurrence,
> Ne m'y ferait trouver aucune répugnance.
>
> (1191–202)

Molière probably wants the audience to be sympathetically amused
by his depiction of the extraordinary tentativeness with which these
characters broach the topic of love. He is likely to invite our amusement at the contradiction between the direct frankness with which
Éliante says she will speak in her first two lines and the clumsiness with
which she goes on to express herself. Deciphered, her lines state that
she is sympathetic to Alceste's love for Célimène and would like to see
them married (is this the self-sacrifice of his fond admirer? or her way

of hinting to Philinte that she is not so keen on Alceste as to want him not to marry Célimène?); but if Célimène were to choose a different marriage partner, Éliante would be willing to marry the rejected Alceste (which seems once again to make her look self-sacrificing, and diminishes any hope that Philinte might have been entertaining for himself). Her speech is not only amusing for the awkwardness of its expression. Molière has prepared a dramatic irony. The audience will remember that Alceste is currently being shown alleged proof of Célimène's infidelity. Unbeknown to Éliante and Philinte, the prospect of Alceste's recourse to her is very imminent.

Éliante's reply has only addressed Philinte's explicit question about her feelings for Alceste. So in his reply to her, Philinte brings his own feelings explicitly, though still hesitantly, into play. We should note that Philinte is unambiguous in his support for an eventual marriage between Éliante and Alceste:

> Et moi, de mon côté, je ne m'oppose pas,
> Madame, à ces bontés qu'ont pour lui vos appas;
> Et lui-même, s'il veut, il peut bien vous instruire
> De ce que là-dessus j'ai pris soin de lui dire.
>
> (1203–6)

This statement is crucial in securing Philinte's reputation as a non-predatory friend of Alceste. He refers accurately to their discussion in the opening scene of the play when he urged Alceste to think of Éliante (243–6), and he does so by way of offering evidence to Éliante of his good intentions towards the two of them. He does, however, take the opportunity to deal with the other possibility that her own speech raised, a marriage between Alceste and Célimène, which would leave Éliante free. For the first time, he explicitly, but with a linguistic awkwardness and hesitancy comparable to Éliante's own, says that, in such an event, he himself would hope to receive her favour:

> Mais si, par un hymen qui les joindrait eux deux,
> Vous étiez hors d'état de recevoir ses vœux,
> Tous les miens tenteraient la faveur éclatante
> Qu'avec tant de bonté votre âme lui présente:
> Heureux si, quand son cœur s'y pourra dérober,
> Elle pouvait sur moi, Madame, retomber.
>
> (1207–12)

Molière maintains the subtlety of their interaction with Éliante's brief reply: 'Vous vous divertissez, Philinte' (1213). Her words say neither yes nor no. They comment instead on the tone and language in which he has expressed himself. The precise tone in which the actress speaks the words will determine the extent to which her words are reserving her position. They must do so to some extent, since Philinte feels the need to reply by making his intentions even more explicit:

> Non, Madame,
> Et je vous parle ici du meilleur de mon âme,
> J'attends l'occasion de m'offrir hautement,
> Et de tous mes souhaits j'en presse le moment.
>
> (1213–16)

But the fact that he is so explicit suggests that Éliante's tone must convey distinct interest in his declaration.

The delicacy of this scene, on which its comic effect depends, leads to no clear conclusion. Mallinson thinks it has shown both Philinte and Éliante move 'from a selfless attitude to a more openly declared personal one' (p. 111). But this is to overstate matters. Philinte's interest in Éliante is certainly explicit by the end of the scene. But Éliante's stated position is that if Célimène does not marry Alceste, she herself would be willing to do so. She has given no clear verbal indication of her response to Philinte's expression of interest in her. We should also be clear that Philinte's interest is conditional on Alceste marrying Célimène. If Philinte's own interests come to the surface here, there is no suggestion that he would press them at the expense of those of Alceste or those of Éliante.

ALCESTE AND ÉLIANTE (4. 2)

Molière is skilful at handling those pivotal points in dramatic performance when the configuration of characters changes with an arrival or a departure. Alceste's irruption on stage at this point is a triumph of comic effect. It is comic because Philinte could not have been interrupted at a more compromising moment, just as he is expressing his own interest in the woman he has been urging Alceste himself to marry. It is comic too because of the contrast between the linguistic tentativeness dominating 4. 1 and the blunt and exaggerated expression of outrage with which Alceste initiates 4. 2: 'Ah! faites-moi raison, Madame, d'une offense / Qui vient de triompher de toute ma constance' (1217–18). Alceste's fury will strike us as all the more impatient and violent if we understand these lines to be addressed to Célimène. He might either assume she is present when he bursts into the room or mistake Éliante for her. His interruption is comic for a third reason. The audience understands from his lines (though Éliante and Philinte, ignorant of the accusation against Célimène, have to wait for a few more lines of explanation) that Alceste thinks he has proof of Célimène's infidelity. The implication is clear: Philinte's so newly expressed hopes for Éliante appear to be dashed and Éliante will now make herself available to Alceste.

Now, Molière cannot end his play with the marriage of his comic fool, but he does need to end it with the prospect of a happy marriage. This means that the position reached at the end of the previous scene (Philinte and Éliante will only marry if Alceste marries Célimène) cannot prevail. Molière has to make something happen that will bring about the wedding of Philinte and Éliante even though Alceste does not marry Célimène. Hence the importance of 4. 2. Apparently betrayed by Célimène, Alceste, for once, listens to the advice of his friend and turns to Éliante (another dramatic irony that operates at Philinte's expense). Crucially, however, his 'façon d'agir' ensures that Éliante, while not refusing him outright, declines his offer amicably by suggesting that he will soon cast aside Célimène's apparent infidelity and be reconciled with her. What makes Éliante reject him? It could be the interest that Philinte has shown in her that can be interpreted as making her prefer him to Alceste. It could be her insight into the relationship of Alceste and Célimène that makes her think Alceste's offer is meaningless bluster: when she assures him that 'Une coupable aimée est bientôt innocente' (1267), this turns out to be an accurate prediction of his attitude to Célimène later in the following scene. Both these probabilities may play a part in Éliante's rejection of Alceste, but the most immediate explanation for it lies in the extraordinarily offensive terms in which he makes it. When he turns to Éliante as a substitute for Célimène, his concern is not love. He envisages her only as an instrument of vengeance:

> Vengez-moi d'une ingrate et perfide parente,
> Qui trahit lâchement une ardeur si constante;
> Vengez-moi de ce trait qui doit vous faire horreur.
>
> (1249–51)

As a proposal of marriage, this could hardly be more at variance with Philinte's. When at the end of the scene, Alceste says he will return to renew his offer after he has dealt with Célimène, it is already too late for him. Molière has prepared the ground for the marriage of Éliante to Philinte at the end of act 5.

Act 4 scene 2 is primarily an interaction between Éliante and Alceste, but Philinte's two brief interventions are important. Significantly, they occur before Alceste asks Éliante to be his wife. After this point, Philinte is silent, a silence which should probably be interpreted as a judicious decision not to interfere on a matter that is properly Éliante's to determine. It is also a silence, of course, that serves Philinte's own interests. If the major source of comic effect in the scene is Alceste's uncontrollable anger and gross conduct, Molière might cause amusement by showing us that behaving in a modest and unassuming way can in fact serve one's own interests. This applies both to Philinte's silence in the last part of the scene, and his two interventions in the middle. Alceste is so outraged at Célimène's alleged infidelity with Oronte that he is variously speechless, spluttering and aggressive. We have seen Philinte repeatedly attempt to moderate Alceste's anger in earlier scenes of the play by suggesting that things might not be as bad as they seem. This is exactly what he does now. Before Alceste's direct accusation of Célimène, Philinte, like Éliante, tries to make him pause and question its reliability: 'Peut-être est-ce un soupçon conçu légèrement, / Et votre esprit jaloux prend parfois des chimères…' (1232–3). And when Alceste says he has incontrovertible evidence in the letter that Arsinoé has given him, Philinte tries again to make him pause and consider: 'Une lettre peut bien tromper par l'apparence, / Et n'est pas quelquefois si coupable qu'on pense' (1241–2). These words are those of a friend, who knows what an inflammably jealous lover of Célimène Alceste is, and they are spoken to help him. Of course, attempting to repair the relationship between Alceste and Célimène is very much in Philinte's own interests given that, at this point, their marriage is the condition on which his own hopes for Éliante might be pursued. The coincidence of Philinte's personal interests and his obligations to Alceste as a friend might make us smile; but it should not lead us to question his status as Alceste's friend.

CRISIS COUNSELS (5. 1)

When act 5 opens with Alceste and Philinte in mid-discussion, the misanthrope has been plunged into a new crisis. He may well have restored relations with Célimène, but he has just learnt that he has lost his lawsuit and is 20,000 francs the poorer. The focus of the discussion is the resolution Alceste has reached and from which no amount of persuasion will make him budge: he is going to withdraw from society and he has come only to deliver to Célimène the ultimatum that she must withdraw with him or stay behind without him. The comedy of the scene lies in the characteristic hyperboles of Alceste as he fulminates against a world which can see him lose his lawsuit when he claims to have justice on his side and as he reveals that his victorious enemy, with the help of Oronte, is spreading the rumour that Alceste is the author of a newly published book of dubious repute ('un livre abominable' (1501)). It lies also in his obstinate refusal to be moved by, or even to listen to, his friend's calming words. For some critics, Philinte's contributions too are subject to comic scrutiny. Peacock laughs off Philinte's main speech in the scene as a 'brief dissertation on the nature of man' using 'the pedant's vocabulary' (p. 305). Mallinson too finds 'comic force' in Philinte's words (p. 121). But to find Philinte comic is to ignore his continuing pattern of friendly behaviour (his words needing to be understood not in absolute terms but as specifically targeted offers of help to Alceste) and to reduce the intensity of the comic spotlight that Molière shines on Alceste. I shall support Thomas' view that 'Philinte is genuinely doing his persuasive best' (p. 90).

The intense focus of laughter at Alceste is suggested by his three rude interruptions of Philinte. In two cases, he hardly lets Philinte say anything before interrupting: 'Mais, quelque soit ce coup, faut-il qu'il vous oblige …?' (1482), 'Mais enfin …' (1151). In the other case, he interrupts just as Philinte is about to give a practical piece of advice about appealing against the verdict: 'Et contre cet arrêt …' (1540).

Critics who find comedy in Philinte's contributions are perhaps too quick to ingest Alceste's view of events. After his long and virulent tirade against his enemies, who are transmuted into the whole of mankind, from whom he wishes to escape, Philinte replies: 'Je trouve un peu bien prompt le dessein où vous êtes' (1525). Parish describes this line as a 'sentence molle, malavisée' (p. 20). Philinte's line certainly strikes a very different note from Alceste's. But it is not a maxim (*sentence*), and it is not ill-advised, in the sense that, for once, Alceste allows him to continue speaking. Philinte is trying to lower Alceste's emotional pressure before giving him a specific example of how he might look at events differently. Crucially the line does not contradict Alceste; it is characteristically moderate in its expression: 'un peu bien prompt'. It should certainly raise a laugh, but one at Alceste's expense, since it punctures the extreme conclusions of his thunderously misanthropic speech. The point that Philinte makes here, by way of soothing Alceste, is that the rumours about Alceste's authorship of the 'livre abominable' have acquired no credit and are indeed more likely to damage their begetter rather than Alceste. When Alceste replies, he does so not on the basis of fact or argument, but by drawing on paranoid speculation: whatever the case, his enemy always comes off better. Philinte's reply reveals him to be calm, patient and persistent, as he firmly repeats as fact that the rumour has not grown in a way that will harm Alceste:

> Enfin il est constant qu'on n'a point trop donné
> Au bruit que contre vous sa malice a tourné:
> De ce côté déjà vous n'avez rien à craindre.
>
> (1535–7)

He then turns systematically to Alceste's other, and major, concern, namely the outcome of his lawsuit:

> Et pour votre procès, dont vous pouvez vous plaindre,
> Il vous est en justice aisé d'y revenir,
> Et contre cet arrêt …
>
> (1538–40)

Whereas Alceste fulminates, Philinte thinks of a practical way forward. If Alceste is so distressed by the outcome as to want to leave all society behind, it seems logical to explore the possibility of an appeal first.

Alceste's interruption at this point is extremely eloquent. It tells us of his ridiculous obsession with, or even preference for, feeling misunderstood and sinned against. He positively wants the verdict to stand as a symbol of the human wickedness of his age. He puts it in more colourful terms:

> Et je veux qu'il demeure à la postérité
> Comme une marque insigne, un fameux témoignage
> De la méchanceté des hommes de notre âge.

> (1544–6)

These lines show how grotesquely comic Alceste is. His retreat from society will not be a quiet one. He wants everyone to know about him and acknowledge his singularity and exemplarity. His egotism has no limits. Finally, Alceste invites Philinte to speak, but he tells him that he will not be persuaded otherwise and asks one of those questions that invite the interlocutor simply to agree with him: 'Aurez-vous bien le front de me vouloir en face / Excuser les horreurs de tout ce qui se passe?' (1553–4).

Philinte's reply is a more cleverly constructed piece of friendly persuasion than some critics have allowed. It is this speech which Peacock thinks is a pedantic dissertation and which prompts Mallinson to find moral fault with Philinte for taking 'pride in his philosophy, not so much because it is right, but because it is a way of distinguishing himself' (p. 121). But, in order to understand his words, we need to interpret them in the precise context of his current encounter with Alceste. Philinte has given practical reasons why Alceste's intention to withdraw from society is an over-reaction to events. It would be odd if the audience was not persuaded by Philinte's practical suggestions, given Alceste's bizarre view of what has happened, the skewed nature of which is suggested by the hyperboles and posturing with which Alceste expresses himself. His dogmatic refusal to hear Philinte out and to insist that his friend agrees with him is what initiates this alleged dissertation. Philinte cannot simply repeat his practical advice, since Alceste has already rejected it. So in order to attempt to modify Alceste's view he returns to an argument that he had sketched out in the first scene of the play: the implication might well be that the recourse to such an argument is a frequent occurrence in the life of Alceste's friend. With rhetorical sensitivity, he begins by answering Alceste's question in the way Alceste wants: that is to say that he agrees with Alceste in his bleak vision of humanity:

> Non, je tombe d'accord de tout ce qu'il vous plaît:
> Tout marche par cabale et par pur intérêt;
> Ce n'est plus que la ruse aujourd'hui qui l'emporte,
> Et le hommes devraient être faits d'autre sorte.
>
> (1555–8)

This opening is clearly intended to disarm Alceste, and to persuade him to let Philinte have his say without interruption.

The strategy works for a while. He then asks a question designed to make Alceste think that his plan to withdraw from society might not be an appropriate response to this vision: 'Mais est-ce une raison que leur peu d'équité / Pour vouloir se tirer de leur société?' (1559–60). He proposes the stoically flavoured response familiar from act 1: 'Tous ces défauts humains nous donnent dans la vie / Des moyens d'exercer notre philosophie' (1561–2). It seems to me inappropriate to read this couplet as a comic puncturing of Philinte's pride. Philinte is not speaking specifically about himself. His 'nous' embraces himself and all others who see society's faults but find ways of tolerating them (including, he hopes, Alceste). When he wants to refer to himself specifically, he says 'je' (1555). Mallinson is unfair in reading these lines as a criticism of Philinte's alleged sense of superiority, because he turns Philinte's direct speech into indirect speech and, in doing so, inadvertently transforms 'notre philosophie' into 'sa philosophie': 'Philinte expresses a similar need of the morally inferior in 5. 1 in order that he might "exercer [sa] philosophie" ' (p. xix). 'Sa' makes it appear as if Philinte actually says 'ma philosophie', which would lend substance to Mallinson's criticism. But Philinte's statement is deliberately general and embracing. He then gives two reasons to recommend this position to Alceste. The first is that 'C'est le plus bel emploi que trouve la vertu' (1563). Again this is not a personal boast. It is a phrase calculated to appeal to Alceste, who thinks himself alone virtuous and wants his virtue to be recognized. Philinte is trying hard to make the non-withdrawal strategy appear the most suited to

Alceste's particular vision of himself (hence the superlative). Philinte then offers a second reason in support of a stoical stance, and he does it wittily: there would be no need for virtues if people did not have to tolerate vice; so, by implication, it is right that Alceste should want to exercise his virtue by remaining in society. Philinte gets no further, because Alceste interrupts him again:

> Je sais que vous parlez, Monsieur, le mieux du monde;
> En beaux raisonnements vous abondez toujours;
> Mais vous perdez le temps et tous vos beaux discours.
>
> (1570–2)

Mallinson reads Alceste's interruption as a deconstruction of Philinte's speech: '[Philinte's] attitude is reduced ironically to empty talk, "beaux raisonnements" and "beaux discours"' (p. 122). Alceste certainly uses sarcasm to dismiss Philinte's arguments. But why should we accept Alceste's view of Philinte? It would be odd for an audience to trust an intemperate egotist rather than a patient friend. Alceste offers no arguments against Philinte other than an assertion of a preoccupation with his personal vanity as a slighted hero. Philinte has patiently used pragmatic arguments relating to Alceste's lawsuit and alleged authorship of the 'livre abominable'; and he has patiently sketched out a more general philosophical argument in terms designed to appeal to Alceste's vanity. That Alceste refuses to listen to all this is more likely to make him, rather than Philinte, look foolish; and he looks all the more foolish if we interpret Philinte's words as sincere and ingenious attempts to persuade and help his friend.

It is clear from Philinte's reactions to him at the end of the scene that he is concerned about Alceste and will continue to try to help even if his own persuasive efforts have been rejected. Alceste asks Philinte to leave, so that he can await Célimène's arrival alone and his opportunity to make his ultimatum. Philinte suggests a different course of action: 'Montons chez Éliante, attendant sa venue' (1581). This simple line conveys a good deal. It shows that Philinte is prepared to leave, as Alceste asks. It reveals Philinte's concern for Alceste, as he asks Alceste to leave with him. The choice of Éliante's rooms as a place to wait is significant. It implies that Philinte thinks Éliante might be able to persuade Alceste when he alone has failed; and it suggests that Philinte is not so personally preoccupied with his own relationship with Éliante as to put it before his concern for Alceste. When Alceste insists on staying behind with only his 'noir chagrin' (1584) for company, Philinte's closing couplet both retains a comic vision of Alceste, with its witty response to his imagery, and demonstrates his determination to help: 'C'est une compagnie étrange pour attendre, / Et je vais obliger Éliante à descendre' (1586). In dramaturgical terms, this expression of his intention to return with Éliante will justify their entrance in 5. 3.

MARRIAGE AND FRIENDSHIP (5. 3–4)

On his return to the stage, Philinte is a spectator of the denouement, speaking only a few lines towards the end of the play. He witnesses the public downfall of Célimène, who has been shown to be playing one suitor off against another. She is deserted first by Acaste and Clitandre, then by Oronte. Molière creates dramatic suspense by showing Alceste with no rivals, but Célimène at her most tainted. Embarrassed as Arsinoé takes his defence and starts to criticize Célimène, Alceste stops her speaking and Molière builds more suspense by making Alceste imply that if he does not persist with Célimène, it is Éliante rather than Arsinoé to whom he will turn: 'Et ce n'est pas à vous que je pourrai songer, / Si par un autre choix je cherche à me venger' (1721–2). It is a more highly charged moment than Alceste can imagine. It is certainly a crisp rejection of Arsinoé, who manifests her pique in her reply. It is a way of suggesting to Célimène that his judgement of her lies in the balance. But whereas he thinks that his third option, marriage to Éliante, is a straightforward matter, it cannot quite be so in the light of the developing relationship of Éliante and Philinte and Éliante's evident shock in 4. 2 at the thought that she would simply be an instrument of vengeance for Alceste. Molière gives no indication of Éliante's or Philinte's reactions to Alceste's words. But the audience can imagine that Alceste's compounded reference here to Éliante's hand as a means of revenge against Célimène is decisive: Éliante's rejection of him is likely to be total, and his attitude serves only to highlight the more loving offer that Philinte has tentatively made her in 4. 1.

Aggravating his insult to Éliante, it is only after he has finally made his ultimatum to Célimène and had it rejected that he offers himself to Éliante. It is true that he no longer speaks of vengeance and presents himself with unaccustomed humility, but her mind was already made up. She interrupts him and, with what is clearly a joyous surprise for Philinte, identifies Alceste's friend as the person whom she would be willing to marry. The surprise of Philinte is evident in his response: 'Ah! cet honneur, Madame, est toute mon envie. / Et j'y sacrifierais et mon sang et ma vie' (1800). The surprise is dramaturgically important, because its signals quite clearly that the pair have not spoken further of a possible marriage since 4. 1 and that they have not therefore, in any sense, been acting deliberately against the interests of Alceste.

Alceste's congratulations, however, are ambiguous: 'Puissiez-vous, pour goûter de vrais contentements, / L'un pour l'autre à jamais garder ces sentiments!' (1801–2). These words could be sincere and indicate Alceste's sensitivity to the good qualities in Éliante and Philinte, even perhaps his appreciation of Philinte's friendship. But his words could also be bitterly sarcastic, interpreting as the ultimate betrayal the marriage of his friend to the woman he had thought of as his reserve partner. Such a reading might be supported by Alceste's immediately succeeding lines:

> Trahi de toutes parts, accablé d'injustices,
> Je vais sortir d'un gouffre où triomphent les vices,
> Et chercher sur la terre un endroit écarté
> Où d'être homme d'honneur on ait la liberté.
>
> (1803–6)

Whining with self-pity, he leaves the stage, followed closely by Éliante and Philinte, who speaks the play's last couplet: 'Allons, Madame, allons employer toute chose, / Pour rompre le dessein que son cœur se propose' (1807–8).

These last few lines of the play have given rise to very varied interpretations. One issue is Alceste's departure. Do Alceste's final lines constitute such a strong sense of persecution that we are encouraged to believe that his withdrawal is definitive? Bourqui seems to think so: 'Il y a fort à parier que l'homme aux rubans verts préférera le désert' (p. 29). The evidence of Donneau de Visé's *Lettre écrite sur la comédie du misanthrope* is that Molière's original performance gave this impression too: 'il fait voir, en finissant, qu'il le conservera [son caractère] toute sa vie, en se retirant' (*OC*, II, 139). Thomas, however, seems to think that Alceste will be persuaded to stay, noting that 'the combination of Philinte/Éliante will be quite formidable' (p. 92), as do Hope and Hammond.[21] Mallinson insists on the irresolvable ambiguity of the text: 'The text leaves open both possibilities, significantly withholding any clearly unambiguous statements of order' (p. xxxii). But in practice, it is likely that a production would need to imply either one or the other. Audiences would be more likely to think Alceste's departure permanent if he delivers his final lines in such a way as to indicate that this is the worst crisis of all, because of the break with Célimène and the perceived treachery of Éliante and Philinte. But they would be more likely to believe that Alceste will not abandon society if they remember the recurrence of the departure motif. The ending of act 5 is modelled on the ending of act 1, when Alceste leaves angrily dismissive ('Plus de société' (442)) and is followed, contrary to instructions, by his anxious friend. Alceste himself is fully aware of the motif and mentions it as a pattern of behaviour in the play's first scene: 'Et parfois il me prend des mouvements soudains / De fuir dans un désert l'approche des humains' (143–4). Audiences would also be more likely to read Alceste's determination as empty words if it was spoken in the same mock-tragic tone as his previous complaints of persecution. They might remember his constant tendency to over-react and see things out of proportion. They know for sure that he has not been betrayed by Philinte, however it might appear to him; so his outrage is likely to strike them as disproportionate.

Some light might be shed on Alceste's departure by the other issue that the ending raises, the interpretation of Philinte's closing couplet. It is possible to find it comic at Philinte's expense. Fargher says that 'if Alceste is incorrigible, so is Philinte [...]. Even after the play is over he will still continue' (p. 106). Guicharnaud dismisses

---

[21] Quentin M. Hope, 'Society in *Le Misanthrope*', *French Review*, 32 (1958–9), 329–36: 'The protagonist who runs off stage [...] is not allowed to withdraw. Someone runs after him.' (p. 336); Nicholas Hammond, 'Authorship and Authority in Molière's *Le Misanthrope*' in *Essays on French Comic Drama from the 1640s to the 1780s*, eds. Derek Connon and George Evans (Oxford: Peter Lang, 2000), pp. 55–70: '[Alceste's] dignified exit is usurped by the happy couple's insistence on the play ending as a comedy' (p. 69).

it as a 'platitude' (p. 497), and Peacock thinks Philinte naive for thinking, in this couplet, that he can bring about a change in Alceste (p. 307). Mallinson too sees the possibility of interpreting weakness in Philinte's position: 'Philinte's own desire to assert his authority is apparent to the last, but his reading of Alceste may be as misguided as Alceste's own reading of Célimène; his confidence may equally imply a lack of comprehension' (p. 130). Potentially such interpretations, if brought out in performance, would make Alceste's departure seem definitive.

But, taken on their own terms, these interpretations seem to me not entirely convincing. I cannot accept that Philinte is naive. He never tries to change Alceste's human nature (whereas Alceste is naive in wanting to change human nature in general). In thinking that he might be able to bring Alceste back, he has evidence of his having done so in the past. I am not persuaded that Philinte is trying to assert specifically his own authority in the last two lines. What is most striking about them is that he uses the first person plural, and very explicitly incorporates Éliante into an envisaged engagement with Alceste. To suggest that Philinte might misjudge Alceste as Alceste misjudges Célimène is to fly in the face of repeated evidence in the play of Alceste's bad, intemperate judgements and Philinte's own patient assessments of people and situations. And to say that Philinte speaks here with confidence (and imply that he therefore speaks with an excess of confidence) is to misrepresent his words, which are about the effort that needs to be expended ('employer toute chose') and not at all an assumption of success. The doubts about the negative interpretation of Philinte's closing lines lead me to prefer Thomas' view that 'it is essentially a happy comment from Philinte, because from now on he is not going to be alone in handling Alceste' (p. 92). The urgency of Philinte's couplet ('Allons [...] allons') and his insistence on the effort that will be required ('toute chose') makes it clear that he is aware that his task will be harder this time than in the past. Molière does not tell us whether or not he will succeed, but, despite the evidence of Donneau de Visé's *Lettre*, implying that Alceste will withdraw, there may be a hint that Philinte will succeed. Molière closes the play with an image of friendship in action, and friendship reinforced. Cicero's treatise on friendship suggests another reason why Philinte's friendship will still prove attractive to Alceste.

Timon of Athens, according to Cicero, was so misanthropic that he fled human contact, but not entirely: 'tousjours auroit-il peine à vivre, s'il n'avoit quelqu'un prés de luy, dans la conversation duquel il pust comme vomir le venin de sa mauvaise humeur' (p. 162 (xxiii.87)). For all Molière's silence on Alceste's future, it is hard to believe that it will be as withdrawn as Alceste asserts.

As Gross says, 'Philinte ends the play as a friend still committed to serving [Alceste]. Instead of celebrating Philinte's engagement to Éliante [...], Molière terminates the play with a statement of this friend's loyalty, a genuine advantage about which Philinte never boasts.'[22] Friendship is frequently foregrounded as a theme in the text of the play and Philinte is explicitly cast in the role of Alceste's long-standing friend. The obligations traditionally associated with true friendship provide a perspective in which to interpret Philinte's speeches throughout the play. It is a perspective that privileges his rhetorical attempts to engage with, and help, his friend rather than to assert himself in opposition to him.

Such an approach to Philinte's role might seem to undermine those critical readings which suggest that we should laugh at him as well as at Alceste and which, thereby, seem superficially to enrich the text by presenting it as inherently ambiguous. But it is also an approach that intensifies the laughter at Alceste, who, in his breathtakingly self-obsessed response to an imperfect world, becomes all the more ridiculous for his refusal to engage politely with an invariably patient and well-intentioned friend, who is entirely in sympathy with Alceste's view of the world, if not with his response to it.

This reading does not ignore the intriguing ambiguities and reflective laughter that the play generates, but situates them differently. The structural relationship between foolish protagonist and *raisonneur* figure works, as in previous plays, to maximize audience laughter at the fool. According to this reading, we laugh in the theatre at Alceste's ill-tempered and excessive *reactions* and we think that Philinte is doing his best to help his bizarre friend. We do not laugh at the *concept* that sincerity is a noble ideal and we do not instantly admire the *concept* of *honnêteté*. It is only when we realize, whether in the

---

[22] Nathan Gross, *From Gesture to Idea: Esthetics and Ethics in Molière's Comedy* (New York: Columbia University Press, 1982), p. 125.

theatre or outside, that Molière has made us laugh at a character who believes in sincerity and made us see him through the eyes of a character who believes in accommodating himself to an imperfect society that we recognize the ambiguities created by the gap between theatrical experience and the complex issues that the play-world has raised; and it is only then that we recognize the power of a dramatist to make us forget, or at least momentarily put aside, our conventional moral responses. If, on reflection, we look for an answer in the play as to where the truth between sincerity and *honnêteté* might lie, we shall not find one, because the play merely suggests the complexity of the issues, while concentrating its energies on the generation of comic structures and comic situations.

6

Le Malade imaginaire: the raisonneur as brother and impresario

J'emploierai toutes choses pour obtenir ce qu'elle souhaite.[1]

In *Le Malade imaginaire* (1673), Béralde is the brother of the eponymous hypochondriac Argan. His role can appear smaller than those of earlier so-called *raisonneur* characters, since he does not appear (indeed is not even mentioned) until the very end of act 2, and critics focus almost exclusively on his meeting with Argan in 3. 3. On the other hand, he is present on stage, without interruption, for the whole of the third and final act. If we bear in mind that he is present too for the final *intermède* (the burlesque degree ceremony) and, possibly, for the second *intermède*, we notice that he is visibly present, alongside Argan, for half the total performance time of the spectacle.[2] It is easy to forget this when we read the text on the page. But in a performance of both the spoken and musical parts of the spectacle, Béralde's substantial presence in Argan's company is likely to reinforce for the spectators the notion of a close fraternal relationship between the two of them.

---

[1] Béralde in *Le Malade imaginaire* (3. 2).

[2] On Molière's use of musical interludes and the significance of the interaction with the spoken parts of the play, see Nicholas Cronk, 'Molière-Charpentier's *Le Malade imaginaire*: The First *Opéra-Comique*?', *Forum for Modern Language Studies*, 29 (1993), 216–31, and 'The Play of Words and Music in Molière-Charpentier's *Le Malade imaginaire*', *French Studies*, 47 (1993), 6–19.

BÉRALDE AND THE CRITICS

The small part of Béralde's role to which critics have attended has provoked no less divergent views than in the case of previous *raisonneurs*. Those who take seriously what Béralde has to say to his brother about medicine explain his views variously as those of Molière or of the period generally. Calder reminds us that his views echo Montaigne's, and assumes that they are also Molière's own views: 'It is an anachronism to view Molière's distrust of medicine as excessive. The views he expresses through Béralde are no more excessive than Montaigne's.'[3] Without claiming that his views are Molière's, Dandrey sees Béralde as the embodiment of lucidity, casting 'l'éclairage de la sagesse sur les délires d'une imagination égarée'.[4] With no evidence, Defaux asserts that Béralde's views are more those of Molière than those of the period: 'il exprime en l'occurrence sur la médecine des credos qui sont davantage ceux de son créateur que ceux de son siècle'.[5] Herzel, who finds other *raisonneurs* comic, approaches Béralde quite differently, claiming that he has 'a more plausible claim that any of the other *raisonneurs* to the title of Molière's spokesman'.[6] Moore, however, takes precisely the opposite view to Herzel: 'Of all the *raisonneurs* Béralde is the only one who does not express moderate views, and there is some evidence that Molière himself did not share them, but took the advice of a doctor.'[7] Eustis finds Béralde the 'jolliest' of the *raisonneurs*, as Peacock does,[8] and is amused when he, allegedly, 'grows hot under the collar despite his philosophy and

---

[3] Andrew Calder, *Molière: The Theory and Practice of Comedy* (London: The Athlone Press, 1993), p. 126.

[4] Patrick Dandrey, *Molière ou l'esthétique du ridicule*, Paris: Klincksieck, 1992, p. 293.

[5] Gérard Defaux, *Molière ou les métamorphoses du comique: de la comédie morale au triomphe de la folie*, Lexington: French Forum, 1980, 2nd edn, Paris: Klincksieck, 1992, p. 295.

[6] Roger W. Herzel, 'The Function of the *Raisonneur* in Molière's Comedy', *Modern Language Notes*, 90 (1975), 564–75, p. 566.

[7] W. G. Moore, *Molière: A New Criticism* (Oxford: Clarendon Press, 1949), p. 74.

[8] Alvin Eustis, *Molière as Ironic Contemplator* (The Hague, Paris: Mouton, 1973), p. 192; Noël Peacock, 'The Comic Role of the *Raisonneur* in Molière's Theatre', *Modern Language Review*, 76 (1981), 298–310, p. 307.

his exhortation to Argan to remain calm'. Peacock also finds Béralde comic for being pedantically obsessed with his scorn for medicine (p. 306). So does Fargher: 'Béralde is almost as irrationally exaggerated in his scorn for medicine as Argan in his passion for it.'[9] Béralde, it would appear, is either the lucid exponent of Molière's or Montaigne's views on medicine, or a risibly pedantic proponent of self-evidently immoderate views.

A dramaturgical perspective on his role helps to cut through these divergent views and understand Béralde's words differently. Molière needs to construct his comedy so as to make it possible for Argan's daughter Angélique to marry Cléante, the young man whom she loves and who loves her. Molière's conception of the character of his foolish protagonist Argan creates two obstacles to this wedding. The first is that Argan's obsession with his health, which makes him rely on his doctor Monsieur Purgon, also makes him want to marry his daughter to a doctor, in the event Purgon's nephew, the grotesquely stupid Thomas Diafoirus. The second obstacle, which pulls him in a different direction from the first, is his blind love for his second wife Bélise, Angélique's step-mother, who, as everyone apart from him can see, is exploiting him for his money. She wants him to send Angélique to a convent, so ensuring that she is likely to be less of a financial drain. Argan's position is that Angélique will marry Thomas within four days; if not, she will go to a convent. He holds this position even though he comes to suspect that she is interested in another man. For the first two acts the comedy focuses on Argan's two obessions, both of which show him to be a fool, utterly blind to Thomas' stupidity and his wife's scheming. In the third act Molière has to organize the dramatic action so that these obstacles can be removed and the happy marriage of Cléante and Angélique can go ahead. To do this, he introduces Béralde, who will work with the enterprising servant Toinette to ensure that the two obstacles are lifted. If Molière had tried to use Toinette alone to achieve this goal, he would not have been able, without sacrificing verisimilitude, to test Argan's intellectual faith in doctors and medicine. Toinette uses

---

[9] Richard Fargher, 'Molière and his Reasoners' in *Studies in French Literature presented to H. W. Lawton*, ed. J. C. Ireson and others (Manchester University Press, 1968), pp. 105–20, p. 113.

trickery to persuade him; Béralde, more plausibly, being his brother
and social equal, uses rhetoric, wittily and inventively.

SURPRISE ENTRANCE (2. 9)

Béralde's sudden appearance at the end of act 2 must come as a
surprise for the audience. Not only has he never been mentioned
before, but he comes on unannounced. Such an entrance is, however,
instructive. Coupled with his opening words ('Hé bien! mon frère,
qu'est-ce?'), it speaks immediately of his fraternal intimacy with
Argan. The audience soon sees, in this short scene, that Béralde
has come to make an intervention that might help Angélique. But
Peacock sees in him 'a partial comic blindness to his chances of
success [...] his unprepared and inopportune proposal of a marriage
between Cléante and Angélique shows a comic unawareness of Argan's
inclinations, and succeeds only in making Argan more irate' (p. 308).
Peacock's words seem to me not adequately to reflect Béralde's words
in this scene or what we learn retrospectively about his arrival at
this juncture. The scene seems rather to establish Béralde as a quick
operator, dealing deftly and knowingly with his brother's folly.

   Although, in its context, Béralde's appearance is certainly unexpected, Molière provides retrospective justification for it, which is
worth pondering. When Cléante returns to the stage in 3. 14, he
mentions to Angélique 'la demande que j'avais conjuré votre oncle
de lui faire [à votre père] pour moi'. We have to assume that Cléante
and Béralde know each other. This mention of Béralde implies that
when Cléante, disguised as a substitute singing teacher for Angélique,
is dismissed by a rather suspicious Argan in 2. 5, we are to assume
that he goes to find Béralde and asks him to support the case for his
marriage to Angélique; we should also assume that he has told Béralde
about Argan's alternative and pressing plan to marry her to Thomas.
So when Béralde appears, he should speak with the confidence of
someone who has had time to prepare a strategy.

   The audience might guess that Béralde is speaking *en connaissance de cause*, but, for Argan, Béralde's words about a marriage for
Angélique are completely unexpected. It is only the evening before

(act 1) that Argan has announced his intention to marry her to Thomas and only during act 2 that he has met Thomas and introduced him to Angélique. So Argan assumes that his brother knows nothing of this match; and Béralde will also assume ignorance on Argan's part.

The audience will believe that Béralde has greater knowledge than Argan thinks and that his initial strategy for dealing with Argan is to surprise him. He begins by flattering Argan's obsession with his health, but does so briefly and in a comically flippant way, ensuring that the audience laughs with him at the protagonist: 'Comment "fort mal"?' and 'Voilà qui est fâcheux.' The calmly routine nature of his concern suggests that he has much practice in this non-committal indulgence of his brother's folly. After these opening niceties, he comes straight to the point: 'J'étais venu ici, mon frère, vous proposer un parti pour ma nièce Angélique.' Contrary to the impression created by Peacock's paraphrase of Béralde's words (p. 308), he does not actually identify as Cléante the young man he has in mind, and this is because Argan interrupts him vigorously. He gets out of his chair, adopts an angry tone, and says: 'Mon frère, ne me parlez point de cette coquine-là. C'est une friponne, une impertinente, une effrontée, que je mettrai dans un couvent avant qu'il soit deux jours.' This sudden display of anger (evident also in Argan's capricious reduction of the time limit from four days to two) is not directed at Béralde, but at Angélique. It must surprise Béralde, however, because it seems quite out of proportion to his own opening gambit. The explanation lies in what Argan learnt immediately before Béralde's entrance, which Béralde clearly cannot know: Argan has found out that the man who presented himself as her substitute singing teacher has attempted to have a private meeting with Angélique in her room. Béralde's suggestion of a match for Angélique makes it seem to Argan as if his daughter has countless suitors. The audience knows that Argan's exasperated outburst is misplaced, but immediately recognizes the cause of his misunderstanding. Béralde is in no position to do so. It is all the more impressive, therefore, that Béralde is not thrown by Argan's strange interjection. Without further ado, he postpones the clearly problematic subject of a match for Angélique and attempts to restore Argan to a better humour. He does this with lightness of touch: 'Ah! voilà qui est bien: je suis bien aise que la force vous revienne un peu, et que ma visite vous fasse du bien. Oh ça! nous parlerons d'affaires tantôt.' Béralde turns impresario.

In a spectacle that so obviously mingles domestic realism and theatrical fantasy, there is no reason to appeal to verisimilitude to explain Béralde's introduction at this moment of some street performers whose dancing and singing constitute the second *intermède*. But Molière does, in fact, make Béralde offer a plausible explanation for his entertaining treat: 'Je vous amène ici un divertissement, que j'ai rencontré, qui dissipera votre chagrin, et vous rendra l'âme mieux disposée aux choses que nous avons à dire.' Béralde implies that on his way to see Argan in order to intervene on Cléante's behalf he came across some performers, whom he asked to accompany him, thinking that it would be very difficult to persuade his irascible brother and that some musical entertainment might support his persuasive strategy. He has to call on the performers sooner than he might have anticipated. He is confident that they will offer Argan pleasure, and with further wit directed at his brother's folly, he assures him that 'cela vaudra bien une ordonnance de Monsieur Purgon'. By presenting the performers as mollifying agents just as Argan's temper has flared up, Molière justifies the intrusion of more spectacular fantasy into his domestic play-world.

The text does not explicitly say that Argan and Béralde are on stage throughout the *intermède*, but the implication is that they are present, because Béralde has brought on the performers specially for Argan's benefit. We might imagine that Béralde negotiated the songs with them in advance, since they are relevant to the cause he has come to plead. The performers sing of the necessity of allowing young love to express itself in full awareness of the pleasures and pains that attend it. Béralde has come precisely to press the case of two people in love, whereas Argan wants to force Angélique to marry a young man whom she does not love. The performance is conceived to offer Argan both pleasure and instruction.

STRATEGIC PLANNING (3. 1–2)

Act 3 seems to start just as the *intermède* ends, though Toinette has now joined Béralde and Argan. Béralde is keen to know Argan's reaction to the entertainment and maintains the humorous tone with which he has introduced it, inviting Argan to confirm that it has done him as much good as a laxative remedy: 'Mon frère, qu'en dites-vous? cela ne vaut-il pas bien une prise de casse?' Toinette maintains the same light-hearted tone: 'Hon, de bonne casse est bonne.' But Argan does not reply. So Béralde attempts to return to the subject which he has come to address. This time he treads very carefully: 'Voulez-vous que nous parlions un peu ensemble?' Argan's reply might look like the avoidance strategy adopted so often by Molière's other foolish protagonists: 'Un peu de patience, mon frère, je vais revenir.' But he is not really trying to avoid his brother. He promises to return, and indeed does so very promptly. For dramaturgical purposes Molière needs to show Béralde and Toinette alone together: the structure of the act depends on their concerted attempt to dispel the obstacles standing in the way of Angélique's and Cléante's wedding; so Molière needs, however briefly, to establish some collusion between them. The justification he finds for Argan's exit, far from being strained, is richly comic. Not only does it show Argan's routine preoccupation with his bowel movements, it also implies that, whereas Béralde had predicted Argan's response to the performance in metaphorical terms (as good an effect as Monsieur Purgon's laxative prescription), Argan's actual response is literal. He hurries off to the toilet. Indeed he is in such a hurry that he even forgets his walking stick. It is as if, in matters medical, Argan is highly, and absurdly, suggestible.

The short scene between Toinette and Béralde (3. 2) is crucial for determining the action of the rest of the act and for establishing the audience's expectations of their subsequent behaviour. Most particularly, it provides the context for interpreting Béralde's words to Argan on the subject of medicine in 3. 3. Critics need to bear this context in mind before asserting that Béralde's apparently authoritative statements about medicine and doctors are either Molière's own seriously held views or views that are patently absurd and that therefore make Béralde look ridiculous.

First of all, Toinette takes the initiative to enlist Béralde's help: 'N'abandonnez pas, s'il vous plaît, les intérêts de votre nièce.' In its very generality, this is deftly phrased by Molière, since it glosses over the problem as to how much Toinette can know about the purposes of Béralde's visit. His reply is decisive: 'J'emploierai toutes choses pour lui obtenir ce qu'elle souhaite.' This must be taken to mean that he will use every means available to him to persuade Argan that his daughter should be allowed to marry Cléante, and what this implies is that everything he proceeds to do and say in Argan's presence has to be interpreted strategically. Béralde knows that there are two obstacles to be demolished: the engagement to Purgon's nephew due to Argan's obsession with medicine; and the alternative obstacle of the convent, the wish of his wife. For her part, Toinette spells out what she thinks the primary obstacle is and how she is going to try to dispel it. In order to persuade Argan to drop the idea of a marriage to Thomas Diafoirus, he needs to have his faith shaken in Monsieur Purgon. Argan's faith in doctors is so strong that she thinks it would take the words of another doctor 'pour le dégoûter de son Monsieur Purgon, et lui décrier sa conduite'. In the absence of another real doctor, Toinette will dress up as one. The scene ends with Toinette's clear instruction that both of them are to act in their different ways to secure the same end: 'Laissez-moi faire: agissez de votre côté.'

BÉRALDE AND ARGAN (3. 3)

Whether they present Béralde as Molière's mouthpiece for negative views of doctors or as a supplementary source of comedy because of the allegedly immoderate advice he gives Argan, critics leave aside a good deal of what is a long and complex scene. In assessing Béralde's role in it, Shaw comes closest to the mark since he recognizes the difficulty of establishing the relationship between Béralde's views and Molière's own and instead puts the emphasis on the interaction that Béralde's views create with those of Argan: 'It would be most unwise to regard [Béralde] as Molière's mouthpiece. He may have sympathized with some of Béralde's remarks: but we cannot be sure. [...] Rather than representing a theory, Béralde's function is to provoke. Argan's love of doctors is underlined by his amazement at encountering someone who has no time for them.'[10] It is certainly the case that,

[10] David Shaw, 'Molière and the Doctors', *Nottingham French Studies*, 33 (1994), 133–42, p. 140.

in response to Béralde, Argan is able to reveal his foolish obsession in such a way that the audience will laugh at his hypochondria; this function of heightening the comic effect at the expense of the foolish protagonist is shared with previous *raisonneur* roles. But even this way of commenting on the scene and Béralde's role does not do justice to the dramaturgical context, established clearly in 3. 2, which gives him an important persuasive function.

The beginning of the scene, after Toinette has left and Argan has returned from performing his bodily functions, shows Béralde to be concerned, as he was at the beginning of 2. 9, with preparing his interlocutor for the unwelcome topic that he is going to raise. The relationship between this pair of characters has a different tonality from that of previous pairs in that Argan is not as subject to anger as such predecessors as Orgon and Alceste (despite the outburst in 2. 9, which is aimed at Angélique) and he is more willing to engage in discussion and even to listen without interrupting. The comic manifestations of Argan's folly lie rather in his extreme gullibility in believing that he needs medical assistance so badly that his daughter must marry a doctor and in the obstinacy with which he holds this belief. So Argan's return to talk to his brother, even though he knows the topic will be the future of Angélique, and his good-humoured assent to talk in a reasonable and dispassionate manner establish Argan's willing participation in Béralde's persuasive purposes.

Peacock finds Béralde's triple insistence on the need to maintain an even temper during the discussion comic on the grounds that he himself loses his own calm (p. 307). It might be possible to perform Béralde as growing heated in the course of the scene, but nothing in the text indicates that he should do so. On the contrary, all the linguistic signals point to his control of the dialogue and his ability to respond calmly to Argan's quirky assertions. What Molière is surely doing in these prefatory remarks, in which, three times, Béralde asks Argan to remain calm and, three times, Argan readily assents, is to set expectations for the audience which will be comically defeated as Argan becomes increasingly incredulous and exasperated before Béralde's claims. Argan makes his third reply of assent as if there were no question about his ability to remain dispassionate: 'Mon Dieu! oui. Voilà bien du préambule.' But the wording of the reply, coupled with the reminder of his outburst in 2. 9, indicate to the audience his comic lack of self-knowledge which the remainder of the scene will expose further.

THE CONVENT (3. 3)

Béralde then broaches his first topic, which is not medicine or Monsieur Purgon, but Argan's idea of sending Angélique to a convent. Why does Béralde start with this? It is the second obstacle to Angélique's wedding to Cléante. Toinette has just told Béralde that she will be tackling the first obstacle by undermining Argan's confidence in Purgon. And the threat of a convent was made explicitly by Argan to Béralde in 2. 9 when Béralde first introduced the topic of a possible match for Angélique. So Béralde is here picking up the thread of their earlier scene in full knowledge that such a strategy will complement Toinette's.

In raising the topic and framing it as a question, Béralde simultaneously and subtly prepares the ground for an attack on the idea of a convent: 'D'où vient, mon frère, qu'ayant le bien que vous avez, et n'ayant d'enfants qu'une fille, car je ne compte pas la petite, d'où vient, dis-je, que vous parlez de la mettre dans un couvent?' The usual reason for sending a daughter to a convent was financial—saving a potentially costly dowry. As Argan is wealthy, that cannot be the reason. Béralde suspects that the reason is the greed of Argan's wife, but rather than make accusations which would anger Argan, he asks the question in an open-ended way. Argan's answer shows that he has already lost any ability to be dispassionate, by parodying Béralde's phraseology in a blocking question, which is none other than an assertion of his right to dispose of his family exactly as he pleases: 'D'où vient, mon frère, que je suis maître dans ma famille pour faire ce que bon me semble?'

Undeterred by such an unhelpful reply, Béralde employs cutting sarcasm to evoke Béline's presumed involvement: 'je ne doute point que, par un esprit de charité, elle ne fût ravie de les voir toutes deux bonnes religieuses'. Argan's reply shows yet again a determination not to engage in argument over his wife. It is worded as if he is familiar with Béralde's attempts to make him see through her alleged scheming: 'Oh ça! nous y voici. Voilà d'abord la pauvre femme en jeu: c'est elle qui fait tout le mal, et tout le monde lui en veut.' This implicit defence of Béline leads Béralde to drop the topic, but not before he has used the rhetorical device of *praeteritio* in order to have a last word on it:

Non, mon frère; laissons-la là; c'est une femme qui a les meilleures intentions du monde pour votre famille, et qui est détachée de toute sorte d'intérêt, qui a pour vous une tendresse merveilleuse, et qui montre pour vos enfants une affection et une bonté qui n'est pas concevable: cela est certain. N'en parlons point, et revenons à votre fille.

There are two ways of interpreting Béralde's words. His praise of Béline, so evidently sarcastic in the audience's eyes, could be intended to appease Argan, who dotes on her and will interpret the eulogy literally, his calm sufficiently restored for Béralde to tackle his task from a new angle. This interpretation has the advantage of intensifying the stupidity of Argan. Alternatively, Béralde's praise could be intended to be so blatantly sarcastic as to be aimed at shaking Argan's faith in his wife. It would then appear to be an aggressive strategy, deployed without giving Argan the opportunity to reply.

A HUSBAND TO SUIT ARGAN (3. 3)

Béralde leaves the threat of the convent and addresses the first obstacle to Angélique's happiness: Argan's desire to marry her to the son of a doctor. Argan does not stop to ask how Béralde knows about this. It is interesting that Béralde's strategy is now different and more direct than when he arrived in 2. 9. Then he was clearly not intending to reveal that he knew Argan's plans, but simply to argue for a preferable match for Angélique. Now, it is as if Toinette's suggestion of the need for concerted effort has determined him to go straight to the heart of the issue. In a series of stichomythic exchanges, he puts to Argan the objections to Angélique's proposed marriage to a doctor's son and Argan responds. Béralde phrases his points politely, using the vocative 'mon frère', as he has done several times before this exchange. When Argan replies, also using the same expression, it is a sign less of his politeness than his recalcitrance. In fact, Argan responds to his brother's objections with comic ease, since—such is his self-obsession—he is quite content simply to assert his own self-interest and authority. So Argan is set on this marriage because the bridegroom suits *him*. If Béralde knows a more suitable partner for Angélique, Argan prefers Thomas Diafoirus as a more suitable son-in-law for *him*. Béralde's witty rejoinder ('Mais le mari qu'elle doit prendre doit-il être, mon frère, ou pour elle, ou pour vous?') can have only one answer as far as the audience is concerned, but Argan, comically, gives a different and tyrannically selfish answer: 'Il doit être, mon frère, et pour elle, et pour moi, et je veux mettre dans ma famille les gens dont j'ai besoin.' Not thrown by his brother's unhelpful responses, Béralde demonstrates further wit by pressing him on this tyrannical claim: 'Par cette raison-là, si votre petite était grande, vous lui donneriez en mariage un apothicaire?' His point is to tease Argan about his obsession with medicine, to which Argan is blind and which he has therefore not himself raised explicitly in any of his answers, by suggesting that if he has one son-in-law who is a doctor, he would want the second to be an apothecary. It would strike a seventeenth-century audience as an absurd wish, as an apothecary (socially inferior to a doctor) would not have been considered a desirable match for the daughter of a rich bourgeois. Argan shows his comic pig-headedness by replying, 'Pourquoi non?'

SATIRIZING PURGON (3. 3)

If Béralde had been hoping to persuade Argan to consider his daughter's future from her point of view rather than from his own, his hopes have been dashed. So yet again he needs to change tactics. Argan's replies have made quite clear his determination to have a doctor in the family. So Béralde tackles him explicitly on his obsession with doctors, and in particular suggests to him that he does not need them as he thinks he does: 'Est-il possible que vous serez toujours embéguiné de vos apothicaires et de vos médecins, et que vous vouliez être malade en dépit des gens et de la nature?' It is a measure of Argan's blindness to his folly that he does not understand his brother's question and needs to ask for an explanation: 'Comment l'entendez-vous, mon frère?' This gives Béralde the opportunity to celebrate Argan's good health and to offer as proof the fact that he is still alive despite all the medicines he has been made to take. As he says this, we should remember that his purpose is to persuade Argan that he can afford to pass over the opportunity to marry his daughter to a doctor. Argan has the perfect reply to Béralde's wit: it is only because of all the medicines he has taken that he is not dead. But again Béralde has a response, confident and witty: 'Si vous n'y prenez garde, [Monsieur Purgon] prendra tant de soin de vous, qu'il vous envoiera en l'autre monde.'

Marking his difference from Molière's previous fools, while also revealing the rootedness of his obsession, Argan takes the initiative to enter into a general discussion about the value of medicine: 'Mais raisonnons un peu, mon frère. Vous ne croyez donc point à la médecine?' The impetus to engage in this more general discussion comes from the fool, and not from the so-called *raisonneur*. The move could be interpreted as a diversionary tactic on Argan's part. He is certainly interested in medicine, but he is likely to be all the happier to explore his brother's views on it if it means that he does not have to keep answering for his choice of a bridegroom for Angélique. From Béralde's point of view, however, this generalization of the topic does not in the least divert him from his main task. In order to dissuade Argan from the match with Diafoirus, he needs to shake his belief in doctors and in Purgon specifically. So when he answers Argan's question about his belief in medicine, we should not interpret the dialogue as a pause from the dramatic action so that Béralde can tell us what he thinks (even less, tell us what Molière thinks). In dramaturgical terms that would be absurd. Béralde shapes his answers to suit his persuasive purpose. By showing Argan that it is possible confidently to assert that doctors do not know how to cure people and that it is just as well not to turn to them when one is ill, Béralde is hoping to convince him that he is not so dependent on Purgon as to want to insist on Angélique's marriage to his nephew. In order for his strategy to carry some plausibility in the mind of the audience, Molière cannot risk making Béralde express ridiculously negative views. And indeed all his points against confidence in medicine had been made by Montaigne. This does not mean that Molière expects the audience to share these views, even less that they are Molière's own views: it means that the audience should recognize them as credible views to put to Argan. As far as Molière himself is concerned, we know that one of his best friends was a doctor, Mauvillain, and that he petitioned the king on his behalf (*OC*, I, 893); we also know that he followed his doctor's advice for treating his tuberculosis: the fresh air of Auteuil, where Molière rented a house, and a milk diet.[11] But we have no statements made by Molière giving his general views on doctors or medicine.

Béralde's technique is to shock Argan into confronting someone who confidently expresses scepticism about medicine. There is a sign to the audience that what he says is tactical, because he insists that he is speaking 'entre nous'. One implication of this intimacy is that other people might not corroborate these as Béralde's views; another is that Argan should feel flattered that Béralde is expressing to him views that he has not expressed to other people. So to Argan's question about believing in medicine, Béralde replies with resolute bluntness: 'Non, mon frère, et je ne vois pas que, pour son salut, il soit nécessaire d'y croire.' When Argan is shocked by such irreverence, Béralde compounds his views with blatant satire: 'à regarder les choses en philosophe, je ne vois point de plus plaisante momerie, je ne vois rien de plus ridicule qu'un homme qui se veut mêler d'en guérir un autre'. Peacock finds Béralde comic, alleging that he 'comes to believe in his role of "philosophe"' (p. 301). But Béralde uses the phrase 'à regarder les choses en philosophe' as a strategic and challenging counter to Argan's superstitious gasps at his apparently irreverent words.

Argan puts a series of questions or observations to Béralde, each time in the expectation that his brother will concede something to medical powers, but each time Béralde is shockingly dismissive. He speaks with urbane humour, and always with Montaigne on his side. So in response to Argan's disbelieving question, 'Les médecins ne savent donc rien, à votre compte?', Béralde appears to make a concession only to satirize the ignorance of doctors more effectively: 'Si fait, mon frère. Ils savent la plupart de fort belles humanités, savent parler en beau latin, savent nommer en grec toutes les maladies, les

---

[11] Virginia Scott, *Molière: A Theatrical Life* (Cambridge University Press, 2000), p. 174.

définir et les diviser; mais, pour ce qui est de les guérir, c'est ce qu'ils ne savent point du tout.' The sentence rises elegantly as it praises doctors for their useless knowledge, before falling abruptly as it punctures them for their ignorance of what they most profess. Montaigne had similarly observed that doctors 'cognoissent bien Galien, mais nullement le malade'.[12]

Argan confronts Béralde with the fact that people do turn to doctors when they are ill. But Béralde replies with relentless rigour: 'C'est une marque de la faiblesse humaine, et non pas de la vérité de leur art.' And when Argan, clutching at straws, suggests that at least doctors believe in what they are doing, since they practise on themselves, Béralde seizes the opportunity to deliver a devastating satirical portrait of Argan's own doctor. His initial response to Argan's point is a general one, distinguishing between those doctors who naively think they do good and those who know they do no good but exploit their patients in any case. Montaigne too had identified this latter category: 'Combien en voyons nous d'entr'eux estre de mon humeur? desdaigner la medecine pour leur service, et prendre une forme de vie libre et toute contraire à celle qu'ils ordonnent à autruy?' (ii, 780–1; bk ii, ch. 37). He puts Purgon in the other category, the naive fool who actually thinks he is doing good. With its satirical bite, Béralde's syntax is as pointedly constructed as that of a La Bruyère portrait:

Votre Monsieur Purgon, par exemple, n'y sait point de finesse: c'est un homme tout médecin, depuis la tête jusqu'aux pieds; un homme qui croit à ses règles plus qu'à toutes les démonstrations des mathématiques, et qui croirait du crime à les vouloir examiner; qui ne voit rien d'obscur dans la médecine, rien de douteux, rien de difficile, et qui, avec une impétuosité de prévention, une roideur de confiance, une brutalité de sens commun et de raison, donne au travers des purgations et des saignées, et ne balance aucune chose. Il ne lui faut point vouloir mal de tout ce qu'il pourra vous faire: c'est de la meilleure foi du monde qu'il vous expédiera, et il ne fera, en vous tuant, que ce qu'il a fait à sa femme et ses enfants, et ce qu'en un besoin il ferait à lui-même.

This extended description of Purgon is superfluous to the general discussion of Béralde's views on medicine that Argan has initiated,

---

[12] Montaigne, *Essais*, 3 vols., ed. Pierre Villey and V.-L. Saulnier (Paris: Presses Universitaires de France, 1965), i, p. 139 (bk i, ch. 25).

but it is absolutely central to the persuasive end to which Béralde is directing the discussion. It is true that Toinette will attempt, by other means, to taint Purgon in Argan's eyes, and Béralde knows of her plans. But the opportunity has arisen for him to demolish Purgon, and he seizes it, and sets about his task with relish. The man in whom Argan puts his trust to the extent of wanting to make his daughter marry into his doctor's family is an unthinking automaton (suggested by the accumulation of relative clauses and repeated syntactic constructions), who, without any ill will and by applying the rigid rules he has been taught, will cheerfully kill off Argan, his own family and himself. For the audience, this is an elegant caricature with a comic climax. For Béralde, it is intended to discredit Purgon in the eyes of Argan and to give his brother pause for thought: the *raisonneur* combines comedy and terror to constitute his persuasive arsenal.

ATTACKING MEDICINE (3. 3)

Béralde's satirical portrait, however, has had no effect on Argan, who dismisses it as a prejudice against the man. But Argan is still interested in Béralde's general views and asks the question that he thinks will demonstrate their serious weakness. If Béralde is right that there is no substance in doctors' claims to offer cures, 'Que faire donc quand on est malade?' This question allows Béralde to make his most shocking reply to Argan: 'Rien, mon frère.' Argan's utter disbelief is comic: 'Rien?' And Béralde capitalizes on the effect with a resolute confirmation of his answer: 'Rien. Il ne faut que demeurer en repos.'

Béralde goes on to elaborate his answer in terms that Fargher thinks comically immoderate (p. 113). But Béralde's views about nature working better than medical remedies, expressed calmly and confidently, are part of his strategy for making Argan question his superstitious need to marry a doctor into his family. The views are not in themselves comic: 'La nature elle-même, quand nous la laissons faire, se tire doucement du désordre où elle est tombée.' This echoes another sentiment of Montaigne: '[je] respons à ceux qui me pressent de prendre medecine, qu'ils attendent au moins que je sois rendu à mes forces et à ma santé, pour avoir plus moyen de soustenir l'effort et le hazart de leur breuvage. Je laisse faire nature' (I, 127; bk I, ch. 24). Béralde sums it up in a witty paradox: 'presque tous les hommes meurent de leurs remèdes, et non pas de leurs maladies'.

Unable to accept his brother's position, Argan tries to force him into making some concession to medicine: surely he would agree that medical intervention can assist nature. The execution of Béralde's rhetorical strategy requires him to give no ground and he accordingly dismisses such a suggestion as 'pures idées' and 'belles imaginations'. By way of support, he paints another satirical portrait of the doctor who claims to help nature along. This too uses syntactical accumulation to tantalize Argan and build up to a pithy climax in which the doctor's claims are brutally punctured:

Lorsqu'un médecin vous parle d'aider, de secourir, de soulager la nature, de lui ôter ce qui lui nuit et lui donner ce qui lui manque, de la rétablir et de la remettre dans une pleine facilité de ses fonctions; lorsqu'il vous parle de rectifier le sang, de tempérer les entrailles et le cerveau, de dégonfler la rate, de raccommoder la poitrine, de réparer le foie, de fortifier le cœur, de rétablir et conserver la chaleur naturelle, et d'avoir des secrets pour étendre la vie à de longues années: il vous dit justement le roman de la médecine.

The comedy lies in Argan's refusal to question his own superstitiously held views in the face of his brother's masterly satirical portrait of the medical profession. Argan's response is comic, since it insists on his naive reverence for doctors and attempts to refute Béralde with only personal insult: 'C'est-à-dire que toute la science du monde est renfermée dans votre tête, et vous voulez en savoir plus que tous les grands médecins de notre siècle.' Eustis finds Béralde funny for his 'inability to convince Argan of his folly' (p. 192). But if by Argan's folly Eustis means his hypochondria and naive faith in doctors, he misunderstands the purpose of this scene within the dramaturgical structure of the play. Béralde's aim is not to change Argan, simply to shake his faith in doctors sufficiently to make it possible for him to contemplate his daughter's marrying a man who is not a doctor.

Béralde paints a final brief satirical portrait of doctors as excellent speakers, but ineffective practitioners: 'Entendez-les parler: les plus habiles gens du monde; voyez-les faire: les plus ignorants de tous les hommes.' He appeals directly to Argan's senses and experience of doctors. He uses sharp antithesis and superlatives that caricature his victims. But Argan's faith in doctors is so entrenched that he is unmoved by Béralde's satire, and replies with yet another personal insult: 'Vous êtes un grand docteur, à ce que je vois.' Confronted with Argan's dogged obstinacy, Béralde changes tack somewhat. He is honest about what he has been doing. He repeats his earlier phrase to the effect that what he has been saying is 'entre nous'. Béralde's views have been framed to have an effect on Argan, and he admits this: 'Ce que j'en dis n'est qu'entre nous, et j'aurais souhaité de pouvoir un peu vous tirer de l'erreur où vous êtes.' The error in question is Argan's dependence on Purgon, which has fixated him on a medical marriage for Angélique.

MOLIÈRE'S COMEDIES (3. 3)

In the light of his own failure to amuse and move Argan with his satirical sketches, he suggests that he would have liked to take him, 'pour vous divertir', to see one of Molière's plays on the topic. Mention of Molière's plays issues in the last series of exchanges between them in this scene. Argan is dismissive of Molière and his allegedly impertinent attacks on doctors, and thinks the doctors should punish him by leaving him to die when he is ill. Béralde defends him, claiming that he does not attack individual doctors, only 'le ridicule de la médecine', and that, in any case, he has the strength to bear his illness, but not the remedies that any doctors might prescribe. Argan's openness to discussion has gradually withered and he closes down their argument abruptly and with mounting exasperation: 'Tenez, mon frère, ne parlons point de cet homme-là davantage, car cela m'échauffe la bile, et vous me donneriez mon mal.'

Interpretation of these exchanges has inevitably been coloured by an irony that Molière cannot have anticipated when he wrote and first performed them. Playing the role of Argan, he fell seriously ill on stage towards the end of the fourth performance on 17 February 1673 and died at home a few hours later.[13] If we set this biographical

---

[13] For a discussion of posterity's various reconstructions of the event, see Henry Phillips, 'Molière: The Empty Chair' in *Dying Words: The Last Moments of Writers and Philosophers*, ed. Martin Crowley (Amsterdam: Rodopi, 2000), pp. 23–38.

circumstance to one side, we can see more easily how Molière is attempting to use this metatheatrical discussion. The audience is entertained by his flirting with a break in the illusion of reality and by the dismissive words about Molière spoken by Molière himself playing Argan (just as Alceste, played by Molière, is dismissive of Philinte's reference to *L'École des maris*). We might be tempted to think of the discussion as a defence against potential objections from the medical profession, though, according to Shaw, there is no record of any real doctors having ever complained about Molière's comic portraits of them (p. 141). In dramaturgical terms, Béralde's introduction of the name of Molière is part of his persuasive weaponry. Watching one of Molière's plays that depict doctors would allow Argan, he claims, to respond humorously rather than reverently to the medical profession: plays like *L'Amour médecin* and *Le Médecin malgré lui* invite audiences to laugh at the ignorance and pretentiousness of the doctor characters. He is suggesting that if his own comic satires have failed, Molière's would hit the mark. It is a way of ensuring that the spectators share Béralde's perspective, since they have voluntarily come along to laugh at one of Molière's plays and Béralde is here aligning himself with them. And that Argan (played originally by Molière) takes against the mention of Molière so angrily is a way of ensuring that the audience will laugh at his evident aberration.

When Argan has closed down the topic of Molière, Béralde, unflagging in his rhetorical efforts, attempts a new strategy. He makes the request, unvarnished by teasing or humour (but benefiting from the teasing and humour that he has deployed so far), that Argan consider his daughter's interests rather than his own obsessions when choosing a son-in-law and that he should not, in any event, think of sending her to a convent. With brilliant comic timing, Molière allows Argan to avoid answering the request, as he engineers the entrance on stage of his apothecary, brandishing a syringe.

If we think that Béralde's persuasive efforts stop here, we might possibly conclude, as Fargher does, that he is 'incompetent' (p. 113), though to do so we would have to have been indifferent to his calm mastery of the techniques of satire and to Argan's rude obstinacy. But just because an apothecary interrupts and another scene starts, this does not mean that Béralde is thwarted. He will continue to deploy every means available to him to shake Argan's belief in the necessity of marrying Angélique to a doctor, and he will deftly support Toinette in her own strategy.

PURGON REMOVED (3. 4–5)

The importunate arrival of Monsieur Fleurant that interrupts Béralde turns out to offer him the decisive weapon in defeating Argan's plans to acquire Thomas Diafoirus as a son-in-law. When Argan politely tells his brother that their discussion has to be interrupted so as to allow him to take Fleurant's enema, Béralde replies vigorously, turning his satire against Argan himself: 'Vous vous moquez. Est-ce que vous ne sauriez être un moment sans lavement ou sans médecine? Remettez cela à une autre fois, et demeurez un peu en repos.' The modest request that he makes for a postponement of the enema succeeds instantly. Molière does not spell out why. Does Argan want to spare himself further satirical attacks in front of Fleurant? Is Argan afraid of Fleurant hearing his brother's apparently hostile views of medicine?

At all events, Argan's response, which is to ask Fleurant to come back later, is highly significant. It implies that his brother's rhetorical efforts have had a greater persuasive impact, even if only momentarily, than the sight of Fleurant and his syringe. Argan will immediately regret the postponement. Fleurant flies into a rage, promises to inform Monsieur Purgon, and leaves, issuing unspecific threats: 'Vous verrez, vous verrez …' Throughout all this, Béralde remains controlled and witty. To the rude apothecary, used to looking at his patients' bottoms, Béralde ripostes: 'Allez, Monsieur, on voit bien que vous n'avez pas accoutumé de parler à des visages.' And to the panic-stricken Argan, he offers the comfort of a life freed from medical tyranny: 'Encore un coup, mon frère, est-il possible qu'il n'y ait pas moyen de vous guérir de la maladie des médecins, et que vous vouliez être, toute votre vie, enseveli dans leurs remèdes?' It is important not to interpret this question as a sign that Béralde's aim is permanently to change Argan's outlook on doctors. It is explicitly to modify his outlook in order to help Angélique. But to do this, he is happy, as here, to work on a broader front, and imply the pleasures of a life without hypochondria.

At the very moment that Argan flies into a rage at the suggestion that he might not be ill, Toinette arrives with an incandescent Monsieur Purgon. Béralde speaks not a word during an encounter in which Purgon, egged on by Toinette, accuses an increasingly terrified Argan of rebellion, withdraws his financial support for Angélique's marriage to his nephew, threatens his patient with an incurable illness to strike him down within four days, and takes his leave without even allowing Argan to make peace. Béralde's silence is rhetorically significant. He positively chooses not to speak, since Purgon's outburst gives concrete support to what he has been arguing. At various points, Argan appeals for his help in responding to Purgon: 'Mon frère?', 'C'est mon frère …', 'Ah, mon frère!' Toinette's support for Purgon's preposterously tyrannical stance and Béralde's silence ensure that there is no reconciliation between Argan and Purgon. So in these two scenes Béralde has prepared and presided over the disintegration of his brother's relations with Purgon and dashed his hopes of Angélique's wedding to Thomas. Far from being ineffective, Béralde is taking every opportunity to achieve his aims.

BÉRALDE AND TOINETTE (3. 6–10)

After Toinette has accompanied Purgon out of the room, Béralde has to offer Argan further comfort in his terrorized state. Argan's response to Purgon's fury suggests what his illness really is. It is a pathological combination of fear of, and reverence for, doctors who, he believes, control his state of health.[14] The authoritarian behaviour of Fleurant and Purgon shows how they have acquired this power over him. Argan's terror is based on his view that Purgon is now taking his revenge.

Béralde has not only to offer comfort; he has also to capitalize on his success. Relations with Purgon may well have broken down,

---

[14] This 'diagnosis' does not preclude the alternative one, that Argan suffers from hypochondriacal melancholia, made by Patrick Dandrey in *Le Cas Argan: Molière et la maladie imaginaire* (Paris: Klincksieck, 1993) and repeated in *La Médecine et la maladie dans l'œuvre de Molière*, 2 vols. (Paris: Klincksieck, 1998).

but Argan needs to recognize that he is not dependent on him if he is to be persuaded to allow Angélique to take a husband who is not a doctor. This comforting persuasion happens in four stages. First, Béralde offers assurance by confidently laughing off Argan's fears: 'Ma foi! mon frère, vous êtes fou.' Secondly, with supreme irony, he diagnoses Argan's problem far better than Purgon has done: 'Il me semble, à vous entendre, que Monsieur Purgon tienne dans ses mains le filet de vos jours, et que, d'autorité suprême, il vous l'allonge et vous le raccourcisse comme il lui plaît' (3. 6). Thirdly, he concludes that 'les principes de votre vie sont en vous-même'. This is no proto-existentialist advice. It is specifically a reassurance that Purgon's threats of illness are empty. And finally he suggests that now is the moment when Argan should realize he can do without doctors.

But he does not stop there. He makes a concession: Argan could find a different doctor. What is the significance of this concession? It could indicate the degree of Béralde's concern for his very anxious brother. It could confirm what we have suspected already, namely that the intransigent stance on medicine that he had adopted in 3. 3 was strategic rather than necessarily sincere. And it could also be yet another strategic move. For Béralde knows that Toinette has a plan to eradicate Argan's dependence on Purgon by dressing up as a doctor herself in order to deride Purgon's claims. Toinette has just accompanied the irate Purgon off stage. So Béralde's mention of an alternative doctor could be interpreted by the audience as his preparation for Toinette's charade. And that indeed is how it appears, as she comes back on stage to announce the arrival of an unknown doctor wanting to see Argan.

Toinette's strategy has, over those that Béralde has deployed, the advantage of appearing to show *medical* opinion denouncing Purgon. It appeals to Argan's weakest spot. But it has the very great disadvantage that the doctor is not a real doctor, only Toinette dressed up as one.[15] If she is found out, her strategy will fail. This is why Béralde's role is crucial in these scenes. He says little, but what he does say is calculated to make Argan believe in Toinette's disguise,

---

[15] On the function of Toinette's cross-dressing, see Joseph Harris, *Hidden Agendas: Cross-dressing in seventeenth-century France* (Güttingen: Gunter Narr, 2005), p. 187.

not least at those moments when Argan becomes most suspicious. And he takes the opportunity to comfort Argan further, offering him hope in the unexpected arrival of this new doctor: 'Vous êtes servi à souhait: un médecin vous quitte, un autre se présente' (3. 7). When Toinette first walks on in doctor's garb and Argan remarks on the resemblance to his servant, Béralde points to the ample reassurance offered by countless precedents: 'Il est vrai que la ressemblance est tout à fait grande. Mais ce n'est pas la première fois qu'on a vu de ces sortes de choses, et les histoires ne sont pleines que de ces jeux de la nature' (3. 8). When Argan's suspicions persist, Béralde repeats his earlier reassurance, but adds examples from contemporary reality: 'J'ai lu des choses surprenantes de ces sortes de ressemblances, et nous en avons vu de notre temps où tout le monde s'est trompé' (3. 9). After Toinette's repeated contradiction of Purgon's diagnosis and then of his prescription, and after she has proposed life-threatening remedies, Béralde offers ironic support: 'Voilà un médecin vraiment qui paraît fort habile' (3. 10). Their combined strategies have worked. Argan will not mention Purgon again.

BÉLINE REMOVED (3. 11–12)

With Purgon out of the way, the other obstacle to Angélique's happiness—life in a convent—becomes more ominous. Béralde tries to brush it aside when he takes stock of the situation and attempts to mention Cléante: 'puisque voilà votre Monsieur Purgon brouillé avec vous, ne voulez-vous pas bien que je vous parle du parti qui s'offre pour ma nièce?' (3. 11). But Argan's response not only reminds him of the second obstacle, it simultaneously re-activates it: 'je veux la remettre dans un couvent […] elle sera religieuse, c'est une chose résolue'.

Again Béralde and Toinette work in concert and successfully remove this obstacle. Both know that the root lies not in any desire of Argan's to see his daughter in religious orders, but in his complete blindness to his wife's plan to exploit him maximally by dispatching her step-daughter to a convent. Béralde tackles the issue head-on, but in a friendly spirit: 'oui, mon frère, puisqu'il faut parler à cœur ouvert,

c'est votre femme que je veux dire; et non plus que l'entêtement de
la médecine, je ne puis vous souffrir l'entêtement où vous êtes pour
elle, et voir que vous donniez tête baissée dans tous les pièges qu'elle
vous tend' (3. 11). This direct criticism of Béline gives Toinette the
cue for a new trick with which to disabuse Argan on his wife's score.
She persuades Argan to pretend to be dead when his wife walks in
so as, allegedly, to disprove Béralde's suspicions about her when she
weeps tenderly over his corpse; he will be disabused, of course, by
her display of joy at his demise. Toinette's strategy is more likely to
succeed than Béralde's direct criticism, because she is appealing to
Argan's desire to score points against his brother (that we observed
in 3. 3) and letting Béline discredit herself. But Toinette would not
have been able to deploy this strategy if Béralde had not taken the
bull by the horns and raised the issue of Béline so frankly. After
Béline's downfall, it is Béralde who points to the truth, over whose
revelation he has patiently presided: 'Hé bien! mon frère, vous le
voyez' (3. 12).

MISSION ACCOMPLISHED (3. 13–14)

As if capitalizing on the success of her trick, Toinette persuades
Argan to play dead again in order to demonstrate, by contrast, the
depth of his daughter's love for him and thereby promote Angélique's
interests. Molière engineers laughter by making Cléante burst in and
start pressing his case just as Angélique is weeping over the corpse of
her apparently dead father, vowing to follow his wishes and retreat to
a convent. It is only at the point of Cléante's entry that the audience
gains a full understanding of Béralde's role, for it is now that we
learn that Béralde's arrival at the end of act 2 was at the behest of
Cléante. And when Argan springs joyously back to life and Angélique
and Cléante go to their knees, she to beg not to be forced to marry
anyone other than Cléante, and he to ask to be allowed to marry
her, it falls to Béralde to prompt Argan: 'Mon frère, pouvez-vous
tenir là contre?' (3. 14). And when Argan half relents, agreeing to the
marriage on condition that Cléante becomes a doctor, it falls again
to Béralde to intervene and suggest a solution that will allow them

to marry with no strings attached. In one sense the solution is not necessary, since Cléante has to say, in order to demonstrate his love for Angélique, that he will happily become a doctor. But in a broader dramaturgical sense, Béralde's alternative solution is essential, since it creates the opportunity for the concluding burlesque degree ceremony in which Argan himself becomes a doctor. Béralde turns impresario once again.

The closing lines of spoken dialogue show Béralde triumphantly in control, still deploying all resources available to him, as he said he would, in order to ensure the untroubled wedding of Cléante and his niece. He is able immediately to give Argan a reason why it would be better for Argan himself rather than Cléante to become a doctor: 'faites-vous médecin vous-même. La commodité sera encore plus grande, d'avoir en vous tout ce qu'il vous faut.' When Argan worries about his competence to study, Béralde is able simultaneously to reassure him and to entertain the audience with an ironical reference to the complementary intellectual limitations of both Argan and the medical profession: 'Vous êtes assez savant; et il y en a beaucoup parmi eux qui ne sont pas plus habiles que vous.' Indeed all Béralde's assurances to Argan function simultaneously as winks and nods to the audience and the other characters, acknowledging the trick that is about to be played on him.

When Argan cannot believe he can become a doctor there and then, Béralde's assurance indicates to the audience that he is about to use the resource he had drawn on at the end of act 2, namely the musical players he had brought with him to soothe his brother's anxieties. This is what 'Je connais une Faculté de mes amies, qui viendra tout à l'heure en faire la cérémonie dans votre salle' means to the alert audience. And as Argan goes off to prepare, Béralde offers assurances to Cléante and Angélique. The players he has brought have a burlesque degree ceremony in their repertory. It is harmless, if helpful, fun.

For the third time in the act, he uses the expression 'entre nous': 'Tout ceci n'est qu'entre nous.' Nothing that Béralde does is for real; it is all a private show designed to promote Angélique's interests. That he uses this expression in connection with the fantasy degree ceremony should alert us retrospectively that when he uses it of his arguments about medicine in 3. 3, they should not be weighed too solemnly. The complete absence of solemnity is underscored by his final point: playing roles and making fun of the master of the household is authorized by the time of year. It is carnival: 'Le carnaval autorise cela.' *Le Malade imaginaire* was first performed in February, so the reference to carnival would have created a momentary 'effet de réel' for the audience just before Argan's domestic interior fills with syringe-bearers, apothecaries, doctors, and surgeons, singing and dancing. Angélique is a little anxious about treating her father in this way, and she needs to be persuaded. The compelling argument, which she articulates in the last line of dialogue, is instructive: 'Oui, puisque mon oncle nous conduit.' In his last play, as in some previous ones, Molière concludes the dramatic action with explicit acknowledgement of the benign, helpful and resourceful role played in it by the so-called *raisonneur*.

In his influential interpretation of the evolution of Molière's plays, Defaux presents *Le Malade imaginaire* as the dramatist's climactic portrayal of the triumph of folly and he repeats the words that Béralde uses in his final speech to sum up his view of the comic vision embodied in Molière's later plays: a fool cannot be corrected, one needs to 's'accommoder à ses fantaisies' (p. 298). A close reading of the final act suggests that there are problems with this view of the play. Argan's folly is two-fold and presents two obstacles to Angélique's wedding. One of his follies is, *pace* Defaux, unambiguously cured. His blindness to his wife's greedy scheming is remedied by Toinette's charade.

The fate of his other folly is harder to assess. If we think of it as a blind devotion to Monsieur Purgon (as Toinette presents it in 3. 2), this too is cured as a result of the combined persuasion and trickery of Béralde and Toinette, and of Purgon's own imprecations. Certainly after Toinette's fake doctor has derided Purgon's competence, Argan calls for him no more. It is only if we think of Argan's folly as a dependence on medicine more generally, that Defaux is right to say that he is not cured by the end of the play.

But why is this folly not cured? In terms of the dramatic action, Molière had no need to insist on this general folly, since removing the obstacles caused by Argan's obsessions with Béline and with Purgon is sufficient to pave the way for Angélique's wedding to Cléante, who is happy to become a doctor. Insisting on Argan's general folly by making Béralde propose that Argan become a doctor himself in the burlesque degree ceremony is, in terms of the overall spectacle, absolutely essential, since Molière wants to end his play with a thematically relevant *intermède*. So Molière's insistence on Argan's general medical folly at the very end of the play is probably less a sign of a moliéresque vision of the ineradicability of human folly than a dramatic convenience (not strictly needed to ensure a happy outcome) allowing him to usher in a musical extravaganza.

This perspective on the dramatic action typifies many of the analyses contained in this and the preceding chapters. Critical opinion of the *raisonneurs* has usually been based on an overall vision of Molière's comedy and supported by a limited number of quotations from the plays. By contrast, this book, interpreting the whole role of each *raisonneur*, has attempted to put Molière's dramaturgical needs and comic structures first. Without such ground work, broad interpretations of Molière's comedy and of his *raisonneurs'* role within it are likely to be built on sand. Fully contextualized dramaturgical analysis often adequately accounts for what characters say and do, as it accounts for Argan's failure to be cured of his more general medical folly. It does not preclude further interpretation, like Defaux's. Indeed it is likely to provide firmer foundations for such interpretations.

Conclusion

Je ne veux qu'un seul mot pour finir nos débats.[1]

Concentrating on those five characters whom modern criticism has most consistently called *raisonneurs*, this book has subjected their roles and the commentaries of the critics to close scrutiny. The perspective adopted has been a dramaturgical one. That is to say that the characters' speeches and actions have been examined in the light of the dramatic action and comic structures to which they contribute. This perspective calls into question existing commentary on these roles. The so-called *raisonneurs* emerge neither as the embodiments of wisdom nor as targets of laughter, but rather as agents through which Molière advances and concludes his plots and through which he sharpens the comic focus on the folly of his protagonists.

This account of their role might seem so bland as to be applicable to most characters in Molière's plays. So we should ask if these five *raisonneurs* have enough specific characteristics in common to justify the continued use of a critical term to identify them.

COMMON CHARACTERISTICS

These roles have a good deal in common. First, they are all male friends of a foolish male protagonist, or, if not friends, they are

---

[1] Oronte in *Le Misanthrope* (1667).

brothers or brothers-in-law enjoying friendly relations with the protagonist: Ariste is Sganarelle's elder brother; Chrysalde, Arnolphe's
friend; Cléante, Orgon's brother-in-law; Philinte, Alceste's friend
since infancy; and Béralde, Argan's brother. The *raisonneurs* are male
because the foolish protagonists are necessarily male—the parts that
Molière wrote for himself—and peers who can speak frankly to these
protagonists need to be male too.

Secondly, they all see clearly the folly of the protagonist; their
interactions with him contribute to the dramatic articulation of this
folly; by word and deed, they try to avert its consequences. Sganarelle
ignores Ariste's words of caution about his repressive upbringing of
Isabelle and he gets his come-uppance when she elopes with Valère.
Arnolphe is deaf to Chrysalde's attempts to temper his obsessive
preoccupation with Agnès's fidelity and suffers humiliation after
humiliation. Orgon rejects Cléante's advice that he should easily see
through Tartuffe's mask of religious hypocrisy until the imposter has
almost cuckolded and fleeced him. Despite his misanthropy, Alceste
wants to live among society, but will not listen to Philinte's suggestions
for making such a life tolerable. And Béralde uses multiple strategies
to dislodge Argan's blind faith in his doctor, Purgon.

Thirdly, all these characters are instrumental in the denouement; in
particular, they ensure that the play ends with the prospect of a happy
marriage which is contrary to the wishes of the foolish protagonist.
Ariste sanctions the marriage of Valère and Isabelle. Chrysalde turns
out to be Agnès's uncle and approves her marriage to Horace. With
Tartuffe unmasked and arrested, Cléante transmutes Orgon's fury at
the imposter's treachery into joy at the prospect of Mariane's wedding
to Valère. When Célimène loses the trust of all her lovers, including
that of Alceste, the well-matched Philinte and Éliante provide the
marriage for the denouement. And Béralde ensures that Angélique
can marry Cléante even if he is not a doctor, by suggesting that, if
Argan really wants to have a doctor in the family, he can become one
himself.

Fourthly, the patience with which they treat the foolish protagonist
is instrumental in making him more than a mere fool. Molière's
formula used to defend his portrayal of Arnolphe in *La Critique de
l'École des femmes*, that he is 'ridicule en de certaines choses et honnête
homme en d'autres' (sc. 6), is generally taken to be the key to his

unique combination of comic ingredients: Molière's comedy gains its power by making us laugh at the farcical depiction of folly, but his fools are not so narrowly farcical as to appear purely theatrical creations divorced from the real world. The *raisonneurs* play an important part in breathing an aura of reality into Molière's gallery of comic fools.

Fifthly, they contribute, along with other characters, to channelling the audience's laughter at the protagonist's folly: the patience, care and resourcefulness with which they attempt to manage their friend's peculiar obsession meet variously with impatience, irascibility or mockery, and this clash of temperaments highlights the folly of the protagonist.

And finally, many of the arguments on which the *raisonneurs* draw have their roots in a long tradition of humanist wisdom. It does not follow that Molière's aim in his plays is to express this wisdom or that the *raisonneurs* function as his mouthpiece, since what they say in any given speech is determined by the needs of the dramatic action and the comic structure. None the less, the presence of such discourse within his plays distinguishes them from the farces on which their comic structures are based and gives them an intellectual dimension. In this connection, the *raisonneurs* can be seen to be important in accounting for the Terentian qualities that many contemporaries found in Molière. Terence's comedies were considered, in the seventeenth century, as models of comic drama, on the grounds that they offered excellent examples of Latinity, which schoolchildren could profitably imitate, that they contained useful moral maxims, and that the dramatic action, apparently imitating real life, offered practical moral lessons.[2] When Molière's enemies and rivals were quick to dismiss his plays as farces, based on the famous French farceur Tabarin, who performed earlier in the century, or copied from Italian players with whom Molière shared a theatre, his supporters celebrated in him the allegedly more elevated qualities of Terence. Boileau famously recognized both qualities in Molière's

---

[2] See Georges Forestier, *Molière en toutes lettres* (Paris: Bordas, 1990), pp. 54–66; Emmanuel Bury, 'Comédie et science des mœurs: le modèle de Térence aux xvie et xviie siècles', *Littératures Classiques*, 27 (1996), 125–35; and David Maskell, 'Terence, Tabarin and Molière's *Fourberies de Scapin*', *French Studies*, 56 (2002), 303–15.

work, but was puzzled at the co-existence of 'le bouffon' and 'l'agréable
et le fin'.[3] La Fontaine, however, came to recognize the importance
of the co-existence of different comic strands in Molière's work and
expressed it in a verse epitaph, in which the Roman poet Plautus
stands for farce and fun and Terence for elegance and intellect: 'Sous
ce tombeau gisent Plaute et Térence, / Et cependant le seul Molière
y gît.'[4] The *raisonneurs* straddle the two traditions that make up
Molière's unique blend of comedy: they are one of the mechanisms
by which Molière intensifies the audience's laughter at the sheer folly
of the protagonist, yet their engagement with the protagonist is of
such a nature as to give the plays a moral dimension that Molière's
contemporaries readily associated with Terence.

DIVERGENCES

If the catalogue of common characteristics seems to make these
five *raisonneurs* look like a clear type, we should not neglect major
differences between them, which, at the very least, tend to blur
their group identity. First, while a dramaturgical reading of their
role undermines any suggestion that they are Molière's mouthpieces,
since their speech and actions are determined by dramatic and comic
principles, nevertheless, in the case of Cléante in *Tartuffe*, the evidence
of the anonymous *Lettre sur la comédie de l'imposteur* suggests that
his role was, in significant ways, conceived as a response to those
who sought to maintain the ban on Molière's play; in other words,
Cléante's lines, or some of them, are at least as much determined
by external factors as by comic and dramaturgical ones. This is not
the same as saying that the views he expresses are Molière's personal
views: we shall never know that. But they are views about true
piety which Molière hoped would satisfy those who had objected to
performances of his play. Among the *raisonneurs*, therefore, Cléante
has a role somewhat apart.

---

[3] Nicolas Boileau, *Art Poétique*, canto 3, line 397, in *Œuvres*, 2 vols (Amsterdam: David Morier, 1718).
[4] Jean de La Fontaine, *Œuvres diverses*, ed. Pierre Clarac (Paris: Gallimard, 1958), p. 609.

Secondly, the extent to which these characters participate in the dramatic action is variable. Cléante and Béralde are both resolutely pro-active. They are both explicitly called upon to intervene in the dramatic action and to attempt to influence the protagonist. In both cases the protagonist wishes to marry his daughter to someone she does not love; the *raisonneurs*, brother-in-law and brother with a vested interest in the family's affairs, try to shake the protagonist's faith in such a marriage and to persuade him to allow his daughter to marry someone she actually loves. In both cases their efforts contribute to a successful outcome, even if the efforts of others are equally, or more, important. By contrast, the role of Ariste, Chrysalde and Philinte in the dramatic action is quite different. Two of them are friends of the protagonist (rather than related by blood ties) and they are essentially reactive. They can foresee disasters resulting from the folly of the protagonist and they attempt, to different extents, to avert them. In these three cases, the wedding in prospect is that of the protagonist to an arguably unsuitable partner. These three *raisonneurs* try variously and vainly to modify the attitude of the protagonist to the woman in question; but the promotion of an alternative wedding is not on the agenda until the end of the play when the alternative wedding provides the denouement. In this respect, moreover, Philinte is different again from both Ariste and Chrysalde, since the alternative wedding is his own; and he marries the woman whom Alceste thought he could keep in reserve for himself. This suggestion of rivalry in love strikes a different note in the relationship between Alceste and Philinte to the one perceptible in other relationships between the *raisonneurs* and the protagonists. And Philinte differs from all the *raisonneurs* by virtue of his aristocratic status.

Thirdly, the *raisonneurs* differ from each other significantly in terms of their presence in the plays. Philinte is Alceste's almost constant companion, present in four of the play's five acts. Chrysalde and Cléante are present in the first, fourth and fifth acts. Ariste, however, appears only at the beginning and end of *L'École des maris*; the dramatic action preceding the denouement evolves without any intervention on his part. And Béralde appears only at the very end of the second act of *Le Malade imaginaire* and is present throughout the third and final act.

DRAMATURGIES

What this list of differences and similarities between the roles of these five *raisonneurs* alerts us to is the variety to be found within apparently similar dramaturgical structures. It is helpful, in understanding the dramaturgical function of the *raisonneurs*, to broaden the perspective to the whole corpus of Molière's plays. In the absence of a full dramaturgical study of Molière the following remarks are inevitably partial and tentative. They are intended to highlight, by contrast with other plays, dramaturgical features of those plays in which the *raisonneurs* appear. No simple dramaturgical formula will embrace the whole of Molière's dramatic output. But a useful way of approaching the different dramaturgies in operation in his plays is to consider the kind of roles he wrote for himself. Two dominant structures emerge that underpin the majority (though certainly not all) of his plays: Molière as servant, and Molière as figure of authority.[5]

In some of his plays, Molière gives himself the role of a servant. These plays fall into two categories: one, in which the servant's role dominates the dramatic action, propelling it along through displays of cunning and resourcefulness (like Mascarille in *L'Étourdi*, Scapin in *Les Fourberies de Scapin*, and Mascarille in *Les Précieuses Ridicules*); the other, in which the servant's role is subsidiary in the dramatic action, but in which he is a constant or episodic, ironic or foolish commentator on the action and its participants (like Sganarelle in *Dom Juan*, Moron in *La Princesse d'Élide*, and Clitidas in *Les Amants magnifiques*).

Sganarelle's role in *Dom Juan* has sometimes been thought of as comparable to that of the *raisonneurs*. Dom Juan behaves in ways that offend conventional morality and Sganarelle questions and taxes him on this. But Sganarelle is, of course, a patently comic character, so different in that respect from the *raisonneurs*; and Peacock deals with him by suggesting that his role is a parody of the *raisonneur*

---

[5] See Roger W. Herzel, *The Original Casting of Molière's Plays* (Ann Arbor, Michigan: UMI Research Press, 1981) and H. Gaston Hall, 'Molière's Roles Written for Himself', *Australian Journal of French Studies*, 33 (1996), 414–27.

role.[6] While this is an attractive view, parody requires that there are significant points of contact between the subject and the object of parody for it to be recognized as such, and Sganarelle's role seems to me to be so different dramaturgically from that of the *raisonneurs* as to be barely perceptible as metatheatrical parody. Sganarelle's was the role originally played by Molière. He consistently attracts audience laughter. He is almost constantly present on stage. There is no relationship of equality between him and Dom Juan; if they discourse in ways surprising for a master-servant relationship, their social difference is emphasized rather than minimized. Sganarelle is invited to argue with his master, but on condition that he does not remonstrate with him: 'vous savez bien que vous me permettez les disputes, et que vous ne me défendez que les remontrances' (3. 1). Above all, he is not in any sense a strategist, trying to engage with the protagonist on behalf of others with an eye to a successful outcome in the dramatic action: he does not try to propose realistic solutions to Dom Juan's problems. The action of the play, in any case, is a series of loosely related comic episodes. Sganarelle is fitfully concerned for his master or for the victims of his master's high-handed whims; but mostly he is concerned with saving his own skin. He is a sustained example of one of those risible, forward, yet cowardly, servants played by Molière, a comic commentator on, rather than an agent in, the dramatic action.

In other plays, Molière gives himself the role of an authority figure, intent on an obviously unsuitable wedding either for himself or for his children, and/or intent on blocking the wedding plans of one or more of his children. These plays can be divided into those in which the actions of the authority figure are governed by his particular delusion or obsession; and those in which his actions are not governed by any such delusion or obsession. In the latter category is a play like *L'Amour médecin*, where Sganarelle is opposed to his daughter's desire to marry for no other reason than that 'je veux garder mon bien et ma fille pour

   6 Noël Peacock, 'The Comic Role of the *Raisonneur* in Molière's Theatre', *Modern Language Review*, 76 (1981), 298–310, p. 309. For a dramaturgical reading of *Dom Juan* see Georges Forestier, 'Langage dramatique et langage symbolique dans le *Dom Juan* de Molière' in *Dramaturgies. Langages dramatiques. Mélanges pour Jacques Scherer* (Paris: Nizet, 1986), pp. 293–305.

moi' (1. 6), which he never elaborates further. The former category, however, includes *L'École des maris*, *L'École des femmes*, *Tartuffe*, *Le Misanthrope* and *Le Malade imaginaire*, precisely those plays in which we find the so-called *raisonneurs*.

The reason we find the *raisonneurs* in this one category of Molière's plays can be understood dramaturgically. Molière needs to frame a dramatic action around the attempts of individuals to persuade the authority figure to relent. Servants, lovers and wives can all attempt such persuasion. In *L'Amour médecin* lovers and servants combine forces and use scheming to overcome Sganarelle's objections to Lucinde's wedding to Clitandre. But if the authority figure's objection is rooted in a delusion or obsession, any techniques of rational persuasion need to include a level of discourse and confrontation with the protagonist that neither wives, lovers nor servants could plausibly initiate or sustain. Close friends and brothers, however, being the social and sexual equals of the protagonists, can provide that additional level of interaction needed to tackle his folly or delusion in explicit terms. This dramaturgical consideration explains the presence of the *raisonneur* in the dramatic action of the five plays that have formed the basis of this book.

But there are other plays that fall into this same dramaturgical category: most notably, *L'Avare* (1668), *Le Bourgeois Gentilhomme* (1670), and *Les Femmes savantes* (1672). Do these plays not also have *raisonneurs*? The answer reveals more about the dramaturgical structures that Molière deploys.

A superficial description of the dramatic action of *L'Avare* suggests that there should be a role for a *raisonneur*. Obsessed with avarice, Harpagon intends to marry his son to a widow and his daughter to a rich widower. He is opposed to the matches that they themselves want: Cléante wishes to marry Mariane (but Harpagon intends to marry her himself) and Élise wishes to marry Valère. The dramatic agents who work against Harpagon (to different degrees and in different ways) are the four young lovers along with the *entremetteuse* Frosine, who has brokered Harpagon's marriage with Mariane, but is prepared to work to undo it in view of his failure to give her a reward. As Defaux says, 'plus aucun raisonneur ne vient sur scène essayer de lui démontrer qu'il a tort'.[7] For Defaux, of course, this is evidence for his view that Molière's later plays are dominated by a celebratory vision of human folly as something which no powers of reasoning can overcome, but which can only be indulged.

There is, however, a dramaturgical explanation for the absence of a *raisonneur* character in *L'Avare*.[8] Molière structures the dramatic action so as to emphasize Harpagon's own plan to marry Mariane. Although he announces his intentions for his children in 1. 5 and although the audience knows (from information about Élise's and Cléante's loves revealed in 1. 1 and 1. 2) that these are contradictory to his children's wishes, Molière organizes the action so that it is only very late in the play when Harpagon discovers that his children wish to marry different people from those he has himself chosen for them: in 4. 3 he learns that Cléante is his rival for Mariane and only in 5. 3 that Valère wishes to marry Élise. Molière has, therefore, created a dramatic structure in which there would be no (or only minimal) space for a *raisonneur* like Cléante or Béralde to intervene on behalf of Harpagon's children by tackling him on the subject of his avarice, since Harpagon does not, until late in the play, become an active obstacle to their desires. Instead, Molière has privileged, in the dramatic action, Harpagon's own projected marriage to Mariane and the young lovers' plans to take anticipatory steps that might ensure a happy outcome whether by indirect persuasion (Valère of Harpagon, Mariane of her non-appearing mother), or by looking for a long-lost rich father (Valère finds Anselme), or by preparing to elope (Cléante), or by trickery (Frosine suggests a scheme to make Harpagon abandon his plans for Mariane, though it is not realized), or by a mixture of theft and blackmail (the servant La Flèche steals Harpagon's 10,000 crowns and Cléante makes agreement to his wedding Mariane the condition of its restitution). What in the end ensures the happy outcome is a combination of Valère's discovery of his rich father (who also turns out to be the father of Mariane) and Cléante's blackmail.

---

[7] Gérard Defaux, *Molière ou les métamorphoses du comique: de la comédie morale au triomphe de la folie* (Lexington: French Forum, 1980; 2nd edn, Paris: Klincksieck, 1992), p. 196.

[8] Jonathan Mallinson notes that the absence of a *raisonneur* makes the foolish protagonist 'unusually prominent' in *Molière: 'L'Avare'* (London: Grant and Cutler Ltd, 1988), p. 84.

Similarly, the dramatic structure and the nature of Harpagon's folly do not allow for a *raisonneur* like Ariste or Chrysalde to engage conflictually with Harpagon at the beginning of the play. Ariste and Chrysalde are able to tackle the folly or mad-cap ideas of Sganarelle and Arnolphe respectively, since these are flagrantly at odds with Sganarelle's and Arnolphe's aspirations for married life. Sganarelle and Arnolphe both think that their strict education of Isabelle and Agnès will ensure that they have faithful and obedient wives, and the *raisonneurs* can question this assumption comically and conflictually. But an early interaction between Harpagon and a *raisonneur* would be dramatically flaccid, because Harpagon's decision to marry Mariane is quite unrelated to his avarice. A *raisonneur* would therefore have to talk about Harpagon's avarice in the abstract. But abstract discussion, unrelated to the contingencies of a specific dramatic action, would be completely at odds with Molière's practice. Alternatively, a *raisonneur* could discuss Harpagon's marriage plans without reference to his avarice, but any such discussion would lack a critical edge, since there would be no reason for a *raisonneur* to object to these plans, as long as Molière keeps Cléante's rivalry for Mariane's hand a secret from Harpagon until act 4. Dramaturgical analysis of this kind does not necessarily invalidate Defaux's views, but it suggests that considerations of dramatic structure should take precedence over statements about Molière's comic vision.

Analysis of *Le Bourgeois Gentilhomme* leads to the same conclusion. Because of his obsession with the aristocracy, Jourdain objects to the marriage of his daughter Lucile to Cléonte on the grounds that Cléonte is not noble. While some critics have suggested that Mme Jourdain fulfils the role of the *raisonneur* in this play,[9] she has none of the common characteristics of the other *raisonneurs*. She is a woman, not a man (though the role was originally played by a man in drag); a wife, not a friend. She is hectoring and not at all patient. And she does nothing herself to ensure a happy outcome. Two reasons might explain why Molière does not write a role for a *raisonneur*. One is that, with the parade of tutors, musicians and dancers that fill the first

---

[9] See, for example, Richard Fargher, 'Molière and his Reasoners' in *Studies in French Literature presented to H. W. Lawton*, ed. J. C. Ireson and others (Manchester University Press, 1968), pp. 105–20, p. 111.

two acts, Molière is more interested in the comic demonstration of Jourdain's folly rather than the attempt to talk him out of it. Another is that the longed-for marriage is adequately safeguarded by the charade whereby Cléonte comes on as a member of the Turkish nobility, and is therefore deemed a suitable match for Lucile by Jourdain.

Again, for Defaux (p. 280), this abandonment of the *raisonneur* and the indulgence of the protagonist's folly is expressive of Molière's later comic vision of an irremediably foolish world. But yet again, the explanation could also be more practical, more dramaturgical: after *L'École des maris*, *L'École des femmes*, *Tartuffe* and *Le Misanthrope*, entirely spoken comedies written for performance on the public stage in Paris though the very first performance of *Tartuffe* was at Versailles, Molière introduces into the same dramaturgical structure as these earlier plays an abundance of music and dancing in a spectacle intended for first performance before the court at Chambord, and this has consequences for the relative balance of the familiar and the new components. In *Le Bourgeois Gentilhomme*, Molière sacrifices the *raisonneur* on the altar of a spectacular musical charade. In dramaturgical terms the *ballet turc* fulfils a similar function to the role of a *raisonneur*, neutralizing the foolish protagonist so that he will allow the marriage of his daughter, though in terms of theatrical presence the two are of course immeasurably different. In *Le Malade imaginaire*, which also has musical interludes, the *raisonneur* is resuscitated, but Molière balances the components differently: though the *raisonneur* is reintroduced, his presence is smaller and his role is intimately bound up with the musical charade, which he himself initiates as the means of persuading Argan to subscribe to the wedding of Angélique and Cléante.

In between *Le Bourgeois Gentilhomme* (1670) and *Le Malade imaginaire* (1673), *Les Femmes savantes* reveals further dramaturgical experimentation with consequences for the role of the *raisonneur*. There is one character in the play who has features in common with the other *raisonneurs*: Ariste. He is the brother of Chrysale, who was played by Molière and whose daughter Henriette wants to marry Clitandre. Ariste is explicitly enlisted by Clitandre to help promote his marriage to Henriette. Making claims that resemble those of the *raisonneurs* Cléante and Béralde in their respective plays, he promises to do all he can to help them and to oppose the marriage of Henriette to the poet Trissotin, whom she does not love: 'J'appuierai, presserai, ferai tout ce qu'il faut' (330), 'J'emploierai toute chose à servir votre amour' (1448). And he invents a trick to remove the obstacle of Trissotin, so ensuring that Henriette and Clitandre can marry.

So why has Ariste not consistently been called a *raisonneur*? The explanation is dramaturgical. It is because the interventions with his brother do not have the same powerfully conflictual and intellectual basis as those of other *raisonneurs*. And this is because of a novelty that Molière has introduced into the dramatic structure of this play. Chrysale himself is only *indirectly* an obstacle to Henriette's wedding to Clitandre; indeed he very much wants the wedding to take place. It is his domineering wife Philaminte, obsessed with ostentatious learning, who wants their daughter to marry a poet. So Chrysale is an obstacle to the wedding which his daughter desires only to the extent that he is spineless before his wife's will. Ariste's role (in 2.2–4) is, therefore, to stiffen his brother's resolve against his wife. The encounter has quite a different tenor from that of previous discussions between *raisonneurs* and protagonists, since Chrysale readily agrees to be firm and is confident that he can stand up to Philaminte. The comic structure deployed by Molière is that of showing a character riding for a fall, because when, moments later, he comes face to face with his wife, his resolve instantly evaporates (2.6–8).

The action, therefore, depends on two conflicting authority figures, but the *raisonneur* engages with the one who is only a subsidiary obstacle in the dramatic action and who is not the victim of a comic obsession. The real obstacle, with delusions to boot, is Philaminte. But it would not be plausible to show Ariste trying to dislodge Philaminte's obsession in private discussion, since such discussions only take place between individuals who enjoy a close and friendly relationship, and not between individuals of the opposite sex. Ariste's role clearly derives from that of previous *raisonneurs*, and Molière retains it because it allows him to depict his own role (Chrysale) engaging comically with a social equal. But Molière's subject matter, women obsessed with showy learning, means that Ariste cannot engage so directly with the deluded authority figure as his predecessors did. For such engagement, the dramatist substitutes Ariste's successful trick at the end of the play, without which a happy denouement would not be possible. While closely modelled on the roles of previous *raisonneurs*,

Ariste has fewer characteristics in common with them than they have with each other, because of the dramaturgical innovation whereby the main obstacle character with a delusion is not Ariste's social or sexual equal.

COMMONPLACE CULTURE

This book has sought to understand the role of the *raisonneurs* by detailed examination of the dramaturgy of the plays and to use this predominantly internal evidence to cut through the conflicting views that critics have hitherto expressed of their roles. There is, however, a broader context in which the phenomenon might be understood and which offers a view of the *raisonneurs'* apparently sententious utterances that happily complements the view offered by dramaturgical analysis. This context is that of the commonplace culture such as it has been presented by Terence Cave.[10] It is a culture in which, from early days at school, individuals become used to reading books with an eye to the nicely phrased maxim and neatly expressed example and to making use of these same commonplaces in their own writing.

Cave's survey of the evolution of the early modern commonplace culture provides a way of understanding how the *raisonneurs* eventually came to be seen as problematic characters. The commonplace culture was at its height in the Renaissance and into the seventeenth century: 'the increasingly labyrinthine modes of organisation of the commonplace book itself are attempts to handle an exponential proliferation of possible opinions and observations' (p. 39); the result is that the doxa became unstable, 'a breeding ground for the orthodox and the heterodox' (p. 39). Prime examples are Rabelais' encyclopaedically learned fictions and Montaigne's *Essais*, all rich in the quotation and citation of commonplaces. By the eighteenth

---

[10] Terence Cave, 'Thinking with Commonplaces: The Example of Rabelais' in *(Re)Inventing the Past: Essays on French Early Modern Culture, Literature and Thought in Honour of Ann Moss*, ed. Gary Ferguson and Catherine Hampton (University of Durham Modern Languages Series, 2003), pp. 35–49.

century, however, 'philosophies and systems of discursive knowledge will become less radically open and plural, and consequently more susceptible of univocal interpretation' (p. 40). This evolution explains the predominance, since the eighteenth century, of a critical desire to know what authors, including Molière, thought; it explains the urge to find globalizing, univocal interpretations of texts that, participating in the commonplace culture, inevitably give voice to many opinions.

Cave specifically mentions Molière's plays as late-flowering examples of this culture, 'where the voice of the so-called *raisonneur* reiterates prudential commonplaces in opposition to what are often themselves deformed commonplaces (Arnolphe's moralizing discourse, the Jesuitical arguments of Tartuffe, the discourse of the doctors and of Argan himself)' (p. 40). This broad cultural context helps to explain why Molière's original audiences were not perplexed by the plurivocalism to be found in his plays; and it particularly helps to put paid to further attempts to discover Molière's own voice amidst the many.

Cave's comments on Molière are suggestive, but need to be treated with the following cautions. They risk entrenching the common view that the role of the *raisonneurs* is to make sententious utterances. But as I have attempted to show, such utterances make up just one of the rhetorical strategies deployed by the *raisonneurs* in the fulfilment of their dramaturgical function. Moreover, it would be misleading to think that Molière's resort to commonplaces is somehow uniquely associated with the *raisonneurs*. In the aristocratic *divertissement* that is *La Princesse d'Élide*, written to entertain king and court in 1664, the eponymous heroine prefers nature and hunting to love and accordingly refuses to participate in the public festivities that her father has organized. Molière writes a scene in which her two cousins try to prevail upon her. It is composed of relentlessly juxtaposed, contradictory sententious (or quasi-sententious) utterances like the following (2. 1):[11]

CYNTHIE   Et serait-ce un bonheur de respirer le jour
               Si d'entre les mortels on bannissait l'amour?

---

[11] Molière was writing the play in verse until the need for haste made him complete it in prose. The switch from verse to prose occurs in the middle of the scene from which these quotations are taken.

> Non, non, tous les plaisirs se goûtent à le suivre,
> Et vivre sans aimer n'est pas proprement vivre. (363–6)

AGLANTE   je tiens que cette passion est la plus agréable affaire de la vie; qu'il est nécessaire d'aimer pour vivre heureusement, et que tous les plaisirs sont fades, s'il ne s'y mêle un peu d'amour.

AGLANTE   l'Amour sait se venger des mépris que l'on fait de lui.

PRINCESSE le grand pouvoir qu'on donne [à l'amour] n'est rien qu'une chimère, qu'une excuse des faibles cœurs, qui le font invincible pour autoriser leur faiblesse.

CYNTHIE   toute la terre reconnaît la puissance [de l'amour].

PRINCESSE Les croyances publiques sont toujours mêlées d'erreur: les dieux ne sont point faits comme se les fait le vulgaire; et c'est leur manquer de respect que de leur attribuer les faiblesses des hommes.

The commonplace culture is a useful framework for considering the richly varied views expressed by characters in Molière's plays—by all his characters, and not only the *raisonneurs*—and for appreciating his contemporary audience's easy acceptance of such a polyphony.

Another, and parallel way of considering this polyphony, is with reference to dramatic form. The commonplace culture is strongly felt in Rabelais' fictions, Montaigne's *Essais* and even La Rochefoucauld's *Maximes*, all the more so as these forms do not generically *require* a polyphony of contradictions, though these particular works do contain radical instances of polyphonic writing that are explicable in terms of the commonplace culture. Drama, however, is different. It is of necessity conflictual: characters with different desires and opinions are constantly set in dialogue with one another. So if the context provided by the commonplace culture helps us to understand the horizons of expectation of Molière's original audiences, only dramaturgical analysis will explain why certain characters appear to advance certain opinions at certain moments in the dramatic action. Among the polyphony of opposing voices to be heard in Molière's plays, there is one that is sufficiently distinctive for critics to have identified it as belonging to the group of characters known as *raisonneurs*. To imply that they speak with one voice would be misleading since the dramaturgical and intellectual divergences between them are as prominent as the similarities. One aim in this book has been to let each of these characters speak in his own voice without seeking to impose a reductionist interpretation of their roles. Even so, the common denominators are striking. The *raisonneurs* are found in that category of play that revolves around a deluded male protagonist with inappropriate marriage plans. They use their friendly relations with the protagonist to engage with him in a way in which no other character can.

The name *raisonneur* was applied to them first in the 1890s. It implies a view of the seventeenth century as a century of reason, to which Molière was allegedly devoted and to the celebration of which his plays allegedly contributed, most notably through this group of characters. Such a view has not been tenable for many years and it finds no comfort in the dramaturgical approach to Molière's plays adopted in this book. Nevertheless, the misleading name is likely to stick since it enjoys overwhelming critical currency, as critics constantly endeavour to attach new senses to it.

My detailed analyses of entire roles in a dramaturgical perspective are a challenge to prevailing views of the *raisonneurs*, whether as primarily exponents of humanist wisdom or as comic figures in their own right. For all that they have consumed large amounts of the attention and energies of Molière's critics, they constitute a quantitively small part of his output, featuring in five or at most six (if we include *Les Femmes savantes*) out of some thirty plays. The plays in question, however, include some of Molière's most lasting, theatrically lively, controversial and intellectually vigorous plays. These characters might have more to do with Molière's contemporary and posthumous success than their unassuming manner and perennially problematic status might suggest. They are, moreover, an original creation of Molière: only Ariste in *L'École des maris* can be said to have a source in the dramatic texts on which Molière possibly drew, but Molière's Ariste is dramaturgically quite different from Terence's Micio in the *Adelphi*.[12] Above all, they are first and foremost rhetorical

---

[12] See Claude Bourqui, *Les Sources de Molière: répertoire critique des sources littéraires et dramatiques* (Paris: SEDES, 1999), pp. 52, 58. Molière's originality in creating the role of the *raisonneur* can be compared to Racine's flexible handling of the dramatic convention of *confident*. On this see Valerie Worth-Stylianou, *Confidential Strategies:*

strategists, ready to use rational argument, but also emotional pressure, humour, ridicule, trickery and deceit; their words and actions are best interpreted in the full context of the dramatic action, to which they contribute in different degrees, always seeking ways to ensure a happy outcome; and their variously patient and teasing engagements with the protagonist serve to maximize audience laughter at some of Molière's most compelling fools.

The Evolving Role of the Confident in French Tragic Drama (1635–77) (Geneva: Droz, 1999), p. 205 (for an assessment of Racine's approach to the role).

Bibliography

Albanese, Ralph, *Molière à l'école républicaine: de la critique universitaire aux manuels scolaires (1870–1914)*, Saratago, CA: ANMA Libri, 1992.

Andrews, Richard, 'Arte Dialogue Structures in the Comedies of Molière' in *The Commedia dell'arte from the Renaissance to Dario Fo*, ed. Christopher Cairns, Lewiston, Queenstown, Lampeter: Edwin Mellen, 1989, pp. 142–76.

Aristotle, *L'Éthique à Nicomaque*, ed. R. A. Gautier and J. Y. Jolif, 2nd edn, Louvain-la-Neuve: Peeters, 2002.

Barnwell, H. T., *Molière: 'Le Malade imaginaire'*, London: Grant and Cutler Ltd, 1982.

_____ *The Tragic Drama of Corneille and Racine: An Old Parallel Revisited*, Oxford: Clarendon Press, 1982.

Baschera, Marco, *Théâtralité dans l'œuvre de Molière*, Tübingen: Gunter Narr Biblio 17, 1998.

Bellegarde, abbé de, *Réflexions sur le ridicule et sur les moyens de l'éviter*, Paris: Jean Guignard, 1696.

Bellenger, Yvonne and others (eds.), *L'Art du théâtre: mélanges en hommage à Robert Garapon*, Paris: Presses Universitaires de France, 1992.

Bergson, Henri, *Le Rire: essai sur la signification du comique*, Paris: Presses Universitaires de France, 1978.

Bertrand, Dominique, 'Bruit et silence: la voix rieuse au XVIIe siècle, ses enjeux scientifiques, sémiotiques, et disciplinaires', *Littératures Classiques*, 12 (1990), 101–15.

_____ *Dire le rire à l'âge classique*, Aix-en-Provence: Publications de l'Université de Provence, 1995.

_____ 'De la légitimité du rire comme critère de la comédie (XVIe–XVIIe siècles)', *Littératures Classiques*, 27 (1996), 161–70.

Bloch, Olivier, *Molière/Philosophie*, Paris: Albin Michel, 2000.

Boileau, Nicolas, *Œuvres*, 2 vols., Amsterdam: David Morier, 1718.

Bourqui, Claude, *Polémiques et stratégies dans le Dom Juan de Molière*, Paris-Seattle-Tübingen: Biblio 17 PFSCL, 1992.

_____ *Les Sources de Molière: répertoire critique des sources littéraires et dramatiques*, Paris: SEDES, 1999.

_____ *La Commedia dell'arte: introduction au théâtre professionnel italien entre le XVIe et le XVIIIe siècles*, Paris: SEDES, 2000.

Bourqui, Claude, and Claudio Vinti, *Molière à l'école italienne: le lazzo dans la création moliéresque*, Paris and Turin: L'Harmattan, 2003.

Bradby, David, and Andrew Calder, *The Cambridge Companion to Molière*, Cambridge University Press, 2006.

Bray, René, *Molière: homme de théâtre*, Paris: Mercure de France, 1954.

Brunetière, Ferdinand, 'Études sur le xviie siècle 4', *Revue des deux mondes*, 100 (1890), 649–87.

Bury, Emmanuel, 'Comédie et science des mœurs: le modèle de Térence aux xvie et xviie siècles', *Littératures Classiques*, 27 (1996), 125–35.

Butler, Philip, '*Tartuffe* et la direction spirituelle', in Cairncross, *L'Humanité de Molière*, 1988, *q.v.*, pp. 57–69.

——— 'Orgon le dirigé', in Cairncross, *L'Humanité de Molière*, 1988, *q.v.*, pp. 125–35.

Cairncross, John, *New Light on Molière*, Geneva: Droz, 1956.

——— (ed.), *L'Humanité de Molière*, Paris: Nizet, 1988.

Calder, Andrew, *Molière: The Theory and Practice of Comedy*, London: The Athlone Press, 1993.

Calder, Ruth, 'Molière, Misanthropy and Forbearance: Éliante's "Lucretian" Diatribe', *French Studies*, 50 (1996), 138–43.

Caldicott, C. E. J., 'La cour, la ville et la province: Molière's Mixed Audiences', *Seventeenth-Century French Studies*, 10 (1988), 72–87.

——— 'L'Inspiration italienne ou la permanence du jeu dans *Le Malade Imaginaire*', in Cairncross, *L'Humanité de Molière*, 1988, *q.v.*, pp. 179–86.

——— *La Carrière de Molière entre protecteurs et éditeurs*, Amsterdam: Rodopi, 1998.

Canova-Green, Marie-Claude, 'Présentation et représentation dans *Le Bourgeois gentilhomme* ou le jeu des images et des rôles', *Littératures Classiques*, 21 (1994), 79–90.

Cave, Terence, 'Thinking with Commonplaces: The Example of Rabelais' in *(Re)Inventing the Past: Essays on French Early Modern Culture, Literature and Thought in Honour of Ann Moss*, ed. Gary Ferguson and Catherine Hampton, University of Durham Modern Languages Series, 2003, pp. 35–49.

Cicero, *Dialogues de la vieillesse et de l'amitié*, Paris: La Veuve Jean Camusat, 1640.

Collinet, Jean-Pierre, *Lectures de Molière*, Paris: Armand Colin, 1974.

Conesa, Gabriel, 'Remarques sur la structure dramatique de *L'École des femmes*', *Revue d'histoire du théâtre*, 30 (1978), 120–6.

——— *Le Dialogue moliéresque: étude stylistique et dramaturgique*, Paris: Presses Universitaires de France, 1983 (2nd edn, Paris: SEDES-CDU, 1992).

_____ 'Molière et l'héritage du jeu comique italien', in Bellenger and others (eds.), *L'Art du théâtre*, 1992, *q.v.*, pp. 177–87.

_____ 'La Question des tons dans *Le Malade imaginaire*', *Littératures Classiques*, supplement (1993), 45–60.

_____ *La Comédie de l'âge classique: 1630–1715*, Paris: Seuil, 1995.

_____ 'Le Misanthrope ou les limites de l'aristotélisme', *Littératures classiques*, 38 (2000), 19–29.

Cronk, Nicholas, 'Molière-Charpentier's *Le Malade imaginaire*: The First Opéra-Comique?', *Forum for Modern Language Studies*, 29 (1993), 216–31.

_____ 'The Play of Words and Music in Molière-Charpentier's *Le Malade imaginaire*', *French Studies*, 47 (1993), 6–19.

Dandrey, Patrick, *Molière ou l'esthétique du ridicule*, Paris: Klincksieck, 1992.

_____ *Le Cas Argan: Molière et la maladie imaginaire*, Paris: Klincksieck, 1993.

_____ 'La Comédie du ridicule', *Littératures classiques*, supplement (1993), 7–23.

_____ *La Médecine et la maladie dans l'œuvre de Molière*, 2 vols., Paris: Klincksieck, 1998.

Defaux, Gérard, 'Un point chaud de la critique moliéresque: Molière et ses raisonneurs', *Travaux de linguistique et de littérature*, 18(2) (1980), 115–32.

_____ *Molière ou les métamorphoses du comique: de la comédie morale au triomphe de la folie*, Lexington: French Forum, 1980 (2nd edn, Paris: Klincksieck, 1992) *Dictionnaire de l'Académie Françoise*, 2 vols., Paris: J.-B. Coignard, 1694.

Dock, Stephen Varick, *Costume and Fashion in the Plays of Jean-Baptiste Poquelin Molière: A Seventeenth-Century Perspective*, Geneva: Slatkine, 1992.

Emelina, Jean, *Les Valets et les servantes dans le théâtre de Molière*, Aix-en-Provence: La Pensée universitaire, 1958.

_____ *Le Comique: essai d'interprétation générale*, Paris: SEDES, 1991.

_____ 'A propos de Molière moraliste', *Seventeenth-Century French Studies*, 16 (1994), 155–60.

_____ *Comédie et tragédie*, Publications de la Faculté des Lettres, Arts et Sciences Humaines de Nice, 1998.

Eustis, Alvin, *Molière as Ironic Comtemplator*, The Hague, Paris: Mouton, 1973.

Faguet, Émile, *En lisant Molière: l'homme et son temps, l'écrivain et son œuvre*, Paris: Hachette, 1914.

Fargher, Richard, 'Molière and his Reasoners', in *Studies in French Literature presented to H.W. Lawton*, ed. J. C. Ireson and others, Manchester University Press, 1968, pp. 105–20.

Ferreyrolles, Gérard, *Molière: Tartuffe*, Paris: Presses Universitaires de France, 1987.

Fleck, Stephen, *Music, Dance and Laughter: Comic Vision in Molière's Comedy-Ballets*, Paris, Seattle, Tübingen: PFSCL, 1995.

Florent, François, *Pour jouer Molière*, Paris: Panama, 2006.

Force, Pierre, *Molière ou le prix des choses: morale, économie, comédie*, Paris: Nathan, 1994.

Forestier, Georges, 'Langage dramatique et langage symbolique dans le *Dom Juan* de Molière', in *Dramaturgies. Langages dramatiques. Mélanges pour Jacques Scherer*, Paris: Nizet, 1986, pp. 293–305.

——— *Molière en toutes lettres*, Paris: Bordas, 1990.

——— 'Le Classicisme de Molière ou la quête de la reconnaissance littéraire', *Information littéraire*, 42 (1990), 17–20.

——— *Essai de génétique théâtrale: Corneille à l'œuvre*, Paris: Klincksieck, 1996.

——— 'Dramaturgie racinienne (petit essai de génétique théâtrale)', *Littératures classiques*, 26 (1996), 13–38.

——— 'Structure de la comédie française classique', *Littératures Classiques*, 27 (1996), 243–57.

Fournier, Nathalie, 'Dialogue et polyphonie conversationnelle dans *Les Fourberies de Scapin*, *La Comtesse d'Escarbagnas*, *Les Femmes savantes* et *Le Malade imaginaire*', *Dix-septième siècle*, 177 (1992), 561–6.

Fumaroli, Marc, 'Aveuglement et désabusement dans *Le Malade imaginaire*' in M. T. Jones-Davies (ed.), *Vérité et illusion dans le théâtre au temps de la Renaissance*, Paris: Jean Touzot, 1983, pp. 105–14.

Gaines, James, *Social Structures in Molière's Theater*, Columbus: Ohio State University Press, 1984.

——— (ed.), *The Molière Encyclopedia*, Westport: Greenwood Press, 2003.

Garapon, Robert, *Le Dernier Molière*, Paris: SEDES-CDU, 1977.

Gossman, Lionel, *Men and Masks: A Study of Molière*, Baltimore: Johns Hopkins Press, 1963.

Grimm, Jürgen, *Molière en son temps*, Paris, Seattle, Tübingen: PFSCL, 1993.

Gross, Nathan, *From Gesture to Idea: Esthetics and Ethics in Molière's Comedy*, New York: Columbia University Press, 1982.

Guicharnaud, Jacques, *Molière: une aventure théâtrale*, Paris: Gallimard, 1963.

Guichemerre, Roger, *La Comédie avant Molière: 1640–60*, Paris: Armand Colin, 1972.

——— 'Situations et personnages pré-moliéresques', *Revue d'histoire littéraire de la France*, 72 (1972), 1007–23.

——— *La Comédie classique en France*, Paris: Presses Universitaires de France, 1978 (2nd edn, 1989).

——— 'L'Amplification comique dans le théâtre de Molière', *Le Nouveau Moliériste*, 1 (1994), 83–94.

_____ *Visages du théâtre français au xviie siècle*, Paris: Klincksieck, 1994.

_____ 'Gratuité et développement ludique dans les comédies de Scarron et Molière', *Littératures Classiques*, 27 (1996), 281–9.

Gutwirth, Marcel, *Molière ou l'invention comique: La Métamorphose des thèmes et la création des types*, Paris: Minard, 1966.

_____ *Laughing Matter: An Essay on the Comic*, Ithaca: Cornell University Press, 1993.

Haight, Jeanne, *The Concept of Reason in French Classical Literature 1635–1690*, University of Toronto Press, 1982.

Hall, H. Gaston, *Molière: 'Tartuffe'*, London: Edward Arnold, 1960.

_____ *Comedy in Context: Essays on Molière*, Jackson: University Press of Mississippi, 1984.

_____ *Molière's 'Bourgeois gentilhomme': Context and Stagecraft*, University of Durham Modern Languages Series, 1990.

_____ 'Molière's Roles Written for Himself', *Australian Journal of French Studies*, 33 (1996), 414–27.

Hammond, Nicholas, 'Authorship and Authority in Molière's Le Misanthrope' in *Essays on French Comic Drama from the 1640s to the 1780s*, eds. Derek Connon and George Evans, Oxford: Peter Lang, 2000, pp. 55–70.

Harris, Joseph, *Hidden Agendas: Cross-dressing in seventeenth-century France*, Güttingen: Gunter Narr, 2005.

Hartley, David, 'Language and Authority in Molière', in *Voices in the Air: French Dramatists and the Resources of Language: Essays in Honour of Charles Chadwick*, ed. J. Dunkley and Bill Kirton, University of Glasgow French and German Publications, 1992, pp. 29–41.

Herzel, Roger W., 'The Function of the "Raisonneur" in Molière's Comedy', *Modern Language Notes*, 90 (1975), 564–75.

_____ 'The Decor of Molière's Stage: The Testimony of Brissart and Chauveau', *Publications of the Modern Language Association of America*, 93 (1978), 925–53.

_____ ' "Much depends on the acting": The Original Cast of Le Misanthrope', *Publications of the Modern Language Association of America*, 95 (1980), 348–66.

_____ *The Original Casting of Molière's Plays*, Ann Arbor, Michigan: UMI Research Press, 1981.

_____ 'Le Jeu "naturel" de Molière et de sa troupe', *Dix-septième siècle*, 132 (1981), 279–84.

Hope, Quentin M., 'Society in Le Misanthrope', *French Review*, 32 (1958–59), 329–36.

_____ 'Philinte's Récit in Le Misanthrope', *Papers on French Seventeenth-Century Literature*, 12 (1985), 511–24.

Howarth, W. D., 'Alceste, ou l'honnête homme imaginaire', *Revue d'histoire du théâtre*, 26 (1974), 93–8.

_____ *Molière: A Playwright and his Audience*, Cambridge University Press, 1982.

_____ and Thomas, M., *Molière: Stage and Study: Essays in Honour of W. G. Moore*, Oxford: Clarendon Press, 1973.

Hubert, J. D., *Molière and the Comedy of Intellect*, Berkeley, Los Angeles, London: University of California Press, 1962.

Jasinski, René, *Le Misanthrope de Molière*, Paris: Armand Colin, 1951.

Jaynes, William, 'Critical Opinions of Cléante in *Tartuffe*', *Œuvres et Critiques*, 6 (1981), 91–7.

Johnson, Samuel, *The Yale Edition of the Works of Samuel Johnson*, vol. 7, ed. Arthur Sherbo, New Haven and London: Yale University Press, 1968.

Jones, D. F., 'Love and Friendship in *Le Misanthrope*', *Romance Notes*, 23 (1982–83), 164–9.

Jouvet, Louis, *Molière et la comédie classique*, Paris: Gallimard, 1965.

Knutson, Harold C., *Molière: An Archetypal Approach*, University of Toronto Press, 1976.

_____ 'Yet Another Last Word on Molière's *Raisonneur*', *Theatre Survey*, 22 (1) (1981), 17–33.

La Fontaine, Jean de, *Œuvres diverses*, ed. Pierre Clarac, Paris: Gallimard, 1958.

La Grange, Charles Varlet de, *Registre de La Grange 1659–1685*, ed. Bert Edward Young and Grace Philputt Young, 2 vols., Paris: Droz, 1947.

La Mothe le Vayer, François de, *Lettre sur la comédie de l'imposteur*, ed. Robert McBride, University of Durham Modern Languages Series, 1994.

Lawrence, Francis L., 'The "Raisonneur" in Molière', *L'Esprit Créateur*, 6 (1966), 158–66.

_____ 'The Norm in *Tartuffe*', *Revue de l'Université d'Ottawa*, 36 (1966), 698–702.

_____ *Molière: The Comedy of Unreason*, Tulane University, 1968.

Lerat, Pierre, *Le Ridicule et son expression dans les comédies françaises de Scarron à Molière*, Lille: Atelier de reproduction des thèses, 1980.

McBride, Robert, 'La Question du *raisonneur* dans les *écoles* de Molière', *Dix-septième siècle*, 113 (1976), 59–73.

_____ *The Sceptical Vision of Molière: A Study in Paradox*, London: Macmillan, 1977.

_____ *The Triumph of Ballet in Molière's Theatre*, Lampeter: The Edwin Mellen Press, 1992.

_____ 'La Musique chez Molière: source dramatique ou simple agrément?', *Littératures Classiques*, 21 (1994), 65–77.

_____ 'Une Philosophie du rire', *Le Nouveau Moliériste*, 1 (1994), 95–117.

_____ 'Une Philosophie du rire (suite)', *Le Nouveau Moliériste*, 2 (1995), 145–61.

_____ 'Le Raisonneur comme déclencheur de l'action comique chez Molière' in *Œuvres de Molière*, ed. N. Akiyama, Tokyo: J. P. Rinsen, 2002, vol. 9, pp. 421–50.

McKenna, Antony, *Molière dramaturge libertin*, Paris: Champion, 2005.

Mallinson, Jonathan, *Molière: 'L'Avare'*, London: Grant and Cutler Ltd, 1988.

_____ 'Vision comique, voix morale: la réception du *Misanthrope* au XVIIIe siècle', *Littératures Classiques*, 27 (1996), 367–77.

Maskell, David, 'Molière's *L'Étourdi*: Signs of Things to Come', *French Studies*, 46 (1992), 11–25.

_____ 'Terence, Tabarin and Molière's *Fourberies de Scapin*', *French Studies*, 56 (2002), 303–15.

Mauriac, François, *D'un bloc-notes à l'autre 1952–69*, ed. Jean Touzot, Paris: Bartillat, 2004.

Mazouer, Charles, 'Molière et la voix de l'acteur', *Littératures Classiques*, 12 (1990), 261–73.

_____ *Molière et ses comédies-ballets*, Paris: Klincksieck, 1993.

Mesnard, Jean, '*Le Misanthrope*: mise en question de l'art de plaire', *Revue d'histoire littéraire de la France*, 72 (1972), 863–89.

Michaut, Gustave, *Les Luttes de Molière*, Paris: Hachette, 1925.

Molière, *Œuvres complètes*, ed. E. Despois and P. Mesnard, 13 vols., Paris: Hachette, 1873–1900.

_____ *Tartufe [sic] ou l'Imposteur*, ed. abbé Figuière, 2nd edition, Paris: Alliance des Maisons d'Édition Chrétienne, 1895.

_____ *Œuvres complètes*, ed. Georges Couton, 2 vols., Paris: Gallimard, 1971.

_____ *Les Femmes savantes*, ed. H.Gaston Hall, Oxford University Press, 1974.

_____ *Œuvres complètes*, ed. Robert Jouanny, 2 vols., Paris: Bordas, 1989–93.

_____ *Le Tartuffe*, ed. Richard Parish, London: Bristol Classical Press, 1994.

_____ *Le Misanthrope*, ed. Jonathan Mallinson, London: Bristol Classical Press, 1996.

_____ *L'Imposteur de 1667 prédécesseur du Tartuffe*, ed. Robert McBride, University of Durham Modern Languages Series, 1999.

_____ *Le Misanthrope*, ed. Claude Bourqui (Paris: Livre de Poche, 2000).

_____ *The Misanthrope, Tartuffe and other Plays*, tr. Maya Slater, Oxford University Press, 2001.

Mongrédien, Georges, *Recueil des textes et des documents relatifs à Molière*, 2 vols., Paris: CNRS, 1973.

Montaigne, Michel de, *Essais*, 3 vols., ed. Pierre Villey and V.-L. Saulnier, Paris: Presses Universitaires de France, 1965.

Moore, W. G., *Molière: A New Criticism*, Oxford: Clarendon Press, 1949.

____ 'Molière's Theory of Comedy', *L'Esprit créateur*, 6 (1966), 137–44.

____ 'Raison et structure dans la comédie de Molière', *Revue d'histoire littéraire de la France*, 72 (1972), 800–5.

Morel, Jacques, 'Molière et la dramaturgie de l'honnêteté', *L'Information littéraire*, 15 (5) (1963), 185–91.

____ 'Médiocrité et perfection dans la France du xviiᵉ siècle', *Revue d'histoire littéraire de la France*, 69 (1969), 441–50.

____ *Agréables Mensonges: essais sur le théâtre français du xviiᵉ siècle*, Paris: Klincksieck, 1991.

Norman, Larry F., *The Public Mirror: Molière and the Social Commerce of Depiction*, Chicago: University of Chicago Press, 1999.

Nurse, Peter H., *Molière and the Comic Spirit*, Geneva: Droz, 1991.

Parish, Richard, '*Le Misanthrope*: des raisonneurs aux rieurs', *French Studies*, 45 (1991), 17–35.

____ 'Tartuf(f)e ou l'imposture', *The Seventeenth Century*, 6 (1991), 73–88.

____ 'Molière en travesti: Transvestite Acting in Molière', *Nottingham French Studies*, 33 (1994), 53–8.

____ 'How (and why) not to take Molière too seriously', in Bradby and Calder, *The Cambridge Companion to Molière*, 2006, q.v., pp. 71–82.

Peacock, Noël, 'The Comic Role of the "Raisonneur" in Molière's Theatre', *Modern Language Review*, 76 (1981), 298–310.

____ 'Verbal Costume in *L'École des femmes*', *Modern Language Review*, 79 (1984), 541–52.

____ 'Verbal Costume in *Le Misanthrope*', *Seventeenth-Century French Studies*, 9 (1987), 74–93.

____ *Molière: 'L'École des femmes'*, University of Glasgow French and German Publications, 1989.

____ *Molière: 'Les Femmes savantes'*, London: Grant and Cutler Ltd, 1990.

____ 'Lessons Unheeded: The Denouement of *Le Misanthrope*', *Nottingham French Studies*, 29 (1990), 10–20.

Pensom, Roger, *Molière l'inventeur: 'c't avec du vieux qu'on fait du neuf'*, Oxford: Peter Lang, 2000.

Phillips, Henry, 'Molière: The Empty Chair' in *Dying Words: The Last Moments of Writers and Philosophers*, ed. Martin Crowley, Amsterdam: Rodopi, 2000, pp. 23–38.

Picard, Raymond, '*Tartuffe*, production impie?', in Cairncross, *L'Humanité de Molière*, 1988, q.v., pp. 43–55.

Plantié, Jacqueline, 'Molière et François de Sales', *Revue d'histoire littéraire de la France*, 72 (1972), 902–27.

Potts, D. C., 'Molière's *Dom Juan* and the Trickster: A Coherent Theatrical Reading', *French Studies*, 49 (1995), 142–54.

Powell, John, 'Making Faces: Character and Physiognomy in *L'École de femmes* and *L'Avare*', *Seventeenth-Century French Studies*, 9 (1987), 94–112.

Rabelais, François, *Œuvres complètes*, ed. Guy Demerson and Michel Renaud, Paris: Seuil, 1995.

Regosin, Richard, 'Ambiguity and Truth in *Le Misanthrope*', *Romanic Review*, 60 (1969), 265–90.

Rey-Flaud, Bernadette, *Molière et la farce*, Geneva: Droz, 1996.

Riggs, Larry W., *Molière and Plurality: Decomposition of the Classical Self*, New York, Bern, Frankfurt am Main, Paris: Lang, 1989.

Sales, Saint François de, *L'Introduction à la vie dévote* in his *Œuvres*, ed. André Ravier and Roger Devos, Paris: Gallimard, 1969.

Scherer, Jacques, *Structures de Tartuffe*, 2nd edition, Paris: SEDES, 1974.

Scott, Virginia, *Molière: A Theatrical Life*, Cambridge University Press, 2000.

Shaw, David, 'Molière and the Doctors', *Nottingham French Studies*, 33 (1994), 133–42.

Taylor, Gary, *Moment by Moment by Shakespeare*, London: Macmillan, 1985.

Taylor, Samuel S., 'Le Geste chez les maîtres italiens de Molière', *Dix-septième siècle*, 33 (1981), 285–301.

Terence, *The Comedies*, tr. Betty Radice, Harmondsworth: Penguin Books, 1965.

Thomas, Merlin, 'Philinte and Éliante' in *Molière: Stage and Study*, ed. W. D. Howarth and Merlin Thomas, Oxford: Clarendon Press, 1973, pp. 73–92

—— 'Farce et réalité', *Revue d'histoire du théâtre*, 26 (1974), 132–9.

Truchet, Jacques, 'Molière et la tradition des fous savants', *Travaux de littérature*, 3 (1990), 75–84.

—— 'Molière ou l'élégance', in Bellenger and others (eds.), *L'Art du théâtre*, 1992, *q.v.*, pp. 189–97.

—— et al., *Thématique de Molière*, Paris: SEDES-CDU, 1985.

Wadsworth, Philip A., *Molière and the Italian Theatrical Tradition*, Columbia, S.C.: French Literature Publications Company, 1977.

Wheatley, K. E., *Molière and Terence: A Study in Molière's Realism*, University of Texas, 1931.

Worth-Stylianou, Valerie, *Confidential Strategies: The Evolving Role of the Confident in French Tragic Drama (1635–77)*, Geneva: Droz, 1999.

Website

www.toutmoliere.net

Index

Italic numbers denote passages that are particularly significant.